FULL CIRCLE

Around the World with a Motorcycle and Sidecar

Richard and Mopsa English

FULL CIRCLE

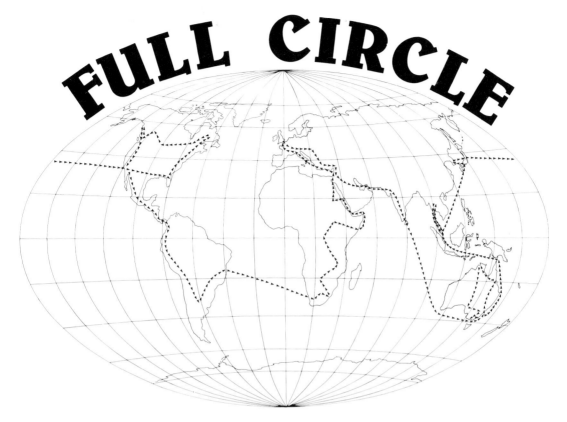

Around the World with a Motorcycle and Sidecar

Richard and Mopsa English

ISBN 0 85429 662 X

A FOULIS Motorcycling Book

First published July 1989
© Richard and Mopsa English 1989

Published by:
Haynes Publishing Group
Sparkford, Near Yeovil, Somerset
BA22 7JJ, England

Haynes Publications Inc.
861 Lawrence Drive, Newbury Park,
California 91320, USA

British Library Cataloguing in Publication Data
English, Richard
   Full circle; around the world by motorcycle and sidecar
   1. Journeys round the world by motorcycles
   I. Title   II. English, Mopsa
   910.4'1

   ISBN 0-85429-662-X

Library of Congress catalog card number
89-80120

Editor: Jeff Clew
Page Layout: Syd Guppy
Printed in England by: J.H. Haynes & Co. Ltd.

Dedication:

For the Grandparents of Joe, who was born nine months after our return to England

Dusk over Lake Atitlan, Guatemala

Acknowledgements

Our thanks go to the many people who helped and befriended us along the way, only some of whom appear in this story. Their kindness, hospitality and help motivated us to continue and complete our journey. We would like, however, specifically to express our gratitude to Overseas Containers Limited and Avon Tyres for the constancy of their support and to mention the unfailing service rendered by our Optimus stove and Ultimate tent which assured we had home comforts wherever we were. Finally, our thanks to Tommy, without whom . . .

Photographs by Richard and Mopsa English.

Contents

Farewell from John Rosamund, Chairman of the Triumph Co-operative at Meriden

Chapter One

First Steps

IN THE small hall of a seventh-floor flat in Camden, London, lay scattered the semi-organised piles of equipment which, in a few hours, would fill a cramped, coffin-shaped box on wheels. Each piece had been studied, weighed, discussed. Some had been rejected only to be redefined later as being essential. Leaning against the wall, I surveyed through tired eyes the culmination of six months' hectic activity. It was 2 am, 19th August 1982, and in the living room at the end of the narrow passage several friends were chatting noisily over a bottle of whisky. They had come to bid farewell and to celebrate our departure. In a corner Mopsa sat curled in an armchair, assiduously sewing trade-name patches onto our Barbour riding suits in preparation for our press launch later that day. Then we were to leave a steady, secure London, our home, our families and friends, for a new life – a life on the road.

I returned to the kitchen to resume pouring oats, dried fruit and rice into their respective plastic containers. An image had been burnt into my subconscious to reappear in these quieter moments of reflection between work and the time spent organising our departure. Two close, bent figures, astride a white motorcycle, lean into the wind, silently crossing a vast plain towards a point far on the horizon where snow-capped peaks glisten in the pale light of a setting sun. As from tomorrow we would be doing just that: every day going around the world, every day travelling through unknown lands towards that intangible point far in the distance. The motorcycle would be the means. It would be our one constant: a journey involving three characters, each dependent on the other two. In a romantic gesture to link us to home and England we chose a British motorcycle for the trip – a new 650cc Triumph Thunderbird to which we attached a white Squire box sidecar to carry the mass of equipment we felt necessary to keep us sound in body and mind, and the motorcycle running. Inevitably it would prove too much, but only experience taught us what was superfluous as we battled to rearrange our luggage over the first few weeks of our journey and sought solutions to lighten the load on a straining engine.

We snatched a few hours' sleep, then at 6 am began the laborious process of ferrying our chattels down to the parking lot below, praying that the rattling, graffiti-covered lift would hold out long enough for us to make good our escape. We laid everything out beside the sidecar.

"How the hell" snapped Mopsa, overwrought, "are we supposed to get all that in there." She pointed first to the immense pile of equipment, then to the shallow, enclosed space revealed as we opened the sidecar lid.

"Only one way to find out" I replied through a forced grin, and thus was instigated a daily routine which developed into a resentful obsession on my part and an after breakfast amusement for my wife – that of getting the sidecar lid securely closed once all our gear was in.

We started to load. A box of spare parts. A bag of tools. A milk crate filled with bottles and cans of chain lubricant, shampoo, WD40, Dettol, cooking oil, soy sauce, hand lotion and Swarfega. Hot weather clothes. Cold weather clothes. Thermal underwear. Waterproof oversuits. Sandals, walking shoes and riding boots. Spare visors for the helmets. A box of dried foodstuffs. Petrol cooker. Unbreakable thermos. A set of saucepans and a frying pan. A small selection of cooking utensils including whisk and garlic crusher. Books on first aid and third world doctoring. Shipping timetables. Maps and guidebooks. Vaccination certificates. Passports, vehicle documents and thirty identical passport-size photographs each. A bulky first-aid kit. A tent. Sleeping bags and inflatable mattresses. A neatly ironed white shirt, tie and jacket and one smart, all-purpose frock. Two cameras, three lenses, eight filters and thirty rolls of film. A monopod. A pair of binoculars. A sewing kit. A make-up bag. An umbrella. Six rolls of lavatory paper. Two spare tyres, and a spare wheel rim.

Two hours passed and somehow the impossible happened. All but the large bag of clothes, the spare tyres, the umbrella, the wheel rim and the tank bag which held the cameras, was inside. As we strapped the excess onto the sidecar's rack, it began to rain. I hurriedly stuck some sponsorship decals onto the bike, then dashed to join Mopsa beneath the shelter of the entrance porch. As sheets of water bounced from the chrome and paintwork, the Triumph stood in rugged anticipation. It looked ungainly with its front wheel thrust forward by the leading link forks, the Perspex screen and the squareness of the topbox and sidecar detracting from the bike's classical lines, but the overall effect one of practicality. This bike looked as though it were going places.

1 pm. The rain continued. Outside the Apollo Theatre in Victoria a small band of friends, family and colleagues gathered beneath the main awning while an announcer from Capital Radio edgily checked her watch. Petula Clark, who was scheduled to press the electric start button, thus officially launching us, was late. The interview started without her. We revved the engine, the small crowd cheered, and we were off. Once around the block, and into a nearby pub to fortify ourselves, to say final fond farewells and to linger a little in the public warmth of a London public house before the ride down to Dover. It was an emotional moment when we finally tore ourselves away. Mopsa sat silent behind me, tears mingled with the streaming rain, and the water on the Old Kent Road rushed past our boots.

We spent that night at my sister's place in Romney and took the following evening's ferry to Ostend. After catching up on a little sleep in a lay-by, we rode into Bruges in search of our first continental breakfast. As we stood by the bike in the centre of town eating chocolate-filled croissants in the early morning sun, an English couple approached on a Honda. They pulled up alongside us and a conversation began. They were on their way home from two weeks in Holland and Belgium.

"Where are you heading?" one of them asked as they both eyed our overloaded outfit. I glanced at Mopsa, who averted her eyes and shuffled her feet. I too was unable to admit to the absurd extravagance of our plans.

"Oh," I replied airily. "East." And so we were.

★   ★   ★

The British have a distinctly reverent attitude to travel, born of a mercantile background and the development into empire. The desire is almost inbred. On the shelves of any self-respecting bookshop you will find titles on the journeys of Elizabethan traders, Victorian gentlewomen and modern day adventurers and travel writers. But, in these modern times, travel usually means leisure and leisure requires a disposable income only got through working forty-eight weeks of the year. Around the world the exotic has been timetabled and packaged and the travelling involved is little more than a drive to the airport. The experience of Getting There, traditionally half the fun, has been reduced to a minimum. But for some the inexpediency and interest of Getting There is still important. Travel for travel's sake is a very personal affair, and those who do it have their own particular reasons, although they will probably be quite uncommunicative or at best very vague if asked to explain them.

The ambitiousness of our design had a very tentative beginning: we were enjoying a meal out one summer evening in Cambridge where I worked as stage manager at the local theatre and Mopsa was running a restaurant in a discotheque. We had known each other only a couple of months, but were both looking to a change of job – perhaps moving back to London. Idle talk of the future developed, and we found that we shared an unsatisfied interest in travel and a vague desire to explore and experience different areas of the world. For Mopsa it was India and Asia. For myself, South America and the Middle East. Parked outside was Mopsa's Honda H100. For many years she had harboured a strong wish to buy a motorcycle and had finally taken the plunge just before we met – something small and manageable to learn on before moving on to a something more adventurous. I had a Yamaha RD200. Just owning a motorcycle had changed my perceptions of travel. Each morning as I rode to the theatre it challenged me: Come on, let's go for a ride. You know you'll enjoy it. Let's head south and see what happens. Find out what's on the other side of the hill.

I had always led a kind of gypsy life. My father was an army officer and I can remember six homes in England and Europe before I left school. My father occasionally let slip glimpses of a strange isolated life in Northern Nigeria during the war years, or arrived back bronzed and heroic from a tour of duty with the UN forces in Cyprus. I was ferried back and forth between boarding schools and army bases, taken on confusing holidays to Venice and Zandvoort. University in Bangor and Cardiff was followed by theatre work in the north, east and south of England. Change held no terror for me – in fact I have always rather relished it. My roots and background are English, but at twenty-six I was not yet chained to the ground. Mopsa, for her part, comes from a family of literate travellers, and even boasts some explorers in her family tree.

We mapped out a projected schedule on the table-cloth. We set a date. In eighteen months we would go travelling, by motorcycle.

Four months later we rode out of Cambridge into the grey light of a February morning. Mopsa had traded her H100 for an older and matronly-looking CB200. The break had been made and our jobs filled by people with different aspirations, different priorities. We were to test our resolve and our relationship against the inclement weather of a British winter. For three weeks we rode through a frozen land, numbed by the cold, through freezing fog in the Pennines, slipping on black ice near Mold then around the snow-covered hills of North Wales.

"It's all good practise for when we cross the Andes" I volunteered as we each shivered over a cup of lukewarm coffee. Mopsa didn't look convinced, but the experience was on the whole more edifying than painful and the raw beauty of the English winter as seen from the seat of a motorcycle was a particular pleasure. The die was cast and we returned to London to begin in earnest the slow process of saving the money which would, at least, start us on our way.

It was 1981 and unemployment was rising fast. The economy was in recession and undergoing a painful restructuring. As the dole queues lengthened, people's attitudes began to polarise. The Conservative employment minister, Norman Tebbit, declared that the unemployed should get on their bikes and go and look for work. His words seemed unnecessarily harsh and uncaring to those people in the midlands and the north who were bearing the brunt of the recession, but in London there was some work for those who were prepared to look for it and who didn't mind what they did. Mopsa found a job running a telephone answering service and in the evenings worked for a music school. I found work through Manpower, mostly in warehouses, and spent my evenings crewing on theatre shows in London's West End. In the precious little time between we concentrated on our plans for the future. One Sunday night, over a quiet beer in a pub near my parents' home in Bedford, I proposed marriage.

"You know, if we are going to do this trip together, we should be married. Rights of access if one of us gets arrested or something. Having the same name on our passports has got to be to our advantage, especially in Muslim countries."

Three months later the deed was done before two witnesses at Marylebone Registry Office. A white Rolls-Royce was waiting outside for the following couple, so we borrowed it as the backdrop for the photographs before I dashed back to work to the Sound of Music and Mopsa went home for tea and champagne with her sisters.

We began to look for suitable motorcycles, reading old copies of bike magazines and scouring the motorcycle press for the latest road tests. Our initial idea was a bike each – preferably identical models to share spare parts, maintenance and knowledge. The choice soon narrowed: there was the new BMW 80GS, heralded as the Range Rover of the biking world and advertised as the motorcycle for the adventurer. When loaded down with equipment it would be hard work, especially for Mopsa who is five foot three and eight stone. Anyway it was just too expensive for our budget. A lightweight trials model – a Honda XL250 or a Yamaha XT might be better. A simple, single cylinder four stroke, competently made by the Japanese. Then while glancing through a motorcycle paper one evening, I started reading a more unusual road test. My imagination was stirred, the moment propitious, and our whole attitude and approach changed. The test was on a 350cc Enfield India. A factory in Madras was still producing this grand old reliable British thumper, based on the 1957 Royal Enfield Bullet, and were even exporting a handful to this country.

"How about Enfield to India on an Enfield India?" I asked Mopsa.

"On a what?"

"An Enfield India."

"Never heard of it."

Over the months which followed I came to wish that I'd never heard of it either. I picked up a cheap demonstration model from Slater Brothers, the importers, in Herefordshire. Just starting this bike was an exercise in patience: Ignition on, tickle the carburettor, open the air lever. Ease the engine over its compression stroke with the aid of the valve lifter. As the ammeter flicks to zero, kick. Ideally, the engine thumps into life. The ride to London was disconcerting, the gear changing ponderous, the brakes all but non-existent, but I was in a different world. As I cruised along at about fifty miles an hour, I listened to the thudding, low-revving engine. It was an education to ride a motorcycle designed for a different time – something I really enjoyed. The love affair, however, didn't last long. Within two months the engine was in bits in the spare room of our seventh floor council flat. Valves were reground and the head gasket replaced, and with a friend to help I had a valuable lesson in engine overhaul. When it was finally back together and we were ready to run it, we found that the lift had broken down so we lugged and dragged the bike down fourteen flights of stairs. We now realised that this machine was unlikely to get us to Dover, let alone to India and on around the world, but somehow the old machine rattled unreliably on until, four weeks before we were due to leave on an altogether different bike, I collided with a determined dispatch rider and it was consigned to a dealer in the East End. There it forlornly sat for two years until it was bought by two strippers from Leytonstone.

Our brief flirtation with the past did, however, have some positive results. We were now strongly attracted to the idea of taking a British motorcycle around the world, and it was with this in mind that we contacted Triumph. The Co-operative at Meriden was the lone survivor of production motorcycles in the UK and they were doggedly continuing to make motorcycles which tried to bridge the gap between the traditions of the past and a new era of rapidly accelerating technology. At the beginning of 1982 we wrote to them, detailing our plans, and were pleasantly surprised when John Rosamund, the Chairman, invited us up to see the factory and talk about our trip. In the meantime we decided against having two bikes, anticipating the increased outlays on petrol, maintenance, shipping, spares, documentation, insurance, etcetera, would prove prohibitive. If we were to succeed in this venture, we had to keep our costs to the absolute minimum. Two up meant we could share the driving, and if one of us fell ill we could still continue. The problem with only one bike, on the other hand, was how to load all the equipment needed to keep the bike running and two average sized Anglo Saxons fed, clothed, housed and healthy for more than three years on the road. We decided to look at sidecars.

Back in the old days before the advent of affordable mass-produced family cars, there were many sidecars on Britain's roads. It was a form of transport born of necessity as a motorcyclist acquired a wife and family, or as a small business needed some extra space to carry goods. The result was a strange deviant, an awkward anomaly, whose characteristics destroy many of the inherent advantages in a motorcycle, which is now increasingly designed as a vehicle for sport and leisure, and for the joy of the ride alone. A motorcyclist's initial reaction when driving a sidecar for the first time is one of fear, distaste and alarm, for it behaves quite differently from its two-wheeled cousin. Some, who persevere, grow fond of its unusual character, but one has to learn how to drive it, and carefully too. During its heyday there were many manufacturers, but now only a very few remain. Two companies dominate the British market. Squire, a relative newcomer, has grown to become one of Europe's main manufacturers, supplying lightweight fibreglass models for a range of different sized bikes. Watsonian has been around a lot longer and among the faithful is almost a legend. We looked at what was available and decided we needed a sidecar for luggage: a lightweight box which could be securely closed and locked, something like the ones the AA once used. Squire make just such a box, so we wrote to them. Neither Mopsa nor I had any desire to sit enclosed by fibreglass, low to the ground and in many countries exposed to oncoming traffic. We would ride two up with our belongings packed away beside us.

When we arrived at Triumph John Rosamund was away in the States, so we were ushered into the boardroom by George Mackay. He came straight to the point.

"As you probably know things are a bit tricky for us financially just now," he told us. "The lads are on a three-day week and there's no way we could justify giving you a Triumph for your trip. But we'd like to help," he continued, "and we've agreed to offer you a factory-prepared bike, to your own specifications, at the ex-works price."

"That's the best offer we've had all day" replied Mopsa, and the choice was made.

Three months later when we walked through the workshop doors at the Squire factory at Bidford-on-Avon, the Triumph had been delivered, and the finishing touches were being put to our sidecar box, before being mounted on the bike. My left hand was heavily bandaged, my arm in a sling, and our departure date delayed by six weeks. My collision on the Enfield had put me in hospital for several days with a badly mangled little finger. Before operating, the duty surgeon had asked whether I was perhaps a pianist or someone whose career depended upon the use of the little finger.

"No," I replied in my pre-operative, half-drugged state. "But I am supposed to be riding a motorcycle around the world next month."

Fortune smiled – he was a Top Finger Specialist, and he worked hard to save it, where another surgeon might just have cut it off.

During the intervening three months we had concentrated on seeing what sponsorship we could raise. Mopsa typed out over fifty individual letters to anybody we could think of who might like to help. We expected nothing, but hoped for a lot. We could fully understand a certain reluctance amongst companies to support a couple of complete novices about to disappear into the far reaches and so were mildly delighted with the response. Full waxed cotton riding suits arrived from Barbour, tyres from Avon, colour slide film from 3M. Optimus donated a petrol pressure stove, a seat and topbox for the bike came from Pulley Brothers of Birmingham, shock absorbers from Girling, brake pads from Dunlop. Renolds sent us chain, Schrader sent us one of their invaluable air pumps which run off one cylinder. We got hefty price reductions on our Damart Thermawear, Peter Storm rainsuits and on our Ultimate tent. And on top of all this we got two Stanley screwdrivers, four Champion spark plugs and six cans of WD40.

Peter Rivers-Fletcher at Squire insisted that Mopsa should be taught to ride an outfit before he would allow her to take our one out onto the roads. He recounted cautionary tales of novices tumbled into ditches as they came upon their first left-hand bend. So we were duly taken down to the local playing fields and there on a battered old MZ two-stroke, she learnt the basic requirements necessary to keep a combination on the road. The most disconcerting characteristic was the tendency for the sidecar wheel to be lifted high into the air when the front wheel is steered too forcefully into the sidecar. To start with Mopsa was tentative and slow, while I stood frustrated on the sidelines, but soon she was swinging back and forth in fast tight circles and figures of eight, and by the afternoon's end was flushed and exhilarated by the whole experience. It boded well for the future, and in the first few months of our ownership of the outfit we argued fiercely over who was to drive it.

Next day came the turn of the Triumph. Keith Wash of Unit Sidecars, who runs a small company from a garage in Essex, and who makes a very professional and classic-looking sidecar himself, had come to fit his leading link forks to the front end of the bike. The general consensus is that modern telescopic forks are unsuited to prolonged sidecar use and that leading links improve the handling considerably. Keith had recently sold one of his Hedingham sidecars to a couple from Kent, who, having attached it to their 1100cc Honda Gold Wing had already set off on their trip around the world. A couple of days before they left we had been down to see them. He was a driving instructor, she a nurse, a

The Bike after fitting the sidecar and leading link forks

combination we thought was well suited to such an expedition. They had applied to emigrate to Australia and confident of success, had sold their house before their applications had been fully processed. Then, at the last moment, they had been refused and so, at a loose end, decided on their trip. All planning done, we felt that we should be able to glean quite a lot of information from them, but we found that their attitude proved very different from ours. They were packing a huge family-sized tent, weighing more than forty pounds – we were worrying that ours was a little over the top at eight pounds! But with such a powerful machine, I suppose it didn't matter. With only a few days before their departure, they seemed blissfully ignorant of what lay ahead. Maybe that wasn't such a bad thing – one's preconception of foreign lands are always over-simplified or highly exaggerated. For our own peace of mind, however, we continued to read whatever we could get our hands on regarding the places we planned to visit, and immersed ourselves in the colourful tales and subjective writings of past travellers.

After a morning spent acquainting herself with our vehicle, Mopsa drove the two of us back to London. The following six weeks were a hectic time as we tied up loose ends, arranged to put our life in England on hold and visited friends around the country while running-in the Triumph. Our old friends, the CB200 and the RD200 were stolen from outside our flat. The police were not surprised – we were living in the highest vehicle theft-rate area in Britain. This left us convinced that our new outfit would be whisked from under our very noses and that all our plans and hopes would come crashing down. We searched for somewhere safe to keep it and eventually rented a lock-up garage nearby. As the day of departure drew nearer we both began to get nervous, pre-occupied and fraught. One night brought a violent hammering at our front door – water was pouring through our downstairs neighbour's ceiling. Mopsa had started to run herself a bath, and forgotten all about it as she assembled the first-aid kit.

Kettles were boiled dry, washing left at the launderette for days. She confided to me a fear that when the time came for leaving she would simply refuse to go.

We returned to the Triumph works at Meriden for a press launch and to collect a box of spare parts which included spokes, air and oil filters, carburettor jets, gaskets, pushrods, piston rings and one spare piston. Why only the one piston for a twin cylinder engine? I had read that Ted Simon, who rode around the world on a Triumph Twin back in the early seventies had packed just one spare. We were determined to keep our weight down, and looked to the experiences of past travellers when deciding what to take. We had chosen the recently introduced 650cc model Triumph, named after its illustrious predecessor of the 1950s, 60s and early 70s, rather than the more powerful 750cc Bonneville. This modern Thunderbird was in effect a destroked 750, and, in our case, when fitted with a single carburettor, electronic ignition, electric start, twin exhaust, large fuel tank, low handlebars, leading link forks, and attached to a box sidecar, was a truly unique machine. One of the main reasons for choosing the 650 was that of economy – both in initial price and running costs. It was only on the morning of our departure, when we were fully loaded for the first time, that I suspected a more powerful engine might have been a better bet.

While we were at Meriden, Brian Jones, the Chief Engineer, organised our first service: we'd already put almost two thousand miles on the clock.

"Your oil level was a bit low" he informed me. "You'll want to keep an eye on that."

"Oh yes, we'll be checking it daily" I replied defensively. But he was right. I was used to riding Japanese motorcycles whose oil consumption was negligible, and had overlooked the fact that this was a very different animal. We would have a lot to learn in the coming months.

The final countdown to departure

Chapter Two

Europe

"I BUY Missis English. Is have good time. Is plenty money . . . you sell . . . is good price . . . just one day." A toothless, grizzled Turk eyed Mopsa appreciatively. A retired sailor, who had learnt his English in ports all around the world, he looked not a day over ninety and little realised that the "Missis English" he wished to buy, or rent, was indeed Mrs English. We were in Istanbul, the colourful and bustling city with one foot in Europe and the other in Asia. Across the silvery waters of the Bosphorus the elegant curve of a suspension bridge joined the continents. In a few days time we would ride across its span and begin our journey through the world's largest and most culturally diverse continent.

We escaped the leering intent of the ancient Turk and struggled through the clattering confusion of activity which was the hub of the sprawling city's transportation system, where overcrowded buses, trains and ferries converged to settle just long enough to disgorge their various hordes before refilling and departing again. This downtown area exhibited all the characteristics one associates with the East: narrow cobbled streets which twisted and turned, lined with makeshift stalls of broken wood and tattered canvas, fronting shops crammed full with all manner of foodstuffs, household goods and general merchandise. Multicoloured plastic buckets and brooms, grains and pulses and spices unknown to our western eyes, sacks of dusty dried fruits and nuts, and row upon row of newly fashioned exhaust pipes, shining and blue from the heat of the welders torch. Hustling hawkers abounded, selling cheap and colourful trinkets at inflated prices, or intent on persuading us and other wandering tourists to visit and view, with of course no obligation to buy, their fathers' or uncles' carpet shop, "just close by". Small boys carried trays of tea into shops and offices or sold, for a penny or two, glasses of water, which they awkwardly poured from great galvanised jugs. Minarets rose tall like well-sharpened pencils from among the jumbled streets, and from these wailed out, at the five appointed hours each day, the amplified and distorted call to prayer, filling the air with tinny insistence. The smell of spices, of grilling meat and of musty drains completed the ambience.

Unwittingly we had arrived at a tourist campsite on the outskirts of the city on a Sunday evening, the eve of the major Muslim festival of Idh al Adaha. On the Monday morning we had boarded an early commuter train into the city centre, only to find that the banks were closed and the doors of the main Post Office firmly locked – for the whole of the week. A holiday atmosphere pervaded and family groups, dressed in their equivalent of Sunday best wandered the crowded bazaars. Through tall gates of small courtyards, or on open ground outside residential tenements, we saw sheep and goats ritually slaughtered, their carcasses hanging from trees with blood draining from their slashed throats – all in bloody celebration of Abraham's sacrifice to God. The meat thus provided by the rich is then distributed among the poor.

The previous morning had seen us still in eastern Europe, encamped by a rainy beach on the shores of the Black Sea in a Bulgarian holiday resort. It was the final week of the summer season, and the grounds were all but empty, with only a handful of Russian and Hungarian holiday makers hoping to soak up a last few days of sun before returning to a long, bleak winter in the north. Our breakfast was interrupted by the approach of two burly Hungarians who helped us to fold our waterlogged tent and pack the sidecar, then escorted us to the Turkish border. One was a truck driver, who claimed to know Turkey well, and all the hazards we would meet: we must be well provided with petrol, he insisted, and also cigarettes; in Turkey we would be unable to get any. To be sure, he bought us a tankful of petrol, and watched over us as we bought several packets of unsmokeable Bulgarian cigarettes: these, he told us, we should throw to the young Turkish boys who line the roads right across the country, lying in wait for foreign trucks and tourists to drive by, a large rock in each hand . . . Thus prepared we left this reserved and austere country, from which our most lasting memory was to be the thick creamy yoghurt on which we breakfasted each day.

As the border post disappeared behind us, obscured by the forests through which this scarcely travelled road ran, swallows appeared, swooping and diving before and around us as we rode down through the scented pineclad hills, leading us forward then vanishing as we emerged onto the sudden fury of a Turkish main road. Stark propagandist billboards extolling the virtues of Marxist-Leninism were replaced by a jumbled display of solidly capitalist advertising slogans: "Coke is it" in Turkey, as is a Toyota car, a box of Persil, a set of SKV bearings or a flight to Germany on Lufthansa airways. After the polite, ordered driving habits of the Bulgarians, who rarely displayed the temerity to push their speedometer needles much above the prescribed 50mph mark, we rode on tattered nerves along the main arterial highway toward Istanbul. We survived the audacious antics of the speeding Turks, and retired, 20 kilometres from the city centre, to the welcome, if relative, peace of a well-signposted campsite. There, on the shores of the Marmara Sea, we pitched our tent on the sun-baked soil, beneath the insufficient shade of a tall and spindly pine. The tent alongside was a vast partitioned one, with porch and freezer and small coloured bird in a wicker cage. It belonged to a sprawling

Iranian family with an air of wealth about them. A Mercedes was parked alongside and from deep within the voluminous folds of the canvas roared a wavering tune from a television playing at full volume, unsettling the quiet atmosphere of the heavy, mid-afternoon heat. The patriarch, with rolling folds of fat displayed above a short wrapped towel, barked sharp orders to his family, shook his vast stomach and gyrated his hips in exuberant participation with the cacophony from within. On the beach, and on the white wrought iron seats of the bar, bronzed Italians lounged. Young European girls in skimpy bikinis lay prone on the narrow strip of sand, in contrast to the groups of Iranian and Syrian women who, covered from neck to wrist to ankle in enveloping folds, sat in tight secluded groups in the available shade.

That evening we decided to stay for a few days. We felt the need to relax a little, to accustom ourselves to the habits and ways of a very different culture. More than this, the motorcycle was in need of attention, and I was unwilling to continue before some essential work was done.

★   ★   ★

The six weeks we had spent riding down through Europe had been a strange affair as we slowly adjusted to the realities of our new life. At times it seemed inconceivable that we should not be turning around in a few days, heading for home along with all the other holidaymakers, our three weeks complete. But all Europe was green, bathed in the softening colours of late summer, and our excitement propelled us optimistically forward. Unused to the open air, breezy existence of motorcycle touring we slept long hours, collapsing into dreamless sleep and lingering over our campsite breakfasts. We were rarely on the road before ten. Slowly and inexorably, Belgium merged into Luxemburg, which then merged into Germany. Under the stolid black Roman arch at Trier, across the Moselle and the Rhine, following the wide sweeping bends of the Neckar river, before reaching the forests of Bavaria. In Salzburg we paused to spend several days with my younger brother, on his way back to England after fifteen months spent wandering on his bicycle through Europe, North Africa and the Middle East. His taut, sunbrowned body and weather beaten, travel-weary face presented us with an image of what we might become, and as his sinewy brown legs began to pedal him home, we continued on, with no more effort than a twist of the throttle, into upper Austria, our pale, indoor faces reddening a little in the early September sun.

It was in Hungary that we encountered our first real difficulties with language. Since leaving England we had relied upon Mopsa's French and my few words of remembered German, and had got by efficiently. In Upper Austria Mopsa decided that our kitchen needed a spatula, and in a small hardware store in Grein acted out an elaborate mime involving the breaking , frying and turning of eggs. The elderly shopkeeper knew precisely what was meant, and sent her grandson up a ladder to rummage among dusty boxes on the top shelf. The article in question was found, carried down with care, unwrapped and ceremoniously presented: a corkscrew!

In Hungary, not only was the language incomprehensible, but the sounds which people uttered were totally unfamiliar to our ears. Hungarian is allied only to Finnish and to a language spoken in an obscure area east of the Urals. We began therefore to learn the basic grammar of international sign language, to which the Hungarians reacted with detached indifference.

In Budapest we stayed with a young couple and their two year old daughter. Gabor was a partner in a private computer software business. Small scale private enterprise was beginning to be allowed in certain limited sectors of the state-controlled economy. This was an experiment. He was enthusiastic about it, dismissive of state bureaucracy and subscribed to *Time* and *Newsweek*. Both Gabor and his wife spoke English, but Susanna, a paediatrician, felt the need to disappear to the kitchen now and then to gulp down several tots of fierce plum brandy in order to loosen her "English tongue". Their dream was to obtain the necessary green passports which allow Hungarians to travel in the west. Then they would take six months sabbatical and travel as far as they could around the Mediterranean seaboard of north Africa, Europe and Turkey.

On a hill overlooking the twin towns of Buda and Pest, we walked around the castle walls, St. Thomas' church and an unfortunate addition, the Budapest Hilton, and were introduced to the ritual greetings of men on the lookout for hard currency and the opportunity to make a reasonable profit on a very simple economic transaction.

"English? Deutsch?" they would cheerfully ask.

"Ah, English, how are you my friend?" Then the eyes would tighten, the voice lower, a furtive look to left and right.

"Change money, my friend?"

"No thank you."

"Pounds, Dollars? Very good rate. In the bank only sixty-five forints, me, I give you ninety."

"I'm sorry, we have no hard currency."

"I give you one hundred."

"No thank you."

With a resentful shrug, they slunk off toward some other conspicuous tourist.

Returning to the motorcycle and sidecar we found it being earnestly inspected by a group of schoolboys. The tallest among them noticed our approach, studied our pale complexions and blond hair, and proceeded to announce our arrival to the assembled. I recognised just one word – Soviet. There are some Russian motorcycles on the roads of Hungary, Romania and Bulgaria. Cumbersome old Urals, 650cc horizontally-opposed twins, based on wartime BMWs, some with monstrously heavy sidecars attached, complete with hand brakes and reverse gear. More common were the East German and Czechoslovakian two-strokes. Our unfamiliar marque was beginning to draw small crowds wherever we stopped – the further east we travelled the greater the crowd. Occasionally a few questions were asked in broken English, always including the sensitive one of the cost of the outfit. In order not to appear too extravagantly consumerist, we unashamedly halved the price when converting to the local currency, and still it usually appeared to our questioners as a vast sum. Explaining the relationship of wages and the cost of living between East and West, with only a handful of commonly understood words, was all but impossible.

At Eger we sighted our first mosque, a visual confirmation of our eastward passage and a legacy of the Turkish expansion into Europe by Suleiman the Magnificent during the sixteenth century. Then across the great flat expanse of the Hartobagy, central Europe's largest grass prairie, the landscape toned brown with the occasional long, squat, whitewashed barn, the ends of their steeply pitched thatch brushed by the billowing grass. Before entering Romania, we spent a day in the spa town of Hajduszoboszlo. Between lengthy soakings in the tepid brownish and sulphurous waters, I carefully checked the outfit. The bike was leaning into the sidecar by about three inches and we readjusted accordingly. The rear spoked wheel was showing signs of warpage and the standard springs on the rear shock absorbers were already proving to be unequal to the task set them. We had a stronger set, held in reserve, but without a spring compressor, we postponed the changeover. In order to keep the chain dust- and dirt-free, and thus prolong its working life, I had fitted an aftermarket enclosed chaincase of moulded fibreglass. It was ill-suited to the compact design of the Triumph and it rubbed against the tyre and rattled against the chain until we threw the thing away in exasperation. In theory we felt that we had prepared and equipped ourselves well, but really we were flying blind and only time would tell us whether our choices had been the right ones.

At the Romanian frontier, guards asked us whether we were carrying any form of firearm, then after no more than a very cursory glance at our box full of belongings, they waved us through into the green hills of Transylvania. Pasture alternated with forest, and fields full of sunflower, corn and tomato. The road surface was deteriorating, and the air was filled with sickly sweet black diesel fumes belching from worn out trucks which seemed to spend as much time in roadside repair as in forward motion. We passed ox- and horse-drawn carts, and trailing groups of noisy gypsy caravans, splashes of colour against the patchwork landscape. During our first night in a cramped and grubby mosquito-ridden A-frame chalet, we were frequently disturbed by people in search of a taste of our western materialism. A wide faced man from Poland, with two white-haired children in tow, asked to buy dollars. A swarthy woman enquired after the possibility of spray-on deodorant or furniture polish, but our aerosol cans were limited to chain lubricant and WD40. Shortages were evident everywhere – we queued for eggs and bread, had to show our passports before being permitted to buy rationed sugar, and on our approach to a petrol station were waved by a long line of patiently waiting motorists to a special pump which supplied the needs of tourists with a fuel of dubious quality which had the bike's engine gently pinking as we accelerated away.

Through my previous work in theatre, we had an introduction to Dan Jitianu who was head of design at Bucharest's Bulandra Theatre. He insisted on taking us out to dinner and as evening fell we followed his determined footsteps around the city's streets in search of something to eat. Our first stop was at a restaurant which had only "strong beef" to offer. What was meant by strong beef: was it tough? Was it old? Rotten? We didn't find out, but carried on to another which had only wine, no food. Finally , at our third stop there was a choice of liver, or kidneys, or sausages. We chose the sausages, chewing valiantly to extract the edible bits while Dan told us about his life in Bucharest, keeping our glasses filled with sharp new red wine.

"I am very fortunate to have a job which allows me to organise my own time" he told us in his precise English. "This means that I am able to join the queues for food and other items as they become available. If I find that there is a shop which one day has chickens for sale, I have the time to stand in line and buy several. In the evening my family will then have a feast, and we will enjoy ourselves. We do not know when we will be able to find chickens again."

When we left the restaurant our plates were by no means empty, for a sizeable pile of pink gristle remained on each, testimony to the main ingredient of our meal.

The following morning we visited the folk museum, a collection of traditional houses, cottages and barns of carved wood, uprooted and brought from all parts of the country. We fought our way through groups of loud American tourists who, bristling with camera equipment, were being herded from one "cute little hut" to the next. Returning to the bike, parked in a street lined with horse chestnut trees whose fallen conkers were left uncollected by the small boys of Bucharest, we found one of our helmets gone. Despite being locked on, the strap had been cut. We searched central Bucharest for a replacement, but without success. At the Bulgarian border it became an issue.

"She cannot go without the 'at." The thick voice of the frontier guard was definite. Our paperwork had been rapidly completed, but this seemed an impassable problem.

"But it was stolen in Romania" we explained. He didn't seem to understand, but our mime was clear enough.

"You go buy one. She stay here."

"But it's past six o'clock. The shops are closed."

"It is the law of our country" he countered. Then with a smile and a shrug he returned to his newspaper. We continued on. Next morning Mopsa fashioned herself a mock helmet out of a scarf and my old tweed cap, which she convinced herself looked like the leather flying helmets worn by many motorcyclists we saw. I encouraged her to hide when she saw policemen, but when we did see one for her to avoid, he was invariably riding a small two-stroke motorcycle in pastel blue or green, his cap of authority firmly on his head and his helmet in a string bag swinging from the handlebars. We didn't find a replacement until Istanbul. It was made of laminated cardboard with a removable polystyrene lining.

After three thousand miles we reached the Black Sea, turned south past the Russian naval base at Sozopol and spent our last night in Europe in the empty seaside camping resort in the last week of its season. We were both now feeling more distanced from our previous life and were accustomed to each other's constant companionship. I treated Mopsa rather carefully, as she did me, for the success of our venture depended during those first few months as much on how our relationship developed as on external factors and on our own will to continue. We established routines in our setting up and striking of camp. Mopsa developed and extended her repertoire of meals cooked over the Optimus petrol pressure stove. We found that we fell into a traditional division of labour between the sexes. Mopsa preferred to drive less than I, and became an efficient navigator, for although the outfit handled reasonably well despite its heavy load, and the steering was fairly light, still we both found it considerably more tiring to drive than a solo motorcycle, especially when the road twisted or was in bad condition. Six hours a day in the saddle was enough – much above that and the arms and shoulders began to ache and the riding ceased to be the pleasure it should. But the three wheels of the outfit made it at least stable, so we could shift our weight at will, thus suffering less from the motorcyclist's main complaint at the end of a long day's ride.

I slowly improved the efficiency of our packing system, an exercise with which Mopsa wisely refused to get involved, knowing it would only lead to argument. Together, however, we found out what we really had little use for and from time to time we sent small packages home. The egg whisk, garlic crusher, impact screw driver and torque wrench were all deemed expendable, as was the Coleman pressure lamp we had bought specially for the trip. Not only did we find it difficult to light, matches always seeming to be too short to reach the fragile mantle, but in any case it had given up working properly after only a week on the road, so we made do with candles instead. The expeditionary nature of

The packing of the sidecar box

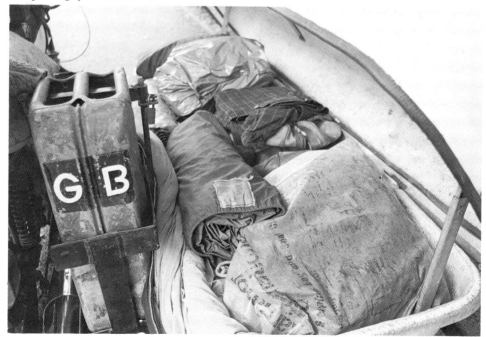

our larder was also dispensed with, we decided to carry only the bare essentials – tea, sugar and salt, rice and pasta, some spices and oil and a couple of tins of sardines for emergencies. Every day or so we shopped, buying bread, eggs, fruit and vegetables enough to last for four or five meals. This arrangement suited Mopsa excellently, for she could happily wander through markets looking for new and exotic products or study the shelves of foreign supermarkets, lost in a comparative study of price and variety. It was only my impatience which kept her from spending long hours doing just that. Many of the clothes we had thought essential, we now found were not, and a bundle of tee-shirts and other extraneous materials were sent back the way we had come. In a gentle and unpressured way we worked out a system of travel which suited both of us, and the bike. If the day was to be spent travelling, and the roads were good, two hundred miles seemed to be a reasonable distance to aim for. Often, though, it was less – especially if we involved ourselves in the intricacies of daily shopping, and stopping at roadside stalls for a drink, talking to those who approached, or exploring the towns, villages or countryside through which we passed on foot. The motorcycle ran quite comfortably at fifty to fifty-five miles per hour. Much above that and it started to consume petrol and oil at a much increased rate. Fuel consumption ranged between forty and forty-five miles per gallon which meant that a full tank and jerry can would take us about three hundred and seventy miles – enough, we felt, for all but the most isolated tracks. Our first six weeks of travel had been untraumatic and quietly educative, a necessary apprenticeship before what we envisaged would be a far more adventurous time in Turkey and the Middle East.

★　★　★

The day following our excursion into Istanbul, we decided to remain at the campsite and began the urgent task of repairing the Triumph's rear wheel. During our initial preparations I had asked Meriden to fit heavy duty spokes to that wheel to help with the stress endemic in sidecar use. Somehow the request was overlooked and we were now suffering the consequences. Increased lateral stresses on the wheel created by the heavily loaded sidecar resulted in it flexing, warping and ultimately breaking several spokes. These spokes I had wired in during the first weeks, but now I had to replace the broken ones and began also to tighten them on one side, correspondingly loosening them on the other in my first attempt at truing up the wheel. All went fairly well, the warpage was all but corrected and I was generally feeling pleased with myself when a resounding crack snapped into my ebbing concentration. I swore gently, then slowly span the wheel, looking for a newly broken spoke. I found none, but saw something far worse. Just beside the spoke I had most recently tightened a split had appeared in the wheel rim. I swore severely this time, just as Mopsa appeared with a dripping bundle of newly scrubbed clothes under her arm.

"I've cracked the bloody rim" I told her.

"Oh dear" she replied mildly. "That's rather serious isn't it?"

She started to hang out the clothes.

"Still, she continued comfortably, "We have a spare one, don't we."

This was not what I wanted to hear. The idea of rebuilding the wheel completely, given the disastrous result of my attempt at realigning the rim, just didn't appeal.

"I met a Hungarian dancer by the wash basins" Mopsa broke into my thoughts. "We've been invited over for coffee"

Outside a long, lace curtained caravan, we were greeted by a towering and angular Turk in the briefest of bathing trunks.

"This," he declared with obvious pride "is my American car." He slapped the roof of a Lincoln Continental, endlessly long and glistening. "See – it has New Jersey plates."

Within the confines of their mobile home we were given iced tea in engraved glasses.

"Why don't you wear a bikini" asked the Hungarian dancer, eyeing the modest one-piece bathing costume which Mopsa had purposely bought so as not to offend the traditions of the more conservative countries through which we might pass. I enquired further about their profession.

"We are entertainers, artistes, exotic dancers" the man exclaimed with theatrical flourish.

"My wife was trained, of course, in Budapest, and we are in huge demand to travel all over Europe with our act. All over Europe."

A poster hung on the wall above our heads, and he looked towards it with further pride. Our eyes followed his. In heavily spangled flesh-toned leotards, the exotic dancers were wound into an erotic embrace.

Full of iced tea and sweet biscuits and somewhat bemused, we returned to our humbler encampment, and together began to remove the spokes from the cracked wheel rim. A large and dusty dog came and sat by us, watching our work. A second one, smaller but dustier also approached, and was chased away by the first, who then complacently sat guard at the entrance to the tent. In the hot afternoon sun we began the tortuous job of relacing the spokes into the spare wheel rim. After several hours, as dusk fell, Mopsa left to prepare supper. Later yet, in total darkness she forced me from my task, so it was not until the following morning that I was able, triumphantly, to spin the wheel, straight and true, on its hub. As an extra precaution, I wired the spokes together to keep them from puncturing the inner tube – should they break – an old trick used by motocross riders, which I had read about during the months of preparation prior to our departure. The dusty dog still sat guard, and seemed to share my pleasure.

Two days later, we left Istanbul. On our way out of town we diverted to an area where we hoped to find a workshop in which to have the springs on our rear shock absorbers changed. Following several misdirections and redirections we finally arrived. The street was lined on either side with rows of cluttered workshops. Battered Fords and Chevrolets and naked truck chassis littered the forecourts, and grease-covered youths hammered vigorously at crumpled sections of bodywork. The dry smell of welded metal permeated the air. We picked a workshop at random and stopped outside. In vivid gesture I explained

A marshy lake on the Great Hungarian Plain

our needs to two young men and the job was taken rapidly in hand. Lacking a spring compressor, the tools used included a bench vice, four large and rusty screwdrivers and a great deal of sheer sweaty brute force, and we handed over the equivalent of £1.50 when the new springs had been fitted. There was an immediate and palpable improvement: the outfit no longer wallowed slightly on bends and the rear tyre had stopped scraping on the mudguard when driving across pot-holes.

So we rode across the Bosphorus, and into Asia. I pulled over at the top of a winding climb high above the straits, and parked on an exposed promontory. Standing separately in the wind we took a long, last look at Europe. Then with a smile between us which confirmed all our joint intentions, we turned east. I released the clutch, the drive engaged and we slowly pulled away: the cord had been cut and we were now to begin our journey in earnest.

Chapter Three

Turkey and the Middle East

THE RAIN, which had been threatening all day, finally arrived. Its delicate threads tumbled through the humid air, releasing the pungent smells of the earth. They were smells I associated with thunderstorms at the end of long hot English summer day, but this was drizzle, it was October and we were at Troy on the northern shores of Turkey's Aegean coast. In contrast to the legend, the ruins were uninspiring: at the entrance a great hideous replica of the wooden horse was being repaired next to a long, squat windowless structure which proclaimed itself the Helen and Paris Discotheque. The Face that Launched a Thousand Ships had been reduced to an ugly caricature painted onto a bare concrete wall.

As we hurriedly struggled into our rainsuits, a VW van pulled into the car park, and the driver strode purposefully toward us.

"Have you had problems yet?" His accent betrayed German origins as he pointed to the bike's engine. A motorcycle enthusiast himself, he was an ex-racer who worked as research engineer for BMW and was now regretting not having brought his own bike, rather than the van, for his holiday. He sighed deeply.

"I love to hear the sound of a British twin" he said, so I kicked over the engine and the Triumph obligingly thumped into life. We left him, a lone figure in the pouring rain, his head cocked to one side, attentively listening. His introductory words were to prove prophetic. During the final months of our preparations, we had sketched out a route through the Middle East. The choice was dictated more by the situation in Iran than by our own preferences, and in order to get as much basic information as possible, I had contacted the RAC and spoken to the Head of Touring there.

"The best advice I can give you is not to go" he curtly responded to my enquiries. His clipped voice continued, explaining the instabilities and dangers of the Middle East as though I were a political naif. His attitude and manner seemed of the old school, possibly colonial, probably ex-army, so I firmly declared that we were not about to be put off by a bunch of turbulent and volatile Arabs. His tone then softened a little, and he proceeded to inform me that the most important document we would need was a Carnet de Passages en Douane for the motorcycle. This large document, printed in triplicate, would exempt us from the payment of import duties or the lodging of bonds when presented at borders. Before the RAC could deliver the document to us, we had to deposit a bond with them, or take out an insurance indemnity, either of which would cover any customs claim should we fail to re-export the motorcycle from any country. For some countries the claim could be as high as three hundred percent of the value of the vehicle. In the years before the Second World War, and for a short period thereafter, a Carnet was required all over Europe but now a passport and a registration document will suffice and it is only when the European driver enters Asia, the Americas or Africa that the need for this document reappears. War zones tend to be excluded, so when our Carnet finally arrived, just two days before our departure, its cover was boldly stamped in red: ex-Israel, -Lebanon, -Syria, -Jordan, -Afghanistan and -Iran. We had, in any case, already decided against Iran: information on entry requirements was sketchy and liable to change, so we planned an alternative, to continue south from Turkey, into Syria and Jordan, across Saudi Arabia to the Arabian Gulf and then find a more or less sea-worthy dhow to sail us through the Straits of Hormuz and on to the Indian sub-continent. We would follow the tracks of one of the ancient trade routes from the east, which had carried the spices of India across the Arabian deserts to the shores of the Mediterranean Sea. It was as viable a route, we believed, as that which passed through the more rugged country on the other side of the Tigris and Euphrates rivers.

We did the rounds of various embassies in London, supplying them with handsful of passport-sized photographs, our marriage certificate and application forms duly completed in triplicate for the visas we needed. Syria and Jordan each provided us with elaborate patchworks of arabic and roman script and several impressively-engraved stamps on the first few pages of our new and unsullied passports. Saudi Arabia regretfully explained that they were unable to furnish us with even a transit visa, and that we should reapply in an adjoining country. As we walked from their embassy, I studied the faces of some the richer London Arabs, who sauntered the capital's streets in their ankle length white shirts, subservient and covered wife just a few steps behind. Their faces seemed too soft, too rounded, their bellies too full, to have been bred in the harsh conditions of a desert environment. I resented their conspicuous wealth, the Cartier watches, chunks of gold on their pudgy fingers, long glossy cars to ride in. They were buying up chunks of London, but were reluctant to allow non-Muslims to travel through their land. But the romance of the desert remained strong, and we were determined, in spite of many threatened difficulties, to find out where myth and reality met, and to ride our motorcycle through to the Indian Ocean.

From Troy we rode southwards down the indented Aegean coast. Straggling lines of women pickers snaked through the cotton fields. If our strange white motorcycle was noticed gliding effortlessly by, then one or two would slowly straighten, questioningly, and then wave to us with undisguised delight. Scores of lorries and horse-drawn carts, laden with tomatoes or cotton,

29

stood in patient line outside canning factories and processing plants. Olive groves covered the higher, less fertile land, and the sun, which shone fierce and bright that day, blanched their dusty green leaves. As we climbed a steep road, our way was slowed by a convoy of trucks hugely burdened with great bales of cotton, their engines shreiking under load and each sending forth into the dry scented air foul-smelling black smoke. We fell in behind this monstrous caravan, slipping the clutch when the speed slowed to a painfully ponderous pace on the steepest gradients, until, with the hill's brow in view, the engine of the Triumph began to stutter and to lose power. I snatched at the clutch lever, pulled over and began to check the fuel lines and taps.

"We seem to have plenty of petrol" I told Mopsa, who liked to be kept informed of all developments, "but this engine is really too hot. I think we should let it cool down a little."

With a nod and a grimace she agreed, and wearily wiped the thin layer of oily grime from her face. When, after half an hour's rest, I kicked over the engine, it fired immediately and we continued on without further stress through the balmy late afternoon heat to a campsite at Bergama. The events of the next two days saw our emotions seesaw between despair and resignation, apprehension and then blessed relief.

The first day started well enough. We collected wood from around the campsite and fed it into a huge, ancient and rusty water heater attached to the side of a wooden hut. This produced lukewarm water which made bathing and washing reasonably pleasant and effective. The campsite attendant, short and effeminate with a nervous gait approached us:

"I have very much worry," he told us. "Tomorrow will come one hundred fifty schoolchild from Uganda eating here. Have you some English discotape?" Mopsa was ready to look in the toolkit but I understood his needs faster, and handed him a Beatles compilation. This became the constant backdrop of sound throughout our stay. After a leisurely morning, followed by sweet black tea in the adjoining restaurant, I began the routine of daily checks on the bike. I was horrified to find the oil level badly reduced and the sparking plugs glossed shiny black. The previous day's overheating had evidently done some damage. We discussed our options. Either we could try to find a workshop, or, although I was mechanically very inexperienced, we could remove the cylinder head here in the campsite to see what state the pistons were in. I had imagined that at some point during our journey we would have to rebuild the engine in some dusty shack, miles from nowhere, but this was far sooner than expected – London was still less than four thousand miles away. But with the various seals and gaskets, rings and tools which we had we could effect a top end overhaul. We proceeded, slowly, to dismantle things, carefully following the instructions in our workshop manual. As the work progressed we became the focus of attention and a small band of men soon gathered around us, tutting sympathetically, ordering trays of tea and beer, and offering endless advice and harsh untipped cigarettes. I hadn't smoked for over a year, but now under pressure from both company and circumstance I succumbed. We carried some cigarettes with us, hidden deep in the sidecar. "You must take some English cigarettes with you," we had been advised before leaving, "to bribe recalcitrant border officials." We hadn't needed them for that purpose yet, and indeed never would, so Mopsa now dug out a couple of packets and handed them around. It seemed that virtually every Turkish man smokes, and it is part of their hospitable nature and tradition to offer cigarettes along with the ubiquitous sweet black tea. The odd non-smoker would tap his chest to indicate a complaint, and embarrassedly mumble apologies at not being able to accept the gift – doctor's orders. He had had to give up. For health reasons.

With the cylinder head removed the extent of the damage was visible: not only had the two middle piston rings seized, but the right hand piston crown was pitted and the barrel scored. As we were dejectedly inspecting the seized parts the camp owner appeared. With the camp attendant acting as interpreter he told us that his brother was a mechanic, and that he would come and mend our motorcycle. And indeed he did: the barrels were whisked away to be honed in a nearby machine shop, the damaged piston was replaced with our spare, and new rings were fitted before the engine was rebuilt. Several more packets of cigarettes were shared, and thirty or so British schoolchildren arrived at the restaurant from an *SS Uganda* educational cruise of the Aegean to eat their packed lunches to the sounds of our Beatles tape. As we prepared to leave the mechanic and the camp interpreter approached:

"He say you going slowly slowly, then you reach England No Problem!" I hadn't the heart to tell them that we were going home the long way.

A dying sun sent shafts of golden light across a flat unmoving sea as we looked down over the town of Kusadasi, spread along the wide arc of a sandy bay. As we started down from our vantage point I slipped into neutral and switched off the engine, so that we were left with only the sound of the soft air and the swish of rubber on tar. We cruised along the beach front and pulled up outside the large BP Mocamp – one of a chain of campsites which dot Turkey. It was heavily fenced and guarded, it would have hot showers, a bar, a restaurant and it would cost the equivalent of five pounds. Our intention had been to camp wild wherever possible, returning only every few days to the relative luxury of an organised campsite for showers and washing. Yet somehow, at the end of each day, we always found ourselves within a fenced off compound, feeling more secure, if less adventurous. The mounting cost of this security was eating into our restricted budget.

"It's a bit expensive," I ventured, wondering whether this might be the day when we took the bull of adventure by the horns.

"It's TOO expensive," Mopsa agreed. "I saw a track leading down to an empty bay on the other side of the hill."

So we returned the way we had come and picked our way through the dusky light over the ruts and furrows of Mopsa's track. The bay was deserted, except for armies of mosquitoes at one end and a corrugated iron hut towards the middle. Furiously barking dogs shot from its door, followed by a young man. He looked at us suspiciously as I asked whether it would be alright for us to camp in the bay, but nodded his head in agreement, and busied himself with two emaciated cows who had appeared from behind the falling down shack.

Within an hour it was dark, no moon and the sky ablaze with stars. Dark figures emerged from the blackness – the Turk carrying a small child in his arms and accompanied by his younger pregnant wife and several mangy dogs. They greeted us solemnly and handed a bowl of still-warm milk from their cows to Mopsa. Though uninvited, still we were their guests, and this was the hospitality they could offer. Sitting on the bare ground they watched as Mopsa prepared our meal, refusing our offer to share with expressions we knew from our own reluctance to taste totally unknown foreign foods. With no language in common, still we sat together for some hours in flickering candlelight, the baby beating out a primitive rhythm with a discarded spoon and plate, and making us laugh with his antics. Eventually they left us, the young man giving stern instructions to one of the dogs, which settled down in the dust beside the tent to keep guard.

For the next ten days we slowly snaked east and south and east again towards the Syrian border. The countryside was as varied as the weather – sometimes harsh, often beautiful and always changing. Torrential rain would send us scuttling for cover, then within minutes the sky would be fresh and blue, the air sweet and the sun shining on the washed landscape. Leaving the ruined grandeur of Ephesus we headed inland to the calcified waterfalls at Pamukkale: industrial pollution from the nearby town of Denizli had tainted this once brilliant monument to nature, but even yellowing as it is, its impression of petrified storm clouds on the hillside is hard to forget.

Later, as evening came in, we sat in a roadside cafe, behind which we had pitched the tent. With us were an Australian couple with whom we had teamed up for a few days. They were living a cramped life in a small Fiat van which had taken them from the cold and barren lands of northern Norway to the southern extremities of Europe and into Asia Minor. We met them at the entrance to Ephesus, when we heard Kathy's strident tones above the shouts of the tour guides and trinket sellers:

"Well g'day. I saw your pommie plates and I just had to come over and check you out."

Now she and David sipped from glasses filled with local wine while Mopsa and I picked at a meagre meal of cheese and salad. The patron had invited us out of the rain for a drink with him and his morose friend.

We had met a few Turkish people who had a little English, and had asked them how they found life under a military government. Invariably they had shrugged noncommittally. They preferred democracy, they told us, but at least under the military most of the shootings had stopped and the buses ran regularly. The patron's friend was not so easily satisfied. Drinking heavily as he was from a bottle of raki, and only semi-coherent, still we were able to piece together the story of a teacher with left wing sympathies, removed from his post, arrested, interrogated in a none too gentle way and then put into a safe job behind a desk where his contact with impressionable youth would be cut off. The patron began to realise that he too was getting very drunk.

"Now we stop," he slurred. "If I drink, my wife she tell me I am no good Muslim. Soon she come from her brother. He arrive from Mecca. She will be very holy."

As we bedded down in the tent, we heard her return and her angry chidings. She didn't sound very holy to us.

From the narrow coastal strip around Antalya, we moved on through the wide fields of cotton, tobacco and tomatoes up into vivid green fir forests which covered the earthy red slopes of the hills of the western edges of the Tarsus mountains. Forest in turn gave way to sparse scrub and pastoralism became the dominant agricultural activity. Slowed by a road which had degenerated from narrow tar to pot-holed gravel, we passed large extended gypsy families who, with carts, donkeys, sheep, goats and cattle lead a nomadic life, settling themselves for a few days with makeshift tents of canvas and polythene beneath spreading trees. Small villages clustered in narrow valleys and on higher open ground solitary teenage shepherds stood sentinel. As protection from the extremes of weather, these young men placed stout sticks across their shoulders, draping billowing swathes of canvas over them. Thus they stood against the bleak landscape: an ungainly combination of scarecrow and grounded kite.

Looking down from grey craggy hills at the jumbled streets of Konya set in a pink desert, we attempted to match our tourist map of the city with the reality which lay ahead. Somewhere down there was the sports stadium and adjacent camp site. We followed Kathy and David in their dusty Fiat into a maze of twisting streets, past Mosques and through bazaars, getting more and more lost until rescued by a police patrol car which escorted us with lights flashing and siren blaring to our chosen site. The Selojuk Turks migrating from their homelands in Central Asia, had arrived on this vast upland plain in the eleventh century. They established a Sultanate in Konya which reached its cultural zenith during the thirteenth century, when the mystic poet Mevlana Celaleddin Rumi founded a sect of Islam whose most singular feature was a hypnotic whirling dance which symbolised the shedding of earthly ties and gave direct access to God. Accused of heresy, the sect was disbanded by Ataturk, but its legacy remains, drawing a steady stream of tourists to the city each December when for three days the modern dervishes are allowed to whirl unrestrained. Small high-hatted representations of dervishes in full whirl were proffered at every turn as we walked the bazaars, mosques and mausoleums. Then we turned to more mundane tasks of routine maintenance – replacing spokes, retorquing the recently rebuilt engine and temporarily stemming our first small seepage of oil – before bidding farewell to the Australians and continuing on towards the Syrian border. Landscape and domestic architecture changed as we went, simpler, squarer, flat-roofed buildings lined our way to Iskenderun where we spent our last night in Turkey comparing notes with Martin, a young German lad who had ridden from Munich on a push-bike. This was something which happened often – we would link up for a few days with some other overland traveller, but even now, three months and several thousand miles from home we still felt diffident about announcing our plans to encircle the globe. Between the two of us, however, there was no such dissembling, our course was set fair and certain.

After breakfasting on fresh hot bread and twisted coils of goat's milk cheese flavoured with cumin we rode to the border. Leaving Turkey was the work of a few minutes. There followed a stretch of no-mans-land where the road followed the barren sandy course of a narrow wadi, the sides littered with the rusting remains of foreign cars which had been dumped to avoid the payment of duty charges at either end. Then Syria, an array of ramshackle buildings of concrete and corrugated iron spread over about an acre and lines of trucks waiting along the approach road. At the barrier the uniformed border officials were clustered together and in their midst a blond head bobbed above the caps. With appreciative noises all were inspecting the fixing apparatus of Martin's panniers. One raised his head long enough to register our presence and then returned to animated discussion. As we felt we were in for a long wait, I went to the bank to exchange our Turkish money and travellers cheques. They would accept neither. A young Syrian in jeans and T-shirt came up to us and in simple English offered his help with negotiating the complexities of importing the bike and changing money.

"How much?" I asked.

"Good rate," he grinned. "Come."

I obediently handed over our passports and documents: we'd been advised by friends of the tangled web of bureaucracy we would meet at this border, and that our best move would be to hire the services of one of the hustlers to ease us through the process in hours instead of days. I rather enjoyed the next couple of hours, shuttling papers between various offices, returning between each procedure to have the forms countersigned by the customs chief. Here and there the boy slipped a little baksheesh, particularly when the impassive officials were faced with hoards of frustrated truck drivers, the air thick with their documents and demands. Our hustler seemed to be tolerated by, or even on friendly terms with, the officers and I was soon able to join Mopsa, now deep in conversation with Martin and the customs inspectors, who had moved on from Martin's packing system to ours. Martin set off ahead – we would meet him later in Aleppo.

Riding into Aleppo was the stressful experience that cities on first meeting nearly always were. A mistake in Mopsa's navigation took us deep into the souk – one of the oldest in the Middle East – where ten miles of cramped lanes meander, overflowing with traditional goods and foodstuffs alongside more modern merchandise. Bolts of lurid synthetics, cheaply produced audio equipment with its tinny musical result, brightly coloured plastic household implements were piled against sacks of nuts and spices and fruits and jumbled stacks of brass or copper trays and jugs and coffee pots. The traffic was as chaotic, so we moved gingerly through in search of the tourist office. Meeting Martin there we explored the city on foot, armed with a list of hotels supplied to us by the loquacious tourist officer. She had talked to us in so rapid a babble of French, moving from subject to subject so fast, that we had no idea where we were bound: only the name of the Baron Hotel had registered in our minds. Its brochure proudly boasted of the scores of the prominent and the notorious who had stayed: Roosevelts, Mountbattens, Lawrence, Ataturk and Agatha Christie among others, but despite the hotel's assurance that the water in its taps was both pure and drinkable, it had seen better days and was anyway beyond our pockets, so we booked instead into an airy if grubby room overlooking the souk, which we shared with Martin and his bicycle.

The highway south towards Damascus passes through the towns of Hama and Homs. Six months earlier an uprising by Muslim fundamentalists in the two towns had been ruthlessly suppressed and we were frequently stopped at roadblocks by civilian militia. Teenaged boys, automatic weapons casually slung over their shoulders, would study our documents with serious self-importance. Once they were satisfied that we were genuine tourists, then the Muslim code, born of a desert culture, would demand that they welcome the weary traveller, and we would be invited to join them for tea. We seldom refused – it would have been impolite, and perhaps even a little rash with the barrels of their guns pointing directly at us.

The narrow section of land in the western part of Syria, although geographically diverse, is reasonably well cultivated and it is here that the majority of the population live. To the east lies the vast expanse of the Syrian desert, stretching over two hundred and fifty miles towards the Iraqi border. From Homs a road runs eastward to the oasis town of Palmyra and on to Baghdad. The road follows a line of wells, served by the Kalamoun hills, which themselves dictated the line of the old trading routes which brought spices and other eastern wares from the Persian Gulf to the shores of the Mediterranean Sea. It was our first venture into the desert, albeit on well surfaced asphalt, when we turned east outside Homs. Riding out into the sandswept country was a release. Travel is tiring at the best of times. On a motorcycle it is often exhausting. In crowded towns or on the busy open road, it required our constant attention. It took time to adjust to each nation's different driving habits, working on the premise that if I drove like the locals they would know what to expect, and would react accordingly. It seemed to me that being overcautious could only cause confusion. In these Arab countries accidents are attributed to the will of Allah, an excuse for all sorts of reckless driving. Our initial reaction to this was one of incredulity – "My God," I thought, "these Arabs are crazy." But we had to accept there was a different attitude to life. Responsibility lay with a higher authority rather than with the individual who was bound to adhere to a set of prescribed rules. So "Inshallah" – "if God wills it" – is the normal response to any question concerned with the future.

The desert was flat and strewn with rocks, not the vast panorama of undulating sand we expected. In the distance the low hills were devoid of the scrubby vegetation which covered the lower land and upon which the Bedouin grazed their sheep. Bleached and monotonous during the day, the landscape took on an eerie beauty as the sun sank low on the horizon. The shadows cast by the hills, the bushes and the rocks, alternated with the brilliant patches of land still highlighted by the dying sun's last rays.

With the sunset behind us, the desert closed in as we entered a range of hills that had for many miles previous appeared as a faint amorphous smudge on a far distant horizon. At the crest of the pass we stopped, for ahead of us, framed by the jagged rock of the hillsides, lay the oasis town of Palmyra. Around the tightly packed forest of vivid green palm, pomegranate and olive stood the scattered remains of a Graeco-Roman city that had reached its zenith of power and prosperity under the legendary Queen Zenobia in the second century BC. Standing midway between the Euphrates and the sea ports of the Lebanon on the very extremities of the Roman Empire it had controlled, as a semi-independent state, the trade between the two hostile powers of the Romans and the Parthians. The first recorded English visitors were merchants who in the blistering summer heat of 1678 had undertaken the arduous and dangerous trek across the desert wastes. On arrival, a suspicious Emir, distrusting their claim to have travelled across such inhospitable land on the mere pretext of viewing the ruins, believed them to be Turkish spies and demanded a hefty ransom before sending them back to Aleppo, whence they had come. Two passing Arab boys gave us a more polite and endearing welcome – a handful of juniper berries.

We camped that night in the garden of the Queen Zenobia Hotel, a fading yellow pre-war building with wide verandahs situated on the edge of the town and right in amongst the ruins. The garden furniture was broken pieces of capital and pillar. On our second evening, after a fiery sky had provided a dramatic backdrop for the few remaining arches and pillars of the central colonnade, and while we were exploring the ruins by the reflected light of the newly installed floodlights which illuminated the solidly impressive Sanctuary of Bel, two men approached and invited us in to view one of the walled gardens of which they were custodians. We entered the garden through a small wooden door in the ancient stone and mud wall, and in the darkness stumbled nervously after our hosts. Although we had started our journey wary of invitations from strangers, mistrustful of their motives, by now we realised that this was how we could make the most of our experiences, and how we could learn something about the countries we visited. Occasionally one the men would gesture into the night air and mumble what I could only assume were the names of the various fruit trees of the garden which were unrecognisable in the pitchy black. We eventually came to a small hut and were ushered inside. A lamp was lit and tea prepared over a small, blackened and smelly kerosene stove. We sat on the mud floor and exchanged pleasantries in a polite and friendly way until one of the men who had been engaging Mopsa in conversation, extended the innocent game they were playing of naming objects about the room, items of clothing and then parts of the body in our respective languages, to those parts of the body considered taboo in both societies. He became somewhat overexcited, and while forcefully attempting to grope her started to shout "Bottim, bosem, bottim, bosem" in gasping breaths. Mopsa's protestations served only to further inflame him and it was not until I stood up and bellowed my indignation that the man came to his senses, retired a couple of feet from her and sat quietly, sheepishly beaming.

The sky was overcast as we left Palmyra the following morning, the colours of the sand and scrub muted. It was late in the afternoon when we left the desert and passing long lines of Russian-made missiles pointing west towards the Golan Heights and Israel arrived at the outskirts of the capital. Damascus boasted a tourist campsite at its northern edge and here we settled for the night. Martin and his bicycle were already there – he had cycled slowly down from Aleppo, taken in at night by locals and fed free of charge at roadside cafes along the way. In one corner of the site stood a London double decker bus. It belonged to Top Deck Travel and was full of Australians, New Zealanders and one or two English. All young people on an overland travel experience to India, they appeared to be stuck in the Middle East having been refused visas to cross Iran. The strains of being a large party in cramped conditions with plans awry were clearly taking their toll. While some of the women were complaining to us of drunkeness and inefficiency, we were invited into the bus for a beer. Tour leader and driver, along with two other chaps, were already extremely drunk and were focusing their attention on building a pyramid with the beer cans they had emptied – it was rising fast.

Riding into Damascus the following morning we fell into conversation at successive traffic lights with a smartly dressed and portly middle aged man driving a battered fifteen year old Mercedes.

"Come to my office," he called over the roar of traffic at the third set of lights and we followed. His office was in the centre of town, near the souk and the Omayadd Mosque. He was a lawyer, and as we sat in his large and opulent office drinking sharp, bitter-tasting coffee he rearranged the day's schedule.

"Today I will show you Damascus," he declared. "Where are you staying?" I explained.

"No, no. You must come and stay at my house." His manner was more commanding than inviting, as if a refusal on our part was unthinkable. When I thanked him for his kindness he beamed proudly and strutted around the office arranging things. Before we got too deeply embroiled in the day's plans, I explained that we had to change travellers cheques and send a telex to our friends in Amman, warning them of our imminent arrival.

"My boy will escort you to wherever you want to go." His boy was his fifteen year old son who helped in the office when not at school. During the next two days we were shown the city by our unexpected host, and were lavishly fed three times a day in restaurants and at home by his wife. The meals we were given in his home were enormous. We were expected to eat three times as much as they and to try every special Syrian dish placed before us. Breakfasts were as sumptuous as dinners. It was not surprising we suffered terribly, not only from extreme flatulence but also from severe diarrhoea and very sore and distended stomachs. It was a relief that on the third morning we finally bade farewell to this kind and overhospitable family, clutching our stomachs and as more pleasant souvenirs an inlaid marquety box, olives from the family grove and a jar of what we were told was macduse – aubergines stuffed with garlic, pine nuts and red peppers and marinated for several months in olive oil. They were marvellous, a favourite for Mopsa, and when bitten into, the smell of garlic filled the room.

Rather than take the main highway south to Jordan, we took a detour to Bosra where stood an almost perfectly preserved Roman theatre. The Arabs in the later years of the first millenium had turned the theatre into a fort, surrounding it with thick, fortified battlements which helped to preserve the interior. Around the edifice were cluttered the makeshift homes of the town's inhabitants which only served to accentuate the timeless grandeur of this theatre-cum-citadel. On the way we got lost amid the confusing collection of minor roads that snaked through the arid land and past several military installations. At a road block outside one of these we were asked into the guard's room and a burly army captain came in to question us. Sitting down opposite us he barked an order for tea to be brought then offered us both a Marlboro cigarette from the packet he had taken from his breast pocket. When we had taken one and thanked him, he threw the packet across the table at us.

"Filthy American cigarettes. I no smoke." He spat heavily onto the floor.

"You like Reagan?" he continued pointedly.

"No, not really." We both shook our heads. It was the right reply for he laughed heartily but followed it up with:

"Mrs Thatcher?"

More shaking heads. An image of the meeting between those first English merchants and the Sheik of Palmyra back in the seventeenth century sprang to mind, and I feared a wrong reply would result in our being arrested as spies. The captain, aware that he had a captured audience, then gave us a political lecture on how good the Russians were to Syria and how bad the Americans were in supporting the Israelis in their oppression of the Palestinian people. He declared that he was a good communist and didn't like God. I was surprised, and a little shocked by this remark which in England would have been a perfectly acceptable thing to say. Since entering Turkey we had been impressed by the high regard the Muslims had for their religion. To hear it damned in such a way seemed very out of character.

From Bosra we drove to the border town of Dera'a, arriving there after dark. The streets of the town were very rutted and while looking for a hotel we blew the main fuse. We had forgotten to pack any before leaving England.

"Improvise," suggested Mopsa. We did have some electrical wire and could easily bypass the fuse. Before I had time to find the wire in the depths of the sidecar, a man, forcing his way through the gathering crowd, asked if we had a problem. I explained. He nodded his head wisely and pulled out his cigarettes, offered us one, then tearing a piece of silver paper from the packet, wrapped it around the fuse and replaced it in its holder. Light. Disowning all credit he then took it upon himself to solve all our other problems, leading us down the long narrow entrance hall of an anonymous building he assured us was a hotel. At a desk a fat man with a shaved head and in grubby underwear gestured to us to share his dish of roasted chicken and flat bread. Mopsa declined and went off to sort out a room. We were joined by an old Palestinian Christian who drove lemons between Amman and Damascus. He looked much older than his declared sixty-two and had learnt his English while working for the British army before and during the war. He had a great liking for the English breakfast and for canteen tea.

The next morning he was waiting for us at the entrance of the hotel. He was to take us out for a good Arab breakfast. After a stroll around the local market, with frequent stops to talk to various stall holders we arrived at a butcher's shop. When seated at the only table fresh kebabs were prepared. They were delicious but we were put off by the pile of bloody goat's heads tossed into the corner by the door, next to the table at which we ate. "Different ways," we would reassure each other when faced with such things. "Different ways."

Our exit from Syria and entry into Jordan was less lengthy and complicated that the Turkey/Syria crossing. Within an hour we were heading south down the main highway to Amman. The change in the countryside was immediate as we climbed into the low rolling hills of northern Jordan. In spring flowers covered the hillsides with a blaze of colour. Now, at the end of October, the pastures were fading. An occasional forest covered the high ground, and the verdant fertility of the valleys below gave the landscape an air of relative fecundity after the desert.

A voluntary stop in Jerash and a fleeting panoramic view of the ruined Roman city there was followed by an involuntary one a few miles south. An accident involving three minibuses had created a scene of frantic bedlam. With much shouting and excitable gesture the crowd was attempting to pull an unfortunate driver from his cab. The arrival of an ambulance forestalled the decision to put our copious and as yet unused first-aid kit to good use. Leaving the scene I kept a close eye on the rash behaviour of the Jordanian drivers and despite three near misses, we survived unscathed arriving at the Royal Cultural Centre where we were to meet Nick James, a British ex-pat, who as Director of the Centre was responsible for opening the prestigious, newly-built theatre. It was a difficult task, he confided as he handed us a welcoming cup of proper English tea, for there was little traditional theatre in Jordan. A government bureaucracy which demanded that even the most minor expenditure (such as a petty cash float for providing tea and coffee to the office) was referred directly to the Minister of Culture himself and in some instances was even passed on to the Council of Ministers, had resulted in delay upon delay.

"Bukara," he groaned, "always Bukara."

Bukara, the Arabic for tomorrow, was a word we came to hear almost as often as Inshallah.

Our most pressing job in Amman was to obtain visas to cross Saudi Arabia. Our friends shook their heads and tutted in sympathy – our journey would surely stop there and then. The Saudis are very tricky they told us. If they can find even the smallest excuse to not give you a visa, they'll use it. So on our second day, armed with a letter of reference from the British Consul, and with instructions not to mention the motorcycle but to infer that we were travelling by car, we approached the Saudi Embassy. We duly presented our documents and filled in the requisite forms: where the type of vehicle was asked I wrote Triumph thankful there was a motorcar with the same name. The clerk perused

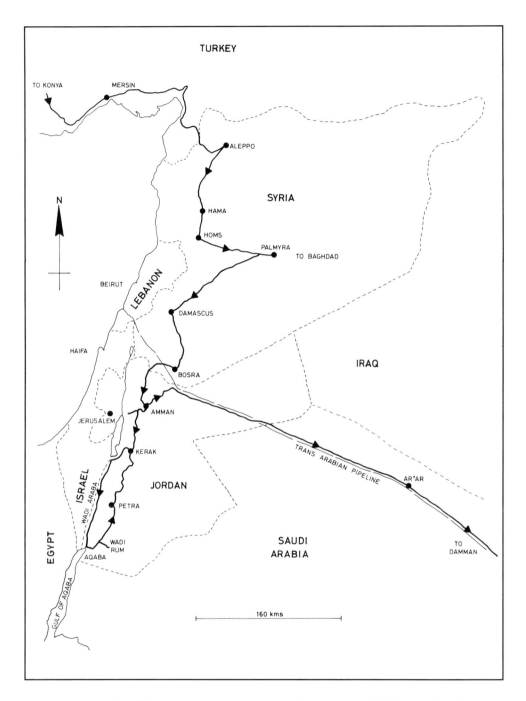

our papers and told us to return at one, when we would learn whether our applications could proceed. When we did return he told us, inevitably, to come back the next day.

"Will we have our visas then?" I asked.

He turned his attention back to his papers, then smiled up at us.

"Inshallah."

The following day our passports were ready, the visas stamped in. The implications of refusal would have involved all sorts of complexities, like returning to Turkey and trying to cross Iran, or continuing down to Egypt, the Sudan and Kenya and seeking a boat from there to India. We might have been forced into the ignominious and prohibitive expense of flying ourselves and the motorcycle over the problem area, straight to the Indian subcontinent. We celebrated that night at a dinner party with a group of British ex-pats. Conversation revolved around the problems of living in Jordan, with particular reference to a shortage of Ribena and the religious education of their children.

Marcel was a short Belgian motorcyclist. He had been riding from Europe on his Honda Silver Wing, en route to India, when the bike was stolen in Amman. We met him at the British Council, whose libraries we used wherever we could to read the British papers and the news from home. With his dreams of overland adventure seemingly at an end, he had publicised his loss in the *Jordan Times*, hoping to get the bike back. Two days later he received a telephone call from the Chief of Protocol at the Royal Palace: the Queen had read of his misfortune, she had brought the matter to the attention of the King. The authorities were doing everything within their power to track down the missing motorcycle. Marcel was delighted. Two further days elapsed before he received another call: the palace had been unable to trace the bike. This was not surprising given that it was certainly the only one of its kind in the country – no thief would have risked riding it or trying to sell it openly. However, the palace was very saddened and apologetic that such a blow should have befallen Marcel in their country, and wanted to make up for it. They hoped he would choose a bike from King Hussein's personal collection, or, if none of these suited, perhaps the local Honda dealer had something appropriate. From the dealer's entire stock – a Gold Wing and a 250cc Dream – Marcel chose the Gold Wing, which was presented to him with great ceremony by the King. As he prepared for his departure to the Gulf, Marcel was like a dog with two tails.

For ourselves we had more of Jordan to see before we followed him, and took the road to Kerak, passing through the dramatic Wadi Mujib on the way. From the high plateau above, we dropped a magnificent 3,600 feet to the valley floor before immediately climbing again on twisting road up the steep sides of this awesome gorge. In Kerak we obtained the necessary permits to go down into the warm, dusty, cushioned atmosphere of the Dead Sea Basin. The recently-completed paved highway, ostensibly for military use only as it paralleled close to the Israeli border, was built along the gentle gradient of the Wadi Araba which rose from minus 400 metres to sea level over a distance of 115 miles. In the sultry, compressed heat of mid-morning we began the imperceptible climb from the potash works near Kerak to Aqaba. This wide wadi, an extension of the African rift valley, was, at its northern end, cultivated in green patches which alternated with large expanses of salt lake. It later became dry and sandy with occasional scrubby bushes and a few wandering camel. The sides of the valley are a combination of sandstone and black basalt, crinkled by the dry tributary river beds that join it. There was no habitation in this extraordinary

The Grocer's shop in Kerak   *At Shobak Castle in Jordan*

landscape between the potash works and Aqaba apart from the Jordanian army who manned a string of check points at which we were required to stop and drink tea. At Aqaba we camped on what was locally known as Saudi beach – it was south of the town and close to the Saudi border. We spent several idyllic days swimming amongst the corals alongside the multicoloured and multivarious fish of the Red Sea. In the evening the sky blazed red over the Sinai Peninsula and we shared our campfire with some Danish travellers, a Swiss couple and a small contingent of the Jordanian army on a recreational weekend by the seaside. It was from them that we heard of Breznev's death.

Wadi Rum lies about 15 miles east of the desert highway which runs from Aqaba to Amman. The small castellated police fort in this wide desert valley is surrounded by a few makeshift buildings and a sprawling encampment of Bedu tents. T. E. Lawrence had, for a short time during the desert campaign against the Turks, made Wadi Rum his base of operations. Then many years later a film crew descended on this peaceful valley and provided lucrative, if short lived employment to the nomadic Bedu. This was followed by the small but steadily increasing stream of interested, and in some cases wealthy, tourists who were innocently commercialising this isolated outpost. The scenery is spectacular. The valley floor is over a mile wide and covered in soft fine sand. When the sun is low, but still strong, the towering sandstone cliffs that rise over 1500 feet above cast striking shadows which contrast with the brilliantly effusive glow of the golden sand.

We entered the valley in the late afternoon with a bitter desert wind chaffing our faces. That morning we had swum for the last time in the warm waters of a coral sea but now that we had left the coast we were experiencing the winter cold of the desert. Snow had fallen the previous night on the upland hills. We reported our presence in the valley at the fort and asked where we could camp. They suggested the camel enclosure as the most sheltered spot. The desert police were mainly recruited from the Bedu tribes and wore the traditional long Arab shirt but made from khaki. With their red and white Arab scarves, red braid and bandoliers they were impressive figures who still patrolled by camel but were now increasingly called upon to escort tourist parties on two-day treks into the desert. No doubt their pride was massaged by middle-aged American divorcees in search of romance and adventure.

Parking the motorcycle in the camel enclosure, we explored the encampment and valley on foot. Before long a young Arab boy beckoned us into one of the tents. We were sat down and two glasses of lukewarm black and sweetened tea were served along with some stale and gritty bread pulled from a grubby piece of sackcloth. Then a wizened old man shuffled in, clutching a battered single stringed oud. He sat down opposite us and began to play, humming a guttural tune intermittently punctuated by fierce bouts of coughing. After about twenty minutes the discomfort of the performance became too much and the old man spluttered to a stop and sat gazing at us intently. I mumbled our appreciation and we made moves to escape, whereupon the young boy who had disappeared for the duration of the impromptu piece of homely entertainment, reappeared. We must stay and sleep in their tent for the night he declared. Such insistent hospitality was difficult to refuse, but having made further excuses, the reason for it became apparent for as we turned to leave the old man thrust out his skeletal hand and from his lips hissed the dreaded word "baksheesh". One couldn't blame them for their opportunism. Their only luxuries were a kerosene lamp and a battered transistor radio. Their penury had led them to beg from the occasional passing tourist, whose conspicuous wealth clashed with their own more meagre existence.

With winter beginning to wrap itself around the high Jordanian plateau we rode on from Wadi Rum heading north on our elliptic tour of the country. We took the high road which followed the route of the ancient King's Highway rather than the fast modern road through the eastern desert along which both imported goods for Amman and military hardware for Iraq, landed at the port of Aqaba, sped dangerously. From the ruined Nabatean city of Petra, where temples and houses had been carved into the solid and soaring sandstone cliffs to the bulky mass of the crusader castle at Shobak and then on again to Kerak. It was exciting riding, some of the best since leaving England, as we rode through the rough pasture of the gently undulating plateau with occasional dramatic glimpses of the Dead Sea Basin, over 6000 feet below. The landscape was cut by deeply incised gorges down whose steep slopes we were delicately led. The ascents were slow and tortuous, the engine of the Triumph having barely enough power to push us, the sidecar, and its load, up to the other side.

We arrived back at Kerak as it was beginning to get dark and at the police station were told to camp on a rocky spot, strewn with rubbish, alongside the castle gate. It would have to do. While buying provisions at a nearby grocery store the owner, his friend and a young boy offered us tea and brought forth some stools and a charcoal burner around which we huddled for it was getting very cold outside. Through the monosyllabic conversation that followed they found out where we were planning to sleep that night. This offended them greatly, and they immediately began to make alternative arrangements. We would sleep in an empty shop nearby. No sooner was this decided when a young, casually dressed middle-class Arab came in to buy cigarettes. He spoke good English and worked as an architectural engineer in the town. He in turn was greatly offended to hear that we planned to spend the night in a deserted shop and invited us to spend the night with him and his recently-wed wife. The shopkeeper thought this a splendid idea and after much vigorous handshaking we followed our host to his mother-in-law's house where in the traditionally draped and vaulted dwelling we were given a traditional greeting of sweet cardamom coffee. Into a small cup was poured a mouthful of coffee. This we drank and then it was refilled twice more. After the third mouthful we were told to gently waggle the empty cup to express our appreciation and the coffee was then whisked away and the tea brought in. The engineer's wife and her younger three sisters, with shy giggling, questioned us on our relationship and life in England. Mopsa tried to explain to them in simplified English my work as a theatre stage manager.

"Ah! Disco!" one of them exclaimed and the latest Jordanian disco hit was found and placed on their turntable. They insisted we show them how the British danced. So to the beat of "Pop Music" and still clad in our waxed cotton Barbours, our muddy riding boots on our feet, we hopped embarrassedly to an appreciative and clapping audience.

The following night we camped on a windy crag near the summit of Mount Nebo overlooking, as Moses had, the promised land, the lights of Jericho twinkling from across the wide depression of the Dead Sea Basin. In the morning a dusty track led us to a small isolated church whose floor displayed an intricate early Christian mosaic of great beauty. The old, stooping Bedu woman who looked after the church, invited us into her stone-built cottage opposite to shelter from the cold and gusty wind. We shared her lunch, a soggy mix of bread, bean, cheese and oil for she had no teeth. Despite knowing no more than a dozen words of each other's language we stayed for more than three hours. With her husband long dead, her only son off fighting the war in Iraq and her five daughters married and settled in Saudi, she lived a lonely life, with the small herd of goats she kept as her only constant companions. With so few common words a misinterpretation became inevitable. She became convinced that Mopsa was pregnant and after taking her into the bedroom applied a thick paste of henna to her hands, wrapping each one in polythene before binding them tightly at the wrist, in time-honoured celebration of the happy event. She then presented Mopsa with a thick woolly sheepskin for the saddle of the motorcycle indicating that it was for her comfort during our long ride home. When we finally left, Mopsa's hands were still wrapped in polythene and when we arrived in Madaba her first priority was to find a tap. It was two months before the stains began to fade.

We delayed our departure from Amman by a further ten days and I spent several of them helping Nick to prepare the cultural centre for its inaugural concert. Then on a piece of waste ground nearby, that had through the traveller's word of mouth become the unofficial campsite in Amman, I gave the bike a thorough service. After six and a half thousand miles of travel I felt we had adjusted well to our new life. Our days on the road had a natural rhythm now, and were uncomplicated by fears or apprehensions as to what lay ahead. We had learnt to be open to passing fancy, to take advantage of the unexpected and above all to accept the hospitality and interest that, on a daily basis, always came our way. The Danes we had met in Aqaba had already set up camp when I arrived to service the bike. Four men living, eating, sleeping and travelling in the cramped conditions of a Ford Transit van. We might not have the few extra luxuries afforded by a van but we did have the infinite sense of space that only a motorcycle, amongst motorised vehicles, could bring.

We left Amman on Saturday, 27th November, and took the paved highway to the oasis at Asraq and then on to the Saudi border. The road was a disaster. One side of it had been completely dug up by the heavily-loaded transport trucks carrying materials and equipment to Saudi Arabia. The right-hand lane of the carriageway was strewn with broken pieces of torn up pavement and gaping holes would suddenly loom up at us. I took to riding on the wrong side of the road to spare both us and the bike from unnecessary damage, only swerving back onto the right side in the face of oncoming traffic. We arrived at the border very tired and bruised to pitch our tent next to the customs hut.

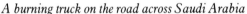

A burning truck on the road across Saudi Arabia

Saudi Arabia is one of the driest countries in the world. The average annual rainfall is around 20 centimetres but most of this falls in the more fertile south west. In summer the temperatures in the desert rise to between 45 and 50 degrees centigrade, sometimes higher, but during the winter nights they will often fall well below freezing. In the cold, misty morning air of 28th November we carefully packed our belongings into the sidecar and drove a few metres to the customs and immigration buildings. Mopsa, in deference to the strict Islamic codes of dress and behaviour for women, sat demurely on the motorcycle, her head covered and wearing her full Barbour riding suit over the bottom half of which she had slipped a long skirt to hide the outline of her legs, while I saw to the formalities of entering the country. Our careful packing of that morning had been unnecessary for the customs officer was determined to search every inch of the sidecar for the illicit alcohol, pornography or packets of bacon he thought might be hidden there. He carefully opened the individually packaged courses of antibiotics to taste the tablets inside, then sniffed with the rolling eyes of a bloodhound the contents of our jerry can and shuffled through the various papers and documents we had carefully filed for future use. It was the first time since leaving England that the contents of the sidecar had been spread out before us and I was amazed at how much we were actually carrying. It was almost an hour before we were repacked and ready for the 1100 mile crossing of Saudi Arabia for which we had been allowed just 72 hours.

The next three days passed in an unending haze of greyish, rocky desert through which the road, and the Trans-Arabian oil pipeline it followed, cut. The route the road and pipeline took was no doubt decided when a surveyor had sat down with pencil and ruler before a map of Saudi Arabia and drawn a straight line from Damman to Turayf across 800 miles of inhospitable desert. The road itself was well surfaced and served by small townships every 80 miles or so. On our right lay the pipeline, often half buried in drifting sand, behind which Mopsa felt obliged to scuttle whenever we stopped to relieve ourselves and to stretch our aching limbs. The three days were little more than an endurance test. On the first day we covered no more than 250 miles, the morning slowed by frequent police checks. We had been advised, and indeed preferred, not to travel at night. Colliding with a wandering camel at 60 mph in the dark would have been highly undesirable. Mopsa was unable to help with the driving for it was an activity forbidden to women in Saudi Arabia. On the second day I managed only 300 miles. The long hours were spent keeping ourselves awake by counting the wrecked cars by the side of the road. They occurred, without fail, at a rate of one per kilometre. Some were almost brand new, their red glossy wings announcing their location as they twinkled in the bright sunlight. Others had been there longer, mere skeletons, from which all recyclable parts had been taken, lying as scarred and sandblown relics of someone's former pride and joy.

The traffic consisted mainly of large trucks heading to and from the Gulf. On this second day we passed two that had been involved in an accident. Plumes of thick black smoke billowed out from them obscuring the road ahead. Sometimes large air-conditioned American Cadillacs sped by, many driven by young boys whose heads were barely visible as they peeped over the dash boards. Occasionally, one of these would veer off into the desert towards an indistinct group of tents on the horizon. Straggling herds of camel and sheep would every hour or so crowd the flattened landscape. Startling mirages would suddenly appear to fuse the earth and sky in a shimmering haze. The early mornings were bitter cold and a freezing mist hung low to the ground waiting for the sun to build up enough strength to burn it away.

We had stopped at around eleven to warm ourselves in the sun when a Toyota Landcruiser roared to a stop and a European jumped out.

"Well, its unusual to see a motorcycle travelling this road" he exclaimed as an introduction. He was British and worked as a technician servicing a string of aerodromes that followed the pipeline. "If you fancy a nice cup of tea and some egg and chips just continue on for another 100 miles and you'll arrive at Rafha. On the left you'll see the airport. Pull in and ask for Brian. He'll look after you."

On the third day we covered over five hundred miles. The road was as endless as the day. As straight as a die until we got to Damman, it gave the impression that we were continually riding down a gentle incline. We cruised at around sixty miles an hour, a little fast for optimum fuel consumption but with petrol on sale at the heavily subsidised price of four pence a litre, we didn't need to consider economies. Bottled water per litre, however, was five times the price. We skirted Damman as it was getting dark, and got lost in a maze of minor roads that linked the oil refineries, whose grotesque illuminations and spurting funnels of flame grazed the cold, dry evening sky. Finally, after 14 hours of continuous riding, broken only by fuel stops, I pulled off the road behind some sand dunes some 50 miles from the Qatari border. I was cold, exhausted, unco-ordinated and incapable of applying myself to even the simplest of tasks and it was left to Mopsa to set up the tent and to brew the sweet nectar that was our end-of-the-day cup of tea, while I wandered about in my dazed state. It was bitter cold that night but the next morning as we approached the Qatari border post at Salwah the moderating influence of the warm Arabian Gulf took effect and we peeled off some of the many layers of clothing that had kept us from freezing through the night. We passed through the Saudi immigration post with an hour to spare.

Over the three days a slight wobble had developed in the steering of the outfit. I assumed that the sidecar fixing clamps had slipped on that terrible road across northern Jordan and the outfit was no longer correctly aligned. The geometry of some motorcycle combinations, however precisely aligned, can still result in the handlebars wobbling on acceleration or deceleration, usually between 20 and 30 mph. To counteract this irritating tendency a steering damper can be fitted. A more expensive alternative is to replace the telescopic front end with leading link forks, which are considerably stronger, more rigid and change the trail geometry, all of which help with wobble. We had wisely invested in a set of Hedingham leading link forks before leaving England and I found that even with the increased drag when the sidecar was fully loaded, the outfit remained easy to steer and was devoid of those dreaded handlebar shakes.

Now after three days of hard, exhaustive riding with the added tension of battling with the steering, I had developed a racking pain in my right shoulder which subsided into a dull ache only when I climbed off the bike and by morning had all but disappeared only to return after an hour or two of riding. Under normal circumstances I would have stopped to investigate the cause and to readjust the sidecar mounts but with only limited time to complete our journey across Saudi I struggled on, cursing the bike, the desert, the road and the country.

The morning after our arrival in Qatar both Mopsa and I were working on the outfit, which we now called Tommy. I was a little sceptical at first over the effect of attributing human characteristics to the Triumph but as our journey progressed and as our dependency on the motorcycle grew, it became increasingly difficult not to regard it as the third character of the party. In a sense the tenacity of its lineage, in the face of a rapidly accelerating technology which the Japanese motorcycle industry were so ably exploiting, which dated back to the glorious years of British motorcycling in the 1930s, became an extension of our own identities in the constantly changing and often confusing world of our journey. We felt the need, and were often forced, to assume a role of unofficial and roving ambassadors for our country, to be representative of ordinary British people, to show to the people we met that there was more to Britain than the reflective glory and misdeeds of past colonialism, the Queen and Margaret Thatcher. This exaggerated sense of our own self-importance would only later be slowly stripped away by the experiences of travel and by the distancing from home. The Triumph was included in this process. At first I would strongly defend our choice of bike to the sceptical European, Australian and North Americans we met who expected us to be disillusioned by constant breakdown. Reliability and the minimum of maintenance were their touchstones and it was only the Japanese and German manufacturers who could provide that. Quirky and idiosyncratic bikes that required time and attention were for the ignorant or the eccentric. We were not interested in giving the Triumph some grand trans-world road test (that had already been done) and our choice of a traditionally-designed British bike over a more modern machine were for reasons of personal expediency and interest. The means by which we travelled I found extremely satisfying and I enjoyed giving the bike the attention it demanded because its fortune and destiny was intricately linked with ours. Without the motorcycle we lacked the impetus and structure around which our plans had been built.

While I was changing the rear tyre Mopsa was inspecting the sidecar fixing clamps to see if they had slipped.

"Hey. Is this a fault in the tubing or a crack?" she asked as I battled to get the new tyre onto the rim without pinching the inner tube.

"Almost certainly a fault in the tubing", I replied and continued to concentrate on the job in hand. But she was not to be put off. I left the rear wheel and walked over to where she was squatting at the front of the bike. She pointed to one of the tubes of the duplex frame just underneath the steering head,

Ken and Maxine Jones with their Honda CBX in Doha, Qatar

directly above one of the sidecar fixing clamps. I pushed the handlebars to the left and watched in horror as a scratch in the paintwork opened up. The break was not quite complete but it would have taken only a few more miles for the frame to have split.

Qatar is an extraordinary state, sticking out into the Arabian Gulf like a sore and desiccated thumb. An arid and sandy peninsula whose only permanent settlements before the discovery of oil had been a handful of fishing communities on the coast. In a few short years it had become one of the richest states per capita in the world and the indiginous Wahibi Arabs were now heavily outnumbered through a massive influx of foreign workers. I had flown into the country earlier in the year on a British Council theatre tour and we had been luxuriously housed as guests of the State in the five star Gulf Hotel. It was with some satisfaction that on my second visit I drove in by motorcycle, dusty and windblown from a drive through the desert, for few of the foreigners who worked there could boast that. One British couple who could were Ken and Maxine. I had met them on my previous visit and we now stayed with them in the capital, Doha. They rode from England on Ken's 1000 cc Honda CBX in only eleven days. Their more direct route had involved over 4500 miles – an average of more than 400 a day. I didn't envy them their feat of endurance, nor the blurred landscapes as they sped south but I would have appreciated seeing the startled faces of the Saudi police as they tore past at over 130 mph. We had taken a more leisurely and scenic route, nearly twice the mileage, and arrived in Qatar 103 days after leaving England.

Through Ken we met Ian, a Scottish mechanic who managed a workshop on the outskirts of the city, and we took him the wounded Triumph. One of his

49

Immigrant workers in Qatar

Pakistani welders wrapped a metal sleeve around the crack and crudely strenghtened the frame with braces between the downtubes. We spent a further frustrating and inactive two weeks attempting and ultimately failing to obtain in reasonable time visas for travelling into Oman. Within two days we had exhausted Doha's limited sights. The city's rapid development had left it a half completed building site and it was only the more prestigous and monumental pieces of modern American-influenced architecture which brought life to an otherwise very dull landscape. Beyond the city limits there was nothing but sand. We idled away the restless hours reading paperback novels, old copies of *Time* and *Newsweek* and watching videos. Expatriate life in Qatar revolved around the swapping of private videos, the illegal selling of one's liquor allowance to the native Qataris and in avoiding the Arab drivers who raced around Doha with an abandon that bordered on insanity. At the main junctions on the approach roads to the city the more enterprising of the garage owners had placed on permanent standby pick-up trucks which casually laid in wait for the accident that would invariably be only a few minutes away. Sidecars were unknown in Qatar and it was with some surprise that a driver, approaching traffic lights at which we had already stopped and having decided to pull up alongside us, found his way obstructed. He grinned an apology when he realised that he had inadvertently pushed us out past the lights and almost into the flow of traffic. On 18th December when we left Qatar for the United Arab Emirates the expatriate community were mumbling their objections to an edict which banned public celebrations of Christmas. An announcement in the *Gulf Times* read "Qatar yesterday banned Christmas and New Year celebrations in hotels, clubs and other public places. A decree issued by the Ministry of Information said that the celebrations were not in line with Moslem traditions and customs."

We spent a month in the UAE. It was the end of a road that had brought us all the way from the Belgian coast, and now we had to cross to the Indian sub-continent. It was more through luck than design, and through a chance encounter with some motorcycling ex-patriates, that in Dubai we found ourselves in the offices of the British shipping company OCL. Robert Wood, the Manager and a British biking enthusiast himself, thought it a splendid and very British thing we were doing on our British motorcycle and pledged his help. A week and several telexes later it was all arranged. They would ship us and the Triumph, free of charge, on the next available sailing to Karachi in Pakistan.

Our time in the Emirates was divided between the two main cities of Abu Dhabi and Dubai and in exploring the few roads that ran through the interior and across to the Batinah coast. At the border post between Qatar and the UAE we were sharing a hastily-prepared meal with two Jordanian truck drivers. The more portly of the two had proudly declared, with some amusement, that he was the "Madame" of the pair – it was his responsibility, among other things, to cook. As we sat with them in the warm sun a small, dusty Honda motorcycle with British plates drew up. Aboard was an equally dusty looking young

The end of the Middle Eastern road – near the Straights of Hormuz

Englishman named Will, who, after two abortive attempts, had finally left London six weeks previously, also on his way overland to Australia. His choice of bike, an eight year old 250 cc Honda, complete with rattles, oil leaks and suspect cam-chain tensioners, eventually got him to Dacca in Bangladesh where he sold it to a dealer for more than he had originally paid for it. Together we travelled on to Dubai and he obtained passage on an Iranian ship that sailed via Banda Abbas to Karachi, arriving there several weeks after us. Our first Christmas away from home was spent in Abu Dhabi where a friend of Mopsa's from Cambridge was the Banqueting Manager at the Abu Dhabi Hilton. Tony treated us to a sumptuous lunchtime meal, including turkey and Christmas pudding which we walked off along the Corniche, singing carols at the tops of our voices (much to the astonishment of passing Arabs) and gulping in the fresh sea air which was tinged by the fishy aroma of the fertiliser that the city authorities liberally spread on the grass, the flower beds and around the fledgling trees which lined the recently-built promenade. These patches of natural colour that daubed an otherwise very faded city canvas required the constant provision of gallon upon gallon of desalinated water in order to survive. In Abu Dhabi, as in other Arab oil-rich states, the gasoline that polluted the crowded and congested cities of North America, Europe and the Third World, was helping to create Garden Cities among desert wastes.

Chapter Four

The Indian Sub-Continent

ONCE WE had passed the perimeter fence that surrounds the grey looming mass of Pakistan's one operational nuclear power station, the road abruptly changed from smooth pavement to dry rutted earth. We followed the road for several more miles and stopped at a point where the tracks split. Ahead the way was indistinct and to our right several tracks veered off into the flat rocky interior. There was little vegetation on this barren coastline which is named Paradise Point. Two youths were each leading a camel up the steep path to our left from a small enclosed bay. It was to them that I turned.

"Do you know where I can find Ali?" I shouted. They shrugged. "Ali and his American wife Jan?" This time they smiled and nodded. The younger of the two left his camel and seating himself on top of the sidecar gestured inland. He directed us to the edge of a village of small, flat-roofed, breeze-block houses. At the first of these buildings, which unlike the others faced towards the sea, our young guide motioned us to a stop. To the old man who sat cross-legged on the wooden verandah tying knots in a bundle of net he explained our needs. The old man was Ali's father and although Ali had gone with his brother into Karachi, he made us welcome – soon tea was brought. We sat with him, in silence, as the sun set and darkness gathered around.

★   ★   ★

Three days previously we had sailed into Karachi port aboard the merchant vessel *Strathfife*. At around ten o'clock I had staggered up on deck with a blinding hangover, the result of a long session in the officers' bar the previous evening. After a large jug of black coffee, Mopsa and I, with the agent's representative, began the long, long process of importing the motorcycle into Pakistan. The bureaucratic procedures were based upon those that had been set up by the British before independence and were by now woefully inadequate for both the massive increase in trade and the temperament of the people. We were entering the country as discharged crew members, having been taken on board not as passengers but as supernumeraries. Our own discharge papers along with the temporary importation documents for the bike had to completed in triplicate and then countersigned by officials whose offices were either at the port or several miles away at the main customs building in the centre of Karachi. The agent helping us formed the opinion that we had more money than time and in line with established practice slipped a little baksheesh to the clerks to ensure that our papers found their way to the top of any pile. It still took us all that day and the greater part of the next before we were finally cleared and rode our motorcycle out through the port gates and into the chaotic streets. There we vied for road space with the rest of the teeming city, with the camel, the donkey and the human-drawn carts, with the brightly painted and tin-plated buses and trucks, with the small Honda motorcycles, with the three-wheeled auto-rickshaws, with the grossly overloaded delivery bicycles, and with the cars and the people. All these seemed totally ignorant of accepted traffic codes and were intent on taking the most direct line across the wide streets, risking, but somehow always miraculously avoiding, damage to life and limb. Our time in the Middle East had made me used to such traffic and I coped pretty well, but Mopsa was loathe even to attempt to drive the outfit under these conditions. She had increasingly, since leaving Europe, felt happier on the back of the bike, and from now on, except in emergencies, there she stayed. My own shoulder muscles had by now developed sufficiently to handle the heavy outfit with reasonable quickness and surety when the roads got rough but a full day's ride was always exhausting. The couple of times when Mopsa did take over in Pakistan, the effect was extraordinary. A woman on the back of a bike was perfectly acceptable in this Muslim country but one actually driving a motorcycle and sidecar was something quite different. Whole busloads would erupt and drivers would hang their heads out of their windows to stare in incredulity as we passed by. On being taken to see the sister of a motorcycling student who had picked us up in Bahawalpur, Mopsa was told that she must be very clever to be able to ride a motorcycle. "But your brother rides a motorcycle", was her reply. "Is he so very clever?" The young girl had to admit he was not. A small seed in the cause of emancipation had perhaps been sown.

Having been rudely dumped from the relative luxury of a fully-equipped European merchant ship into the swirling mass of Pakistan's largest city, we sought out our one tenuous contact. Mopsa's sister had known Jan, who had married Ali who lived at Paradise Point. It was with surprising ease that we found ourselves at Ali's father's house awaiting his return. As we were laying out our sleeping bags on the verandah he finally returned, but it was not until the following morning over a breakfast of fried chicken and chapati that we pieced together the fabric of their lives. Ali had recently returned from the States, where he had lived for five years with Jan and their two daughters, working with dolphins in a Californian aqua park. He had returned to Paradise Point to spend some time with his family, fishing, diving for lobster – leading the quiet life. He was very laid back and with a hint of a West Coast drawl would address us as "you guys". His father Haji Ali was an expert fisherman and their family, which spread for some miles along the coast, had held fishing rights here for over two hundred years. With some pride Haji Ali showed us letters of introduction and recommendation along with some very faded newspaper cuttings dated 1945 and 1947 respectively. He had been sent by the Pakistani Government to teach nylon net making and fishing techniques to the fishermen of Ceylon. Not to be outdone, his son brought out a clipping detailing the time when he saved the lives of two people who had been washed out to sea. We stayed for two further days, sleeping in an empty house which was only used during the main fishing season, perched above the crumbling sandstone cliffs facing the western sky. The sunsets were magnificent and by the time we left we were more appreciative of the name Paradise Point.

There was only one crossing from Pakistan to India by road, via the main highway from Lahore to Delhi which is still known, as it was when the British ruled India, as the Grand Trunk Road. It lies in the north of the country and it was there that we had necessarily to ride. Pakistani immigration had given us three months but the motorcycle's temporary importation was limited to one. We therefore had a time limit around which to organise. We decided to ride up the Indus valley as far as Multan before branching off to Lahore and then to continue north to the Swat Valley in the foothills of the Hindu Kush mountain range, before returning to the Grand Trunk Road and into India. It was not too difficult to acclimatise to Pakistan – after all the great majority of Pakistanis practiced the same religion as the people of the Middle East. It was the same call to prayer that rang out daily at the appointed hours. There were, however, deep divisions in Pakistan, and not just between rich and poor. The people of the fertile Sind province in the south, through which we first rode, were resentful of the Punjabis. The late President Bhutto had come from the Sind and he had been overthrown by General Zia, and then hung for treason. The Sindis with whom we became acquainted would express grave concern when we told them where we were venturing. "Oh, Mr. Richard you must be very careful in the Punjab – all are bandits and thieves up there."

The road north from Karachi was hardly less busy than the city itself. Between the open stretches that ran through the green and highly irrigated corn and rice fields of the river basin were bustling towns full of the decorated trucks and the tin-plated buses that disgorged their travelling hoardes into the tea houses, which served a sweet and milky tea, very different to what we had become accustomed to in the Middle East. Whenever we stopped outside a teahouse or in front of one of the towns' hotels we were soon surrounded by an inquisitive crowd, mainly youths or men with an idle hour or two. From out of this crowd invariably came an invitation to drink chai or an offer of help. The men who asked were middle class or professional men, and English was an essential second language. On our first day out from Karachi it was Mr. Abassi, the Irrigation Engineer for the area around Thatta, who invited us to stay at the Irrigation Department's rest house on the edge of Haleji lake. On our second evening, at Dadu, two Hindu students took us to the government rest house and arranged for food to be brought to our rooms. On the third day at Larkana we were befriended by Inayatullah, who introduced himself as the only university-

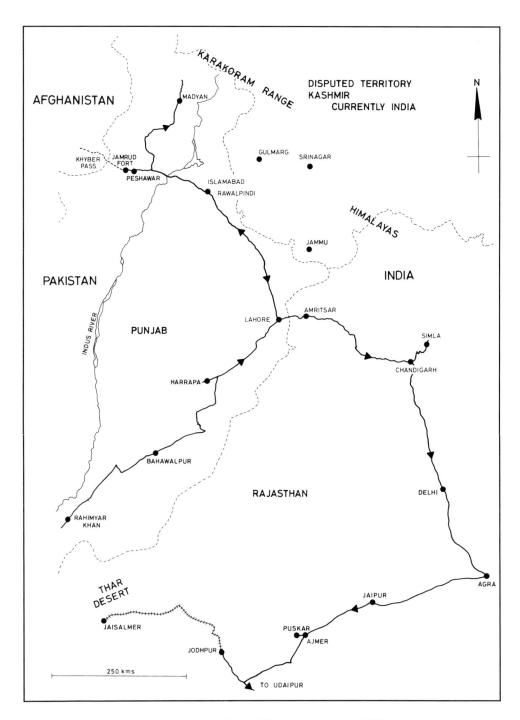

trained motorcyle mechanic in the Sind. He owned a small Honda workshop and was delighted with the colour of our Triumph. He was slowly restoring his own small, white Triumph Tiger Cub. Having arranged a hotel for us, the manager of which insisted that we ride the outfit up some old planks placed over the front steps into the courtyard where it would be safe from possible thieves, Inayatullah took us on a grand tour to show us off to his friends and family, with a proud air of "look what I've just found". Tradition dictated that the women lived a separated life, many were in purdah and wore the burka, a large voluminous all over covering with a small fabric lattice through which they peeped. When taken to a family's house we were sat down and talked to and fed by the men in a separate room set aside for just such a purpose. Mopsa, as a western woman, was treated very much as an honorary man, but would also be taken to meet the women of the household, an invitation that was never extended to me. On this ocassion the women made her up with Kohl and lipstick in traditional Sind fashion, adorned her with earings, necklaces and a shawl and then they all lined up to have a photograph taken by Inayatullah with our camera. It was only much later, when the film had been developed, that I could see the whole family. The Bhutto family lived near Larkana and it seemed a highly politicised town – twice while out walking with Inayatullah we were approached by young Sind radicals, who openly lectured us on the need for a separate Sind state.

We crossed the Indus at Sukkar and then entered the Punjab. Here the road north runs between the river and the western edge of the Thar desert. Where the irrigation canals did not flow the landscape was dry and arid. On our fourth night we stopped at Rahimyarkhan. We arrived after dark and were taken by a student on a small motorcycle to a catholic mission. It was run by four fathers of The Holy Ghost and the Immaculate Virgin order, two of whom were Irish, one English, and one Pakistani. The westerners had taken to wearing Pakistani clothes – baggy trousers, long cotton shirt, sleeveless woollen jumper and a blanket to wrap around them when it was cold. The Pakistani priest, on the

Mopsa with a family group of Sindi women in Larkana, Pakistan

other hand, determinedly stuck to western fashion. Together they served the pastoral needs of the eight hundred very poor Christian families in the area. The Christians came mainly from the lowest classes, and many were deeply in debt to their Muslim landlords who were exerting pressure on them to convert to Islam.

"Their lives would probably be better if they did convert," one of the young priests told us, "but we can hardly encourage them, can we?"

Our fifth night was passed on the bare floor of a small room attached to a petrol station which was looked after by a round, jolly, economics student, whose family owned a string of six stations around Bahawalpur. Here again we were rushed around town on a series of visits, we on the outfit and he, with two college friends, on a small Honda step-thru. We planned to stay at the government rest house at Harappa on our final night before reaching Lahore. Despite it being empty, the caretaker was adamant that we could not stay, since we hadn't booked. He suggested the railway station. There the Assistant Station Master was only too delighted to have our company. Only two trains stopped each day at the small, cream-coloured station. The bike was brought onto the platform, and after unlocking the tall double doors of the Ladies Upper Class Waiting Room, he ushered us in and showed us our room for the night. There were only two pieces of furniture, a long heavy wooden bench and an old wicker lounge chair. Both these and the floor were covered in a thick layer of dust – it seemed the room hadn't been used in years. During the evening we sat with the Assistant Station Master, huddled around a single electric ring which took hours to warm both us and a pan of tea, in the station office. The room was filled with ancient equipment, outdated but still functioning, made of mahogany and brass and Bakelite, which had been installed by the British in the early part of the century.

We arrived in Lahore battered and aching, our faces covered in a thick layer of dust and diesel emissions. The last hundred miles of road was under repair, which meant long sections had been dug up, to be prepared for resurfacing. It had taken us six hours to cover the distance. As we had three weeks before we needed to cross into India, we continued north on the Grand Trunk Road to Peshawar, close to the border with Afghanistan. It was a little disconcerting now we were on the Indian sub-continent – if we put our minds to it we could be in Madras within three weeks, boarding a boat to Penang in Malaysia. Although we had taken the journey through Europe and the Middle East quite slowly, we had always had the next country firmly within view and getting through to India had been the main aim. Our route had been dictated by circumstance. Now we could choose. We had a huge and extraordinarily diverse country to explore with an almost infinite choice of roads and directions in which to go.

The bazaar in Peshawar was Dickensian in aspect. The narrow, muddied streets were made narrower by the goods that piled out of the cramped stalls and muddier by the creaking carts loaded with carcasses on top of which sat cadaverous men. Smoke from the fires, which heated great vats of steaming milk or sizzled small fried sweetmeats, hung heavy in the air. Men crouched over large pieces of brass, beating them into shape with a continual clatter. The variety of goods ranged from the more mundane foodstuffs, blankets, skinned sheeps heads, fur hats and spices to parakeets, bandoliers, guns, samovars and sequins. As we walked the streets, weaving between the carts, bicycles and scooters we were followed by the continual cries of "Com'on" and "hello" from the men seated at their stalls. We had come to Peshawar, at the far edge of the North West Frontier province, to try and ride up the Khyber Pass to the Afghan border. To do this we needed a permit from the Political Agent's office but due to recent tensions in the semi-autonomous tribal area that bordered Afghanistan, none were being issued. The rumour was that several heroin factories had recently been raided and the Pathans of the area, who almost to a man carried a gun, were unhappy with this interference by central government. The next day we tried to reach the pass without a permit and after talking our way through the first checkpoint arrived at the large arch which marks the entrance to the pass. From here, however, our way was firmly barred and we had to make do with the view of the road that snaked its way up into the rocky mountains. Before returning to Lahore we rode into the Swat valley as far as Madyan and spent several days in the high mountain air. It was mid-February and the roads that led still higher into the Hindu Kush and Karakoram ranges were firmly blocked with snow. Returning eastwards we stopped at the American Express office in Islamabad to change money. As befitted an office that was sited in the administrative capital of the country, it was plush and modern, a symbol of the efficiency of international travel and exchange. As I waited in line, three elderly

Mopsa with armed Pathans at the entrance to the Khyber Pass

The road into the Kashmir Valley, India

The Khan family – men and children – our hosts in Madyan, North Pakistan

men from the hills were squatting on the floor in a circle. Between them lay an ink pad and a pile of travellers cheques and one of them was methodically thumb-printing each cheque with slow meticulous actions. The money to buy the cheques would have been collected from among their families and their village, and they were about to embark on the one great journey of their lives – to Mecca, for the Haj.

★　★　★

"But Mr English, you are trying to import twenty rolls and I am telling you that only five can be allowed." It was the customs officer at the Indian border post speaking. He had found the camera films I had packed at the very bottom of the sidecar. After scribbling some calculations on a notepad he continued.

"You must pay one hundred pounds sterling."

I was astonished. "But that is more than they originally cost. I can't pay that. You'll have to confiscate them."

The officer shifted uncomfortably in his seat. He had called me in to his office, out of earshot, to see to this delicate matter. He scribbled some more.

"The lowest duty, Mr English, is forty pounds sterling."

"It's still too much, I'm afraid. I can't afford to pay. You can have them."

He coughed nervously. "I shall have to see my superior officer about this matter." He got up and walked to the door, then changed his mind. "I am taking just these two films," he said as he placed them in his drawer. "The rest you can have but no-one must be knowing." Outside his office Mopsa was still repacking the box. On the road a long line of porters carried huge bales and sacks and were overloading a high-sided truck. Commercial vehicles were not allowed across the border. Relations between India and Pakistan had been strained since partition and the territorial disputes over Kashmir and the Rann of Kutch in the middle sixties were still unresolved. The porters who shifted the goods across the border were divided into three gangs. On the Pakistani side they wore green shirts, in no-mans' land red and in India blue. Beady-eyed vultures sat glowering in the trees and gave the place a most forbidding feel.

Considering that only thirty-five years previously the two countries had been one, the changes on entering India were immediate and palpable. The road to Amritsar was surprisingly empty but when we entered the town we were thrown into the full confusion of an Indian town. Unlike Pakistan, where only the buses and trucks were domestically manufactured, India produced all the vehicles on the roads itself. There was our old friend the Enfield 350 Bullet, smaller two-stroke motorcycles based on Eastern European designs, and Indian-made Lambretta scooters. It was unusual to see less than two people on these machines, more likely it would be three or four, sometimes even a family of five. Crash helmets were not obligatory and so were seldom worn, the only exception being in the City of Bangalore in the south where a more enlightened administration had made them compulsory. This did mean, however, that the cheap moulded plastic hard hats of the type used on building sites all over the world were preferred there. The three-wheeled auto-rickshaws operated as cheap taxis around the towns, and there were the cycle-rickshaws, the bicycles, the carts, the trucks and the buses. Private cars were few, still too expensive for the majority of the Indian middle classes, and consisted of two models. There was the Ambassador, an Indian-made copy of the 1957 Morris Oxford, and an Indian-made Fiat. Some of the three-wheeled vehicles that operated as collective taxis had been improvised from available materials and scavenged parts in back street workshops. The power unit was often a multi-purpose 600 cc diesel engine and the bodywork hammered together from scrap metal. The small fleet that operated in the capital, Delhi, were of a more refined nature. They used the diesel engine with a Harley-Davidson gearbox, clutch, transmission, final drive and front end, with a compartment at the back large enough to seat eight. In Goa we met one motorcycling enthusiast who wanted economy above all else and had placed one of these diesel engines into a Enfield frame.

One of the more immediate differences on entering India was that the women were not in purdah. Bright saris, bare midriffs, uncovered heads – a most welcome sight. We had been dealing almost exclusively with men for nearly five months. The inquisitive crowds which elsewhere had surrounded us whenever we were with the bike, here in India became more inquisitive and more crowded. There were thousands of young western tourists travelling all over India by public transport, and when we were away from the bike we became indistinguishable from them. Then as soon as we returned to the vehicle people clamoured around, talkative, excited and acting as a magnet to those who passed by.

We stayed at the Youth Hostel in Amritsar and there met Jack and Jo Middle, a retired couple from England who had driven down overland in their camper van. They had passed through Iran with little difficulty but some expense and arrived at the Indian border without a carnet. There the van had to stay for five weeks while they arranged for a carnet to be sent out from England. They had finally picked up the van two days previously and were busy scrubbing off the thick layer of encrusted vulture guano that covered it. Around the Golden Temple in Amritsar the atmosphere was tense. The temple attracted the more radical element of Sikh seperatism and was considered a safe haven for those at odds with the authorities. As yet the army had not dared to move into this holy place but they were much in evidence patrolling the streets around. Inside the temple complex, and around the Pool of Nectar – the stagnant and fetid looking lake in which the temple stood – were various holy trees, their bark worn smooth by constant touching. Beside one of these stood a shrine to a sikh warrior who had fought in one of the ancient battles to recapture the temple from heathens. He had taken a blow to the neck which had half-severed his head but holding it in place with one hand he continued to fight on and was able to die within the holy sanctuary. At the youth hostel that day a wedding reception was in progress. We were invited by some of the young, educated and wealthy Sikhs attending, to join the celebations. When the party was over we continued to drink whisky with them. Their attitude was as arrogant and heartless towards the plight of their fellow Indians, in particular the poor, as it was kind and hospitable to us and they seemed over-sensitive to our reactions to the great contrasts between the rich and poor that existed in this teeming country.

"Those vagabonds who sleep on the streets" said one, "they do not want to work." We were discussing a harsh spell of cold weather which had suddenly gripped Delhi the previous month.

"No people died in that weather" another added, "Only vagabonds."

Once we had arrived in Delhi we had to decide on how to organise our tour of the country. Mopsa was all for flying herself direct to Sri Lanka, where we had friends with whom she could stay, leaving me to ride on alone. Her reaction to the sheer volume of people, the very evident poverty and indignity of life for many of the poorer people, and the absolute lack of the western conception of privacy and personal space, was vehement and took me by surprise. As days passed, however, she relaxed and began to enjoy India's diversity.

Although the Himalayan foothills were still in winter's grip we very much wanted to see something of the mountains and particularly Srinagar, where houseboats line the shores of Dal Lake. The road to Kashmir was clear, but landslides and new falls of snow were still possible and traffic was restricted to alternate days in each direction. With petrol in India relatively expensive and public transport very cheap, we left the bike in a friend's garage in Delhi and headed for the hills by train and by bus. A slow and cramped but far from uninteresting journey, our first experience of Indian trains, took us overnight to Jammu, where in the morning we boarded one of a convoy of some thirty buses to Srinagar. Before leaving Jammu we booked one night on a houseboat from a small travel agent, thus saving ourselves the inconvience of finding somewhere to stay when arriving at the dead of night. The bus ride over the snow covered mountains and into the Kashmir valley took all day and as we reached the outskirts of Srinagar, at about ten o clock, the bus was flagged down. A man, draped in a heavy woollen blanket against the bitter cold, climbed aboard:

"I am looking for English," he called down the bus. "For houseboat *Springflower*." As we were the only Europeans and had indeed booked for the *Springflower*, we assumed he meant us. We were bundled into a taxi and driven down to the lake shore where a small canopied paddling boat, a shikara, was waiting for us. Cold rose from the water's surface, as we drifted across to a group of boats with brightly painted name boards at their sterns.

"Which one is *Springflower*?" we asked.

"Oh, *Springflower* is not yet ready for this season, so you are coming to a better boat, a first class boat."

This seemed reasonable enough, and the boat did look very comfortable as we boarded and were seated at a large polished table and fed a large warming dinner.

"You agreed in Jammu to pay three hundred rupees, yes?"

Well, no, we'd agreed to pay eighty, and said so firmly. Indeed we'd already paid it. Mr Khan looked a little sheepish.

"Please," he asked us, "do not tell this to our other guests. They are paying too much more."

When we returned to our bedroom, we saw that several little luxuries, such as toilet paper and soap in the bathroom, had been removed.

Next morning I went, through lightly falling snow, into town, leaving Mopsa asleep with a nasty cold. The streets were covered in a layer of mud, slush

On the road in Rajasthan

and rubbish, a squalor that contrasted with the romantic image created by the lines of carved wooden boats along the reflective waters of the lake. At the tourist information office I was surprised to hear my name called:

"Mr Richard, where have you been. We waited right until the very last bus. We were worrying too much for your safety."

Embarrassed, I told him I was grateful for his concern, but who was he?

"I am from Houseboat *Springflower* of course. Where did you sleep? Where is your good wife?"

Back at the first class boat, Mr Khan was bemused by my anger as I pulled Mopsa from the bed and began packing our belongings. "But why are you so angry? You don't like my boat?"

"That," I said, "is not the point. You kidnapped us. Your actions were dishonest. Dishonourable."

This seemed to strike home – the honour of the Kashmiri is a precious thing – but not for long.

"So you are going to *Springflower*. How much will you pay there? Here you can pay less."

Sitting in the shikara, I was still gently seething as I strained to hear Mr Khan's final words:

"It's business, Mr Richard. Only business."

The time we spent away from the bike recharged our desire to take to the road again, and to explore more of the country. The Indian buses and trains had been an unusual experience but the cramped and uncomfortable conditions, and the frustrating delays were something neither of us would have chosen to endure for long. We repacked the sidecar and, as Delhi began to get hot, headed south. I fitted a small electric dashboard fan, which would run off the battery, to one of the front sidecar struts and pointed it directly at the engine. With summer approaching I feared, after our experience in Turkey, the engine would overheat in the congested traffic of the Indian cities. The fan would maintain air movement through the fins however slowly we travelled.

After the delicate beauty of the Taj Mahal in both morning and evening light we rode into Rajasthan. Between the princely splendour of its pastel shaded cities, the road was dry and dusty. In contrast to the pale landscape the women wore clothes in radiant reds, the men brightly coloured turbans. At Ranakpur, in the south of the State, we stopped at the intricately carved Jain temple and met Diana Wordsworth. A tall, strong woman of seventy-one she had lived in India for fourteen years, but returned to her cottage in Devon each summer during the wet season, she found the rains, upon which the Indian farmers depended, depressing.

"Had any punctures yet?" she asked. I was pleased to be able to answer no, and she was impressed, but next morning, as we walked together to the hotel car park, we found all three of our tyres as flat as pancakes. The previous day we had been forced by roadworks to make a detour over rough ground, and failed to avoid several thorny branches which lay across our path. I had expected punctures, but the tyres remained inflated as we rode the twenty miles to

A final farewell to Chris in Salzburg

Ruined coastal fort in Turkey

Al Dair, Petra, Jordan

Modern offices in Qatar

A wadi in Jordan

On the edge of the Empty Quarter in the United Arab Emirates

A dust storm in Puskar, India

◄ *Madyan in the Swat Valley, Pakistan*

Cattle Market, Southern India ►

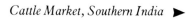

◄ *A Gopuram in Southern India*

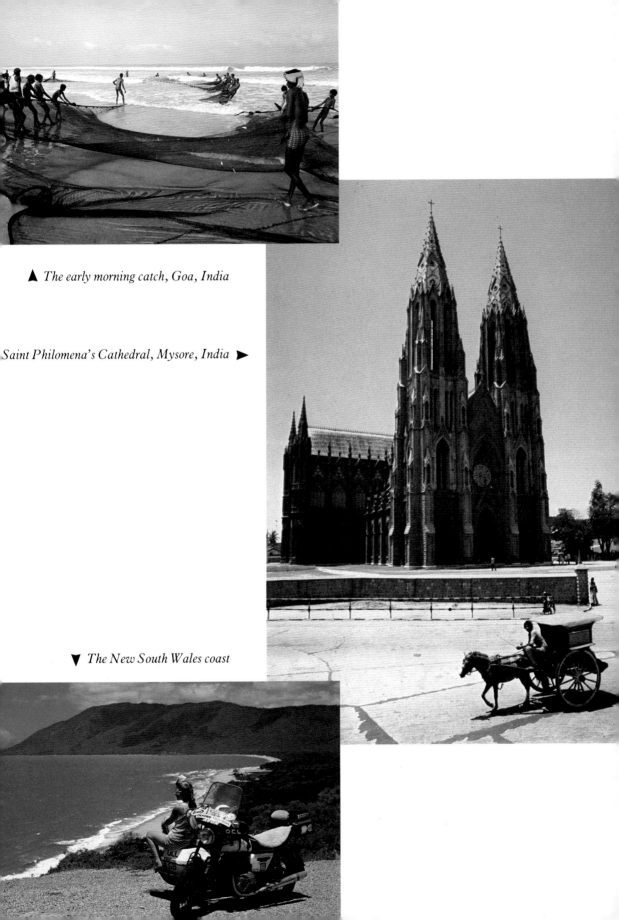

▲ *The early morning catch, Goa, India*

Saint Philomena's Cathedral, Mysore, India ▶

▼ *The New South Wales coast*

◄ *In far north tropical Queensland*

▼ *Pig-shooting in outback Queensland*

In the Kakadu, Northern Territory

Triumph and Durian Shop, Bangkok

Hill Tribe woman,
Northern Thailand

◄ *Downtown Tokyo at dusk – buildings reflected in tinted glass.*

Japanese Festival ►

Ranakpur. It took us more than an hour to remove the numerous slithers of thorn.

Diana invited us to stay at her house in Mount Abu, a hill station close to the Gujarat state border. At four thousand feet it was pleasantly cool and evergreens clothed the hillsides. The town is a holiday retreat for the wealthier Gujaratis, with private schools, hospitals and hotels. It is a traditional place for honeymooners and young well-dressed Indian couples strolled arm-in-arm down the leafy streets. We slept on the open verandah of her large, unfinished house which sat high on a hill overlooking her land, and woke in the mornings to the noisy chirpings of the red-vented bulbuls in the coral tree above our heads. She called the house her white elephant. There was not enough water in her wells to keep it supplied and she lived in a small cottage below. The land was surrounded by jungle where bear and panther roamed and a spirit called Vir Baba lived under one of her banyan trees. One night when she was away the spirit had appeared to one of her Indian boys in his sleep and instructed him to go out into the jungle where her dog Dibu was in trouble – dog is a favourite food of the panther. Despite his great fear of the jungle at night, he did as the spirit asked, and found Dibu caught by his choke chain on a root. An extreme sect of Sadhus had once lived in caves in the hills surrounding Mount Abu. Called the Aghori, they survived on a diet of human flesh: stealing burnt remains from funeral pyres and eating excrement and garbage. They believed that anything created by God could do no harm and set out to prove it. During the Indian mutiny, the Aghori were reputed to have roamed the land feeding like vultures on the bodies of those who had fallen in battle. The practice of suttee, where widows cast themselves onto their dead husbands' funeral pyres to be burnt with them had been banned by the government but still sporadically occurred. One such widow who lived close by and had been forcibly prevented from committing suttee by her family, had refused to eat and drink from that moment on. When, several months later, she was still alive, she became Suttee Mata, the object of much veneration, to whom people flocked as she was believed to have acquired special powers.

When we reached the Gujarati Plain the heat hit us like a hammer. In Ahmedabad it was hovering around 115°C. We rearranged our daily routine, and rose early to ride through the relative cool of the morning, stopping at around eleven to rest or to find a hotel. At four we either continued on for a couple more hours or explored the town in which we had stopped. The road south from Ahmedabad to Bombay was straight, well-surfaced, fast and consequently dangerous. After Baroda it was built up above the surrounding fields, where the corn was being harvested by hand, before being threshed under the hooves of oxen and winnowed in the breeze. We travelling at about 40 mph, wedged between two trucks, when a speeding Fiat began to overtake in the face of oncoming traffic. When level with the motorcycle, the driver realised he wasn't going to make it and swerved towards us. We had nowhere to go but off the road. We shot down the embankment – coming to a stop between two trees, with only inches to spare on either side. We were both still seated and unharmed but I

The Palace of the Winds, Jaipur in India

A home-made Indian three wheeled taxi, with belt drive to the front wheel

A motorised cycle-rickshaw in Southern India

Mopsa in the cool corridors of the Itmud-Ad-Daulah in Agra

was furious. The frustrations of dealing with driving habits that often bordered on the insane, which I had previously managed to blithely ignore, came straight to the surface. The truck behind us stopped to check we were all right and it was on the unfortunate Sikhs who climbed from the cab that I vented my anger. As I launched into a lengthy invective against Indian drivers in general, they stood opened mouthed, unable to understand even half of what I was saying and imagining, no doubt, that I was a beserk. When I calmed down a little, they helped us to pull the bike back up onto the road. Damage to the bike was minimal and turning to them I apologised for the harangue. They grinned at us and at each other, agreeing that the Indian driver was indeed a very dangerous man.

Bombay was immensely sweaty. The monsoon was soon due so although the heat was less than further north, it was the humidity that sapped our energy. We checked into a hotel which had started life as a Maharajah's town-house, became a brothel and then government offices. Although decaying fast it still stood proud and seemed to be a base for Bahaini drug pushers and their couriers. We saw them from across the balcony cutting open the backs of flip-flops, hollowing them out and filling them with drugs. The hotel's main advantage was a constant supply of warm water, which Mopsa used to shower several times each day.

Akbar's Mausoleum, on the road to Agra

Top end overhaul, Bombay

Every movement in the damp air created cascades of perspiration and our walks around town were langourous and reluctant. The hazards of life where people lived on their wits, where the disparity between rich and poor was discomfortingly glaring with shanty dwellings erected at the foot of plush air-conditioned office and apartment blocks, made us very wary of the pickpockets and con-artists for which the city was renowned. The image we had of ourselves as seasoned and aware travellers took a knock when we were stung, on a smallish scale, and we reverted, for a while, to suspicion of the motives behind any gesture of friendship. Despite our wariness we still made friends, one of whom was a freelance photographer who wanted to take shots of us, with and without the bike, in various locations throughout the city, which he would try to sell to newspapers back in England. He was due to photograph the newly-crowned Miss India and persuaded her to pose with us. The day was fearfully sticky when we arrived at the studio, smartly dressed in our riding suits and boots to be placed under the lights on either side of the more coolly dressed beauty queen. As the sweat poured, our Barbour suits began to soften, and oozed wax over her expensive silk sari.

Before leaving Bombay we decided to check the top end of the engine and by the front steps of the hotel we removed the cylinder head. It was 10,000 miles since our breakdown in Turkey and I was feeling nervous as to how well the pistons were coping, given that the fuel we were using was of such a low octane. At many of the petrol stations were government signs warning motorists to guard against the possible wilful adulteration of the fuel. Apart from a sizeable build up of carbon, which we carefully chipped off with the aluminium spatula we had bought in Austria, and the fact that the rings were a little worn, the bore was still good. It took a day to clean and rebuild it and I was confident that the bike would make it through India without breaking down. We wanted to be well away from the coast when the monsoons finally swept in from the south-west so rode quickly to Goa for a few days' rest on a sandy beach. Reinvigorated by the freshening pre-monsoon wind that made the sea almost too choppy in which to swim and by the lush tropical greenery and fruit trees which provided the backdrop against which the white Goan cottages and old Portuguese churches were set, we turned eastward again to cross the sub-continent to Madras, where we would learn which way we were to go next.

We rode though forests of sandalwood and teak, past Jog Falls – the highest in India – and into the coffee-growing district around Chikmagalur. We were passing through the town of that name in the late afternoon, intent on making Belur by dark when we were chased by two young men on a motor scooter. They flagged us down and told us that Mister Gopinath Siva would be pleased to meet us and would we accompany them to their shop. The shop was a chemist's and Mr. Gopinath Siva a coffee grower. He had in a past life been a dealer in motorcycles and remembered with affection several visits to the Midlands before the collapse. He insisted we stay in Chikmagalur that night and took us to his Club. The Kadur Club had been built by British Planters for their own exclusive use. It was not until 1962, fifteen years after independence, that the first Indian

*Temple carving in Belur,
Karnataka State*

Mopsa and the bike surrounded by an inquisitive crowd in India

was admitted. By then the number of European planters had dwindled to no more than a handful for after independence they were required to sell off sixty percent of their holdings to an Indian or have the whole lot confiscated. The decor within this elite club for the major landowners of the area was one of the more endearing legacies of British colonialism. Deep, comfortable armchairs in the lounge, Peter Scott bird prints on the walls. The dining room had a long extending banqueting table and game trophies stared down at the three of us sat at one end for supper. The bar was a perfect copy of an English country inn. After breakfast the next morning Gopinath suggested that we might like to meet Winnie Middleton, an English planter, who was well over eighty and had lived in India all her life. He gave us directions to the estate on which she still lived. When we pulled up outside her bungalow, set on a hill overlooking her flower garden that led the eye to a rolling vista of coffee that stretched to the horizon, she was seated on the verandah and rose to greet us. She took us on a long walk around the estate, which she had managed herself during and after the war until she sold her final share in 1972 to a rich Parsee from Bombay, before we sat down for afternoon tea. A silver teapot, bone china tea cups, drop scones, meat paste sandwiches, bread and honey. It was a proper English tea. We were joined by Ada, her sister-in-law, also staying on in India, sharing the bungalow, until she could arrange to export her savings to England. Winnie had no desire to spend her final days in England. She had been born in India, had lived here all her life, and would feel lost anywhere else. The two of them talked non-stop the whole evening and through the majority of the following day about their lives as colonial planters. The stories were initially about duck shoots, riotous weekend parties, riding fifty miles for a game of tennis, the fun of being young and privileged. As we sat on the verandah at dusk, enjoying a beer, her bearer quietly arrived to announce that four baths were ready. The water had been heated in giant coppers over a wood fire and carried to each bathroom. Mopsa treated herself that evening by putting on the one smart dress she kept in the bottom of the sidecar for just such an occasion. She was the first to enter the dining room.

"Oh, my dear, we don't dress for dinner anymore," exclaimed Winnie somewhat alarmed. I followed wearing a clean T-shirt and pair of jeans, rather than the expected black tie.

"Oh! Thank goodness for that," she sighed. Dinner was boiled mutton and vegetables, followed by a stodgy English pudding, then chocolate and liqueurs.

"I never eat curry," declared Winnie, "I had quite enough of that at school." She was of the opinion that the civil servants and soldiers sent over to help govern India between the wars were a bad bunch who didn't act in a respectful way towards the Indians and treated them like dogs. This had done much damage to British standing and had helped hasten independence. Her own attitude to her coolies was paternalistic. She had looked after their interests and interceded when they quarrelled. On one occasion an irate coolie had come to her door brandishing two large knives to ask her permission for him to kill the foreman. She disarmed him by asking if she could check that his knives were sharp enough for the job.

The ride across Karnataka took us from Mysore to Bangalore. We left the main highway and on a less busy route, passed through a large, sprawling cattle fair on the outskirts of the small town of Terakanambi. Stopping to look at the stalls and livestock we soon became Pied Pipers as we walked, for an ever-increasing crowd of young boys, then youths, and then men followed in our wake. When they numbered over fifty and were becoming excited we decided it would be best to leave, but in the short time it took to return to the bike their number had quadrupled. They crowded around the bike, the ones at the back pushing forward for a better view of these extraordinary white people putting on their helmets and gloves. There was only one way out – to drive, so I inched toward the road as the mass moved forward with us on all sides. It was several hundred yards before the noisy gathering had thinned sufficiently for us to increase our speed and escape. When we reached the next village we had to pull in to the side and stop for there, rolling towards us in the middle of the dusty road, was a naked man with long matted hair. Behind him walked a bare-footed woman holding out a begging bowl. The man was an itinerent sadhu who had, presumably, decided to roll around the roads of India, an extreme ascetic of his faith.

As we crossed from Bangalore into Tamil Nadu, the effects of a prolonged drought in this southern state were very evident. In the towns beggars crouched outside the eating houses and water was rationed. Once in Madras we investigated the alternatives for the next stage of the journey. The agents, who acted on behalf of OCL, were doubtful as to whether they could help us ship out from an Indian port. This left us with only two real possibilities. We could buy tickets on the Indian Steamship Company boat that plied between Madras and Penang in Malaysia or we could ride on down to Sri Lanka and see if we could arrange shipping from there. We decided on Sri Lanka – even if we failed to

Riding the outfit onto a barge/ferry in South-western India

obtain passage in Colombo, we could still return to Madras and take the boat to Malaysia.

The road south passed through the holy cities of Tanjore and Madurai where the soaring goporams of the temple complexes dominated their skylines. The dome on top of the main Brihadeshwara temple in Tanjore, built at the very end of the last millenium, was a solid piece of granite that weighed an estimated eighty-one tons. To raise such a massive stone to a height of over two hundred feet an earthwork ramp was constructed four miles long. Madurai was possibly our last great Indian city. When we were not riding in India, it was in the towns and cities where we spent the majority of our time. The fascination of every teeming street, every bustling market, and every majestic temple and palace had drawn us back again and again. The country created in us whirlpools of conflicting emotion, at the same time both magnificent and unbearable. Our senses had been battered by ever-changing landscape, language, food, architecture and costume, and a continual thread of wonder, inquisitiveness, hospitality, frustration, heat, poverty, richness, squalor and dust wound through the shaded courtyards, the muddy rivers, the parched countryside and the narrow streets. We were to leave with feelings of immense relief and great regret.

The road from Madurai ends in a line of corrugated huts and tea stalls at Mandapam rail station. The ferry to Sri Lanka moors off the port of Ramaswaram, which stands on a thin island projecting out into the Gulf of Mannar. The only way to get from the one to the other was by train and then barge. When we bought train tickets we were told by the station master that if we separated the bike from the sidecar both would fit into the goods wagon, so relieving us of the cost and him of the work involved in attaching an extra vehicle carrier to the train. I then haggled with the head porter to lift our goods into the wagon and we settled on thirty rupees. In situations such as these it was essential to keep control and a cool head. The six porters were willing but not strong men and quite naturally shied away from grease and oil and towards the more readily available handholds, like indicators and exhaust pipes which had a tendency to bend and break. We took the loading slowly and lifted the bike and sidecar from the track, five foot into the air and slid them across the slippery floor of the wagon which had just been emptied of fish. At Rameswaram the process was reversed. Another thirty rupees and we re-attached the sidecar and rode into town to find a bed for the night. At the Shipping Corporation office the agent was dubious as to whether we could board the following morning but he agreed to meet us outside the port gates at eight o'clock. When we arrived he was nowhere to be seen so after waiting an hour we returned to the office and found him sulking behind a cup of sweetened tea. "You bring me nothing but trouble," he complained as we dragged him outside and drove him aloft the sidecar to the port. Once there he reluctantly did the rounds of the various officials to check that all was in order for us to proceed and on handing us our tickets demanded his baksheesh. We cleared customs, and haggled with the crew of the barge we had hired to take the outfit out to the Ramajunan, previously known as the Irwin

Loading at Rameswaram

A new statue of Buddha, yet to be unveiled, in a Temple at the foot of Adam's Peak, Sri Lanka

and built in Partick in 1929, which lay with decaying splendour in the bay. With the barge alongside, the ship-board crane graunched into life and trussed in a huge net the outfit was slowly winched on board. It was dark, when we arrived in Sri Lanka but the boat moored alongside a jetty and again the crane was swung out. Pier charges paid, we rattled along the rail tracks that led into the customs shed. With the final formalities over, the shed door was opened and out we rode, straight down a flight of three stairs, invisible in the darkness.

Within two weeks of our arrival in Sri Lanka our future was assured. We were to be allowed to board a German container ship, on charter to OCL, bound for Australia. The majority of our time on the island was necessarily spent in Colombo but we managed a four-day ride from the lowland coconut estates, through rubber plantations and up into the hills where tea is grown. With the northern Tamil areas closed to tourists, there was only a limited amount of road. After we'd been to Kandy, to the Buddhist shrines at Annuradapura, to the cool hill resort of Nuwaru Eliya and climbed the majestic Adam's Peak at night in time to see the rising sun cast the triangular shadow of its perfect peak across the shifting clouds which hung loosely around the hills below, we returned to Colombo. We left agreeing that once the Tamil problem had been resolved, that once literacy and health had been improved and poverty eased, the island would indeed be close to paradise. Within three days of our departure a Singalese backlash occured that resulted in communal riots in Colombo and fighting in the streets.

A roadside meeting with Charles Batham and his Honda Gold Wing with giant trailer, eight years into his ten year tour of the world.

Chapter Five

Australia

OUR FIRST sight of Australia was uninspiring. Low, sombre, grey hills ran down to a flat and colourless sea as we rounded Cape Leeuwin, the continent's most south-westerly point, and headed out across the Australian Bight towards the eastern seaboard. The motorcycle was carefully stowed away in the Bosun's store to protect it from the ravages of the salt sea spray while we lounged in the artificial, air-conditioned atmosphere of cabin and dining room, decompressing after six months on the Indian subcontinent. During the first few days of this two-week voyage we had battled in vain against the movements of a lightly loaded and heavily pitching ship in order to keep down an over-rich and overabundant supply of German food, served up to us with regular monotony three times during the short day. Then, our sea legs gained, we each relentlessly reapplied the surplus fat we had shed travelling through India. A healthy diet of rice and curried vegetables, several bouts of prolonged diarrhoea and the subtropical heat had made us positively gaunt compared to the rotund outlines of the German officers and crew who were determined to fatten us up before we arrived in Sydney.

The sun shone brightly from the north as we sailed more smoothly now along Australia's southern coast. Above the boat albatrosses occasionally wafted by, effortlessly immobile. Along the ragged Victoria coastline, with its rocky islands, steep cliffs and detached and pounded stacks, through the Bass Straight we arrived at the neat, clean and orderly container port at Botany Bay. Before 1770, when Captain Cook, more by accident than design, first landed at Botany Bay, the Dutch had visited the northern and western coasts in search of gold and the mythical unknown southland. So disillusioned were they, however, by the general aspect of the bleak land and its aboriginal people that they declined to establish a foothold and concentrated their efforts instead on the seemingly richer islands to the north. It was Cook's more favourable description of the potentials of the land and its people that led to the British deciding on the extraordinary venture of establishing a penal settlement at Botany Bay. Since the landing of the first settlers in 1788 the history of Australia has proved to be a triumph of European colonialism – but to the indigenous population of aboriginals it was nothing short of a disaster.

Our own entry into this young, optimistic land of opportunity couldn't have been more informal. After we had docked and the motorcycle had been quickly and efficiently off-loaded and parked beneath one of the monstrous gantry cranes, we were called up to the Officers' saloon, where over a cold beer we were processed by two friendly customs and immigration officials.

"Now then, what about this motorcycle you're importing?" one of them twanged. "Is it clean?"

"Well, sort of clean," I replied hopefully. There were very strict importation requirements designed to keep out alien and destructive animal and crop pests.

"Should be spotless," he countered.

"Okay, it's spotless."

"Well that's alright then," and smiling, he stamped our carnet before buying another round of beers.

Like many others before us we arrived with empty pockets, our funds spent on the journey down through Asia. On our second day in Sydney we heard of the sad and final demise of the Triumph Co-operative at Meriden. We had chosen the one British motorcycle still in production and felt that our fortunes were in many ways linked with theirs. It seemed a rug had been pulled from under our feet. The idea, before we left England, had been for the journey to become self-financing. If we were to achieve this, then Australia would be the place to start. It would require a necessary, if undesirable, break in the momentum of the journey.

It was the very British nature of the trip that enabled us to generate the interest we needed. Help came from Avon Tyres, Australia, and then from Travis Nugara who owned a successful Triumph dealership in Melbourne. The motorcycle was overhauled in his workshop, engine rebored, new pistons fitted and a badly leaking gearbox seal replaced. With the promise of future payments for magazine articles on our journey to date we decided to leave Sydney on 3rd September. We had 400 dollars in our pockets, a recently-arranged overdraft facility with our bank in England, and a carrier bag full of maps and tourist brochures. We were on the road again. At first glance the familiar names of Liverpool, Windsor, Richmond and Newcastle sprang from the map but on closer inspection stranger, more alien names came to light: Quirindi, Woolgoola, Woy Woy, and Goonoo Goonoo. In Sydney friends began our initiation into Australian ways – barbecued steaks, endless cans of ice-cold beer, apple pie and ice cream. Light hearted banter about whingeing poms revealed a strong nationalistic pride among the long established families.

"You'll never see Australia so green" we were told as we headed up through New South Wales towards the Queensland border. Three years of partial drought had been followed by a good amount of rain and the countryside had responded splendidly, but through our eyes, accustomed to the lush rolling pastures of England, it still looked very baked. We decided we could afford a four month elliptical tour of the eastern half of the country. Australia's reputation for offering the overland tourer both adventure and interest demanded that we travel her roads. The grazing land of northern New South Wales, scattered with the stocky forms of unsheared sheep, Angus and Hereford cattle, alternated with forests of gum tree in which we camped at night. The moon blazed bright through their branches and the noisy chirping of the crickets was accompanied by an occasional nightjar or by the startling cry of the rarer and more exotic whiplash bird. The small towns with their wide main streets and their classical Australian architecture of pillared verandas and wrought iron balconies revealed a homely parochialism. As we approached the Queensland border the countryside changed. We were captivated by the light and space. Vast panoramic views stretched endlessly along the coastline and inland rolling, greener hills were interspersed with fields of banana, avocado and macadamia nuts. Our combination, with its British plates and the sidecar on the wrong side, aroused continual interest and made us many friends. We were passed from household to household all the way up the Queensland coast. The State Government of Queensland was intensely conservative and dominated by 'Premier Joh' Bjelke-Peterson whose renowned gerrymandering had assured him uninterrupted power for many years despite only ever receiving 28 percent of the vote. The homely recipes of his wife, 'Senator Flo', for such delights as pumpkin scones had achieved notoriety throughout Australia. Politics on a national and state level were always controversial and accusations of corruption and dishonesty were flung at opponents from both sides of the political spectrum. Political life in Australia seemed to be based more on the principles of the bar room brawl than on any of the loftier ideals inherent in a liberal democracy.

On 20th September we crossed the Tropic of Capricorn and followed the Bruce Highway which hugged the coastline. The tourist potential of this tropical coast had not gone unrecognised: tee shirts, thongs and shorts were everywhere. Grotesque replicas of animate and inanimate objects lined the road. A giant pineapple or banana advertised a plantation open to the public. A giant golf ball, a golf course. A giant cow, a steak house. A giant lobster, a fish restaurant. The enormous amount of space demanded that advertisers think big. Desultory unemployed youths from Brisbane toured the free campsites in plush internally-padded utility vans surviving on a diet of beer and cheap wine, and keeping the more traditional tourers awake until the small hours with their raucous partying. We rode from fruit plantation to long grassed cattle country to sugar cane field to rainforest, enjoying the warm outdoor life. Passing storms failed to dampen our spirits. After dusk cane toads gathered on the warm tarmac and our passage was accompanied by a gentle and continuous squelching, so great were their numbers. Fireflies hovered over our camp fires at night and from the darkness we heard the scratchings and grunts of strange marsupial creatures wandering in the night.

When we arrived in Cairns, Australia had just won the Americas Cup. The pubs were overflowing with satisfied revellers and we stayed with Rod and

An Australian pub, Townsville, Queensland

Michelle whose large, disorganised house on stilts was dedicated to the greater glory of the motorcycle. Beneath their floor boards were gathered a host of Harley-Davidson, BMW and Triumph motorcycles in various states of disrepair. Rod had one leg, rode a Harley and was a skydiving parachutist. We took a boat ride out to the clear colour streaked waters of the Great Barrier Reef where on one sandy cay, more than twelve miles from the coast, had been posted a sign which asked visitors to take nothing but photographs, to leave nothing but footprints. Further up the coast, the unplundered rain forest of the Cape York peninsula ended where the sea began, on long stretches of deserted white sand beach. At Cape Tribulation we were lectured by an eccentric straw-hatted environmentalist who roundly condemned the highly controversial plan to build a road from the Cape to Cooktown and so begin the destruction of an ancient ecological balance that existed in this untouched section of one of the last wetland coastal forests in Australia. Parts of the rain forest date back more than two hundred million years and botanists have identified there some of the first flowering plants to evolve on earth. A damp morning mist lingered in the trees and the chorus from the many forest birds at daybreak was deafening. We too felt that it was worth protecting.

Two days after leaving the splendours of the tropical Queensland coast we were stuck in a dried-up creek bed 10 miles outside Mount Surprise on the Gulf Development road off which we had pulled to camp the previous night, surrounded by a sparse bush of squat gum trees and dry red earth and bedevilled by clusters of flies which clung to our backs and arms with the obstinacy of limpets. We had, for the first time, temporarily reversed our circumvolution of the globe and were heading west into the centre of Australia. The motorcycle was suffering from a drastic reduction in power and refused to pull up the steep bank and back onto the road. The previous morning we had left Innot Hot Springs, a tiny eponymous township situated on the border of the tablelands where forest gave way to bush and where the pre-war telephone exchange still relied on manual power. A recently arrived Belgian immigrant had entertained us to morning tea (a strangely Australian custom) in his tumble-down corrugated shack where he stuffed cane toads, mounting them on plinths and dressing them up as swagmen complete with cork-hung hats and boiling billies to sell as ornaments or paperweights to tourists on the coast. I suspected a slipping clutch as the reason for the motorcycle's sudden mule-like qualities and tinkered accordingly. Despite failing to solve the problem, we managed to extricate the motorcycle from the creek bed by off-loading the greater part of our belongings from the sidecar. It was gone eleven when the three of us stood again on terra tarmac and under a fierce mid-day sun we decided on our next move, which was philosophically backwards to Mount Surprise in search of a mechanic who might enlighten us as to the bike's misbehaviour.

The most surprising thing about Mount Surprise was that it was there at all. A petrol pump, a pub, a store, half a dozen houses and a mechanic to whom we were soon directed. The Country Workshop lay a mile from the town, a ramshackle collection of structures made from old tarpaulins, corrugated iron and fencing wood. Old trucks and half-stripped cars scattered the yard. The resident mechanic and owner was Dennis Jones, a wiry Englishman in his mid fifties who had been in Australia for 35 years.

A welcome cool-off in a ford in North Queensland

"Have you had your lunch yet?" he asked when I explained our visit. Lunch turned into tea which turned into supper which turned into a four day stay. During the afternoon Den and I extricated the clutch plates from the Triumph, cleaned them up and replaced the slightly worn clutch springs with new ones. I took the outfit for a short test ride down the bumpy track that led back to the main road. The bike seemed to have regained some of its lost power. I still wasn't sure that we'd completely solved the problem but Den was, and he soon set us to other jobs. In return for our helping him around the workshop he offered to take us pig shooting at the weekend. Much to Mopsa's chagrin she was assigned the job of cooking and cleaning. Den was a solid traditionalist, set in his ways and a little startled at Mopsa's belligerence in the face of his orders and his assumptions about the role of the sexes. The issue was never resolved and the tension between them would heighten each day as the temperature rose. Mopsa found it surprising that many men, in a country which produced such strong-minded and independent women, should be incapable of coming to terms with a change in attitudes. The insensitivities of the ocker male were reviled by liberal women throughout the country.

On the Saturday afternoon we threw our sleeping bags, Den's guns and several billy-cans and packets of tea into his battered Toyota Land Cruiser and drove forty miles into the bush to the Dagworth cattle ranch. Here approximately three thousand kangaroos and three hundred wild horses coexisted with some three thousand head of cattle over a huge tract of land without adversely affecting the fortunes of the cattle station. It was the thousand wild boar which had to be culled. Descendants of escaped domestic pigs imported into the country in the last century, they caused considerable destruction by tearing up the fragile soil in search of roots. It is an interesting although not necessarily pleasurable pastime, stalking pig in the Australian outback. Throughout that Sunday we trudged our dusty way through the bush, while the temperature rose into the high forties centigrade. Sweat poured, our legs and arms were lacerated by the spiky undergrowth and our bodies blackened by the incessantly settling flies. The arguments between Den and Mopsa escalated and became more petty by the hour. They argued about the heat, whether or not to drink water, wear hats, shoot pigs. Every hour or so a disturbed boar crashed an escape through tangled undergrowth and we let off a couple of wayward shots at its fleeing rump. By the end of the dispiriting day we had shot nothing and it was only while returning home in the truck that we unexpectedly came across an old, confused and sickly boar. Our trophy was won, and Den, after cutting out the tusks and boiling them clean, presented them to us as a souvenir. The carcass, too infested for human consumption, was left to rot in the bush.

Sixty miles to the west of Mount Surprise lies Georgetown. A town of more than one street it boasts a police station, a landing field, a hospital and is subject to flooding when the rains fall. The work on the clutch at Den's workshop seemed to have solved the problem and the motorcycle pulled well as we left Mount Surprise but within a few miles it suffered a dramatic relapse and again displayed the symptoms that had previously had us stuck in a dried up river bed for several hours. My diagnosis had been wrong so in Georgetown I checked everything that could be checked without pulling apart the engine and realised our troubles were the result of a loss of compression. We retired to the town's large corrugated iron workshop-cum-storage warehouse to dismantle the top-end. Being an untutored and inexperienced mechanic any change in the bike's performance and behaviour had me imagining all sorts of horrific catastrophes. On this occasion it was nothing more than a blown head gasket which was replaced the next day. The uncluttered simplicity of the Triumph engine meant that even I could cope, unaided, with an engine rebuild. It was with growing confidence that we continued to take the Triumph where many other motorcyclists would not have thought wise. "She'll be right," a passing gold prospector declared when the engine was reassembled. It was an attitude gained from years of optimism and from having to keep vehicles running in a harsh environment with the minimum of spares. We took it as our own.

Across the Gilbert river the road became rutted dirt with patches of bull dust, a talc-fine sand which settles in pot-holes, disguising them as smooth level road. I cut our speed to around thirty-five mph and the dry, unrelenting heat made riding uncomfortably sticky. If any of the creeks we passed contained enough residual water we stopped for a quick murky dip. Bolts on the motorcycle began to loosen as we rattled and slid along and very occasionally we would be showered with grit and sand as a double trailered "road-train" roared by. The countryside levelled as we approached the Gulf of Carpentaria, the landscape become an endless dusty horizon. At Normanton we turned south and back onto welcomed tar. Camping that night on the banks of the Flinders River

Road Train

we were greeted with a congenial "G'day" by Mike and Evan, two coastal Queenslanders on a shooting holiday. As we prepared for a swim Mike handed me one of his rifles.

"One of you swims, the other stands guard. There's a lot of crocs in these waters." We didn't linger long in the cool muddy water.

With the mid-day temperatures creeping towards fifty degrees centigrade we woke early and were riding as the sun rose. Past Poverty Knob and Bang Bang Jump Up and across a huge golden grassed plain where emu strolled and plains turkeys broke into short bursts of wide-winged flight. A brief stop for petrol and a cold drink at the Burke and Wills Roadhouse broke the monotony of two hundred miles of empty road. Burke and Wills had led an expedition that blazed a tortuous trail across the centre of Australia from Adelaide in the south to the Gulf of Carpentaria in the north, in search of good grazing land and a fabled, non-existent, inland sea. The first white men to make this journey, they have become part of Australian folklore, but it ended in disorganised tragedy when, desperately weak after the privations of the trek and having reached the Gulf in February 1861, they decided to retrace their steps. Burke, an Irishman of uneven temper, soundly thrashed one of his colleagues whom he suspected of feigning illness in order to receive more of their meagre rations and was subsequently racked with remorse when the man died several days later. They arrived back at Coopers Creek to find that the holding party that awaited their return had departed just nine and a half hours previously, having held on for a month longer than they had been instructed. Burke and Wills later died trying to reach Mount Hopeless in South Australia and King, the only survivor, was kept alive by aboriginals until eventually found by a search party sent to discover what had become of the expedition.

On these flat, heat-shimmering roads I pushed our speed up to an uneconomical 65-70 mph in a vain attempt to increase the cooling around the roasting engine. A dry, searing wind from the south chapped our faces and to our astonishment we found it cooler to be stationary thus destroying an unquestioning belief in the wind chill factor. The heat and the haze and the endless horizon made lead of the eyelids and encouraged sleep. I became fixated on the cold beer I knew was waiting at the Quamby Hotel just 90 miles to the south and was oblivious to the pleas of my companion, who was dehydrating fast, for us to stop for water. Violent pounding on my back eventually made me pull reluctantly over and the heated argument that ensued was only brought to an hysterical end when Mopsa poured our last remaining cup of precious drinking water over my perspiring head.

At Cloncurry we joined the Barkley Highway and continued on through Mary Katherine to Mount Isa. Only six years after Burke and Wills had passed nearby the Great Australia Mine opened at Cloncurry. It was later to become the largest supplier of copper in the British Commonwealth. The uranium mine at Mary Katherine didn't last so long, less than thirty years, and we had only missed by months the great auction in which the entire contents of the town and mine, including the very bricks and mortar, had been sold off. Under the

Australian Mining Act a closed site had to be left as it was found and all that remained when we passed by were the overgrown service roads and the concrete bases on which the houses had been constructed. Mount Isa was a thriving town of 28,000 people whose livelihood was completely dependent on the modern efficiencies and paternalistic beneficence of a mine that was one of the world's largest producers of silver and lead and a major supplier of copper and zinc. The mine's massive conglomeration of structured steel, storage tank and slag heap, elegantly topped by a $5.8 million, 270 metre high lead smelter stack completely dominated the surrounding countryside. When the mine eventually runs out of ore it will be an extremely expensive exercise to return the land to its previous rugged glory.

The severe conditions of the last few days had made me nervous of the possibility of the motorcycle's engine seizing, so we found and then fitted an oil cooler in Mount Isa to replace the dashboard fan we had used in Pakistan and India. It was over a thousand more road miles to Darwin on Australia's northern coast with little in between except the great expanse of the arid Northern Territory. Every hundred miles or so, a small service town or hotel would relieve our thirsts and reassure our spirits. It was the distances between places that I found so alien and a need to travel much further than we normally found comfortable. After we crossed the border into the Northern Territory the land flattened out after the rocky hills of Mount Isa and the Barkley Tablelands. The soil turned red and sprouted shorter yellower grass and even squatter gum trees. The hot, rough bitumen surface of the highway tore into our softened tyres and rapidly increased their rate of wear. We continued to camp out by shallow water holes and passed the carcasses of cattle and kangaroo, bloated by the heat, that had been brushed off the highway by the unstoppable road trains. As we approached Darwin tall termite mounds scattered the ground. The city was modern, hot and sticky, waiting with an air of languid transience for the first of the season's rains.

In Darwin we stayed with Suzy, the sister of a passing stranger we had met in Townsville. In her last year at the university she had already been married and divorced, with two children in the custody of her ex-husband. Her consuming interest was in making anthropological films and she financed this by earning over $1000 a week as a call girl. Her enthusiasm and sympathy for the aboriginal people was tinged with lighthearted humour. She told us of the time she had sat in on the interviewing of an old aboriginal from Arnheim Land by a documentary film-maker. Much to their dismay the old man recalled the time in his youth when his kin-group had sometimes indulged in cannibalism. "Chinamen were the tastiest," he had grinned as the interviewer shifted uneasily in his chair. "Once we'd caught them we wouldn't eat them at once but break their legs to stop them escaping and keep them fresh."

Leaving the oppressive humidity of Darwin we rode across the giant termite mounded plains towards Arnheim Land and the Kakadu National Park. A dry and dusty dirt road followed the high sandstone escarpment where hidden in cool caves and overhangs were aboriginal rock paintings that spanned 20,000

An empty road in Central Australia

years of human history. An extensive wildlife of birds, crocodiles, goannas and more recently imported water buffalo crowded the creeks and lakes now at their lowest ebb as the dry season drew to a close. We took the more isolated road back to the north-south highway. One hundred miles of fearful corrugations that shook both bike and bones so ferociously that we were forced to ride at an angle of thirty degrees with our motorcycle wheels on the banked sand verges. We paddled across creeks to check their depth and choose the smoothest line of attack. It was the sort of riding we expected to face in Africa rather than Australia.

An outsider would be wrong to believe that Australia has a uniformity in language, customs and scenery. Coming from England I found it a fascinating combination of the alien and the familiar. Outside the major cities life has a timeless, provincial air that stirred in both Mopsa and I almost forgotten memories of a life in England in the late fifties. Spending long stretches of time alone together, we recounted tales of childhood holidays with scratched legs and midgie bites and adventures in river pools on long sunny afternoons which had grown greater and bolder with the passing of time. But in contrast to the small town stillness which brought back images of being driven through the English countryside on summer outings, the environment in which we now found ourselves was unique and uncompromising. Idling away the long hours on the highway down to Alice Springs I tried to imagine how it might have been for the white explorers who first charted this barren land. Men and women, who had either been transported or had come for reasons of opportunism or merely to escape a desperate poverty in nineteenth century Britain, had in 1871 built, and

85

then serviced, the overland telegraph line between Adelaide and Darwin that greatly reduced the isolation from their colonial motherland. It was a remarkable achievement to construct in less than two years a line that stretched across such rugged and inhospitable land. Simple markers by the side of the road were modest reminders of their endeavours. We stopped at one, near Central Mount Stuart, the geographical centre of the continent – only to find that the plaque had been removed and in its place had been written in beautifully painted script the plaintive and irreverent question: "Which way to the beach?"

With the telegraph line came settlers and cattle, fences and boundaries. As elsewhere in Australia the aborigines were pushed out to the margins, on occasions unmercifully hunted, deprived of access to the land they had wandered for centuries. Our journey around Australia was dependent upon the settlement patterns of the more dominant European civilisation of which we were a part. The aborigines conceived of territory in lines which ran between campsites and waterholes and they were uninterested in anything that lay beyond. Although tied to the white mans' road we did feel an affinity with another culture which was based not on settlement but on movement.

In Darwin shorts and sarongs had been worn. In Alice Springs it was blue jeans, checked shirts and stetsons. The town seemed in political uproar with radical feminists besieging the American tracking station at Pine Gap and aboriginal land rights, uranium mining and tourist industry investments the current political flashpoints. It seemed extraordinary that all these contentious issues should be focused in a town like Alice. We escaped the heat for a circular tour of the western Macdonnell Ranges. Rugged and spectacular these low jagged hills, surrounded by the desert oaks, mulga, sand and shrub, lay bathed in a tonal light that only existed deep within the interior of this vast, island continent. The landscape reflected the spiritual history the aboriginal people had assigned it. The natural features were the permanent manifestations of the actions of their mythical ancestors. When a redbacked parrot woman had cried out the warning that the dreamtime was about to end, the legendary creatures who were half human, half animal or plant turned into the boulders, caves, trees and the forms of the land. The desert oaks were the Liru snake people who at the time of the creation had come to slaughter the peaceful Kunia snake people. These strange landforms at which we gazed with studied awe were sacred sites used for ritual ceremony. When the aborigines lost their lands to the white man, they lost their culture. In loosing their culture they lost themselves, and became a people in shock. Only now was a mutual understanding beginning to develop between the races. Stopping for lunch by a dry creek bed outside the aboriginal settlement of Hermansberg, we were surprised by three young aborigine boys who came roaring out of the bush on dirt bikes of varying sizes, wearing full riding gear and helmets. With huge beams and awkward waves they passed us by and I wondered how their grandfathers would have viewed these extraordinary machines in terms of the creation and the dreamtime.

"When I was only two miles distant, and the hill, for the first time coming into view, what was my astonishment to find it an immense pebble arising

An isolated pub in the Northern Territory

abruptly from the plain . . ." So wrote W. G. Gosse on 17th July 1873, the first white man to view Uluru, the place of the howling dingo, which he subsequently renamed Ayers Rock. Our own first view of it was no less astonishing. Approaching at dusk we were suddenly engulfed by a fierce electrical storm, the centres of which lay on either side of the road, with lightning arcing across the sky above. The looming mass of this giant pebble lay dramatically framed before us. The following day we climbed the 1,140 feet to view the curving horizon of this flat, flat land, and visited the sacred spots where the captured spirits of the dead were sung into the very heart of the rock and where maidens waited for the souls of the unborn to emerge and choose their mothers. That afternoon we tried to concern ourselves with the more mundane tasks involved in travelling by motorcycle, but as we were changing the rear tyre of the bike in the campsite attached to the unfinished and controversial multi-million dollar tourist complex a vicious dust storm blew up and forced us to take shelter. That night torrential rain poured down and the morning saw us dismantling the carburettor to empty it of accumulated water. The Rock was shrouded in mist as we rode down the bright red dirt road to visit the equally impressive Olgas, a collection of more than thirty massive domes of conglomerate stone, before returning to the highway and turning south.

At the Northern Territory and South Australia border, just south of the small service town of Kulgera, the Stuart Highway ran out of tarmac. Since 1966 the politicians had been promising at every election that the sealing of the road was a major priority but there was still a four hundred and fifty mile stretch which held a formidable reputation throughout Australia as a route that left vehicles stranded with broken axles and wheel rims. Its reputation grew as more people used it as the only viable way to or from Alice Springs, apart from the train. The alternative Oodnadatta track which was longer, more isolated and skirted around the Simpson desert and Lake Eyre was little known to the average Australian. It was only when we arrived in Alice Springs that we learnt that this track was both easier and more interesting than the direct "highway" south through the opal town of Coober Pedy.

For the first ninety miles after leaving Kulgera we took an access road that followed the rail line which brought us to the beginning of the track. Our map encouragingly declared that it was inadvisable and hazardous to tour the area in summer due to the extreme heat. It was 17th November and summer had already begun in this part of the southern hemisphere, but the sky was cloudy and with a brisk wind from the south west we were well wrapped up in our Barbour riding suits. The first hundred miles were distressingly slow as the constant shock waves sent out by successive corrugations made the sidecar fixing clamps slip to such an extent that the bike leant dramatically towards the sidecar. Three times we had to stop to readjust, after driving the outfit at an impossible angle, and it was only after smearing a liberal amount of grease over the offending bolts that finally gave enough torque for the clamps to hold firm and the outfit true. Then the welds holding the top box snapped, and it flew into the dust-filled air before bouncing down the road behind us. By eleven the next morning we arrived at Oodnadatta, the only town on the track for over four hundred miles. With a population of around a hundred its wide, wind-blown and dusty main street displayed the forlorn air of the forgotten. A hunched and shabby figure shuffled along the street and outside the hotel and general store a small group of men huddled waiting for the bar to open. We filled up with petrol and drinking water while an old, grey-haired aborigine wandered over to the bike. "Gone with the wind, gone with the wind" he chuckled repeatedly to us with a flap of his hand and so we went, with the wind, towards the largest of Australia's great salt lakes following the rusty and disused single track of the old Ghan railway which had until fairly recently been the main link between the south and the centre. The name of the railway derived from the camels which, along with their keepers, had been imported from Afghanistan to carry and drag and help build the line across the most arid of land. On this second day we covered more miles, over two hundred and fifty, passing the lonely hotel at William Creek (population, two men, one woman and a dog) where on a huge notice board in the bar were pinned the faded and curling calling cards of the many travellers who had visited over the years. We camped one night in the shelter of the veranda of a ruined railway station and showered for the first time in a week under a permanently gushing pipe of sulphurous bore water from the artesian basin that the railway engineers had tapped so many years before. These deserted buildings every twenty miles or so increased the eerie loneliness that hung over the land. Several cattle ranches had somehow managed to survive but they required vast amounts of land on which to graze their herds. The largest covered more than 4,500 square miles. Nearing the southern shore of Lake Eyre we stopped to watch cattle being

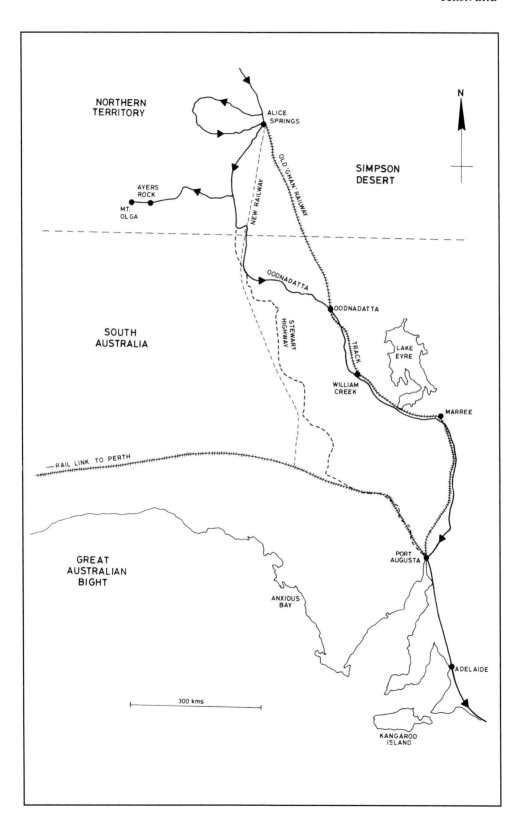

*The Oodnadatta Drive-in
Picture Theatre – showings
fortnightly*

loaded onto trucks. The recent drought meant they could no longer survive here and they were being shipped to the greener pastures of North Queensland. At the tip of the lake, the view across the salt encrusted depression was endless, with what seemed like water shimmering on the far horizon. The land around was now devoid of all vegetation. At Maree the track officially ended but we still had another 70 miles of dirt until at Leigh Creek we once again felt a smooth, sealed road beneath our wheels.

With the hills of the Flinders Range to the east the road ran on toward the southern coast at Port Augusta, and the softness of a rolling landscape filled with golden barley fields was a blessed change after the harsh lines of the bush. The rigours of our cross-continental journey had, however, taken their toll and the engine had begun to drink oil at an ever-increasing and alarming rate. We limped into Adelaide and into George Bolton's motorcycle workshop where I pulled apart the engine and under the expert guidance of their resident mechanic replaced worn valves and guides after some twenty-eight thousand miles of service.

The return to Sydney was anticlimactic after our inland tour. When we had set out we had felt like children let loose in a huge and unknown adventure playground. It had been all breezy and colourful on the eastern coast. But once inland the country took on a more menacing aspect that required one's respect as well as one's admiration. The interior was too vast and too inhospitable to allow man anything more than the scattering of a few livestock and some digging around for stones. But with its light and its skies and the red, red earth – with a moon so big and so bright that it hurt one's eyes – it was a landscape with soul.

With part of our hearts left behind we rode the Great Ocean Road to Melbourne. It was an exhilarating ride as we rose, twisted and fell along a road that followed the very cliffs, bays, islands and stacks upon which we had gazed from the ship that had brought us from Sri Lanka. With the smell of the sea came a renewal of purpose. Our tour around Australia had given us a fascinating glimpse of this strange land but now we had another journey to continue. Back in Sydney we were sheltered under the warm wing of the Byrne family, whose son and daughter-in-law we had met in Turkey. For three month's Mopsa sold first-aid kits over the telephone and I became the Bedford Painting and Decorating Company, cruising the suburbs with ladders, buckets and pots of paint strapped to the sidecar. On Friday 23rd March 1984 the motorcycle was loaded onto a ship of the Australian National Lines bound for Singapore. On 3rd April we flew out of Sydney. The air was unsurprisingly clear. The city's now familiar skyline gave way to the neatly lined properties of one acre plots and then to the five acre plots. We passed over the mountains of the Great Divide and the extensive cattle ranches of the Darling River basin. Flying directly over the shifting sands of the Simpson Desert to Alice Springs, we saw once more the true isolation of the town. On and on, over seemingly endless stretches of arid bush and then at last the landscape changed again as the wide, pale grey delta of the Fitzroy River snaked its many paths to the Indian Ocean. We had flown for five hours over the great expanse of the Australian landmass, then after only a short hour over the sea, we landed at Denpasar, capital of Bali. We alighted into the humid air, into the familiar crowding bustle of Asian life, and taking a communal taxi, twelve people jammed into benches along the sides of a noisy Japanese pick-up truck, grinning at each other, foolishly happy to be back on the exotic roads of the east.

Chapter Six

The Far East

ONCE THE channel tunnel has been completed one should be able to drive from London to Singapore direct, without one's wheels leaving the road. In practice, unless world relationships change considerably, this will not be so. Arriving in Singapore we were returning to the mainland, which – apart from a couple of bridges – spread as far as Ostend but we could travel only some two thousand miles north through peninsular Malaysia and Thailand before we were cut off as surely as by some vast ocean. The Burmese, Laotian and Kampuchean borders are all impassable to the western tourist, so we were obliged to start immediately on a search for onward passage by sea. OCL had agents in Singapore, so we began there. We set in motion a stream of telexes between London, Sydney and Tokyo, and then embarked upon a limited tour of the south east Asian mainland.

★　★　★

Singapore seems determined to build a modern utopia before the century is over. High rise flats, multi-storey shopping centres, prestigous modern hotels and office blocks and sweeping fly-overs smothering the older parts of the city where one felt its heart must lie. Arriving into Changi airport's hushed lobby felt like stepping into the twenty-first century. Earlier that morning, while it was still dark, we had been uncomfortably crushed between baggage and people at the back of a rattling bus, delayed by an overturned truck and a landslide, on our way through the Java hills to Jakarta. We had a plane to catch at seven, and I, for once, applauded the speed and the recklessness of the driver in his manic attempt to make up lost time. We made it to the bus station at six and running for a taxi, were rushed around the outskirts of the city arriving at the airport in time to hear the flight being called. The bike was still en route from Sydney to Singapore, and although we had enjoyed our ten days in Indonesia, we were longing for the freedom to ride our own road. From the palm-fringed beaches and the quiet tropical beauty of the inland regions of Bali, we took a ferry and several buses and reached Surabaya, a place Mopsa had wished to see since

Georgetown, Malaysia

Plate spinning in Kota Baharu, Malaysia

hearing in her teens Kurt Weil's romantic song – Surabaya Johnny. The city was worse than disappointing – crowded, fume-filled, totally without charm. We left as soon as we could find a train to take us to Jogjakarta, which was better, and from there embarked on the bus journey which ended with our headlong rush for the plane.

It took some days getting organised in Singapore, days spent in air conditioned offices and humid streets, noisy food centres where all types of meals could be had under one roof – I indulged my craving for curries from one stall while Mopsa ate Chinese delicacies from another, both of us drinking exotic fruit juices from a third. We drank Singapore Slings in the colonial splendour of the Raffles Hotel but stayed on the top floor of a Chinese boarding house whose manager sat all day in blue pyjama trousers and a string vest dispensing tea and overseeing noisy games of Ma-jong that clattered on until dawn.

While Singapore was busy creating an homogeneous City State, Malaysia remained mixed. The Chinese on the west coast considered themselves businessmen, the true entrepreneurs, and felt increasingly shackled by the Malay majority. In Batu Pahar, on our first night in the country, we were rescued from the sweaty grasp of a dingy hotel by Mr Hoe, who took us to his home. Having inherited a firearms store from his father, he moved on to vehicle accessories and insurance.

"We Chinese," he complained, "we build a row of shops but the law says we can only own a third. So we sell them to the Malays and the shops remain empty or they rent them back to us."

In Malacca the dark salmon-coloured square contains the oldest Dutch building in the east, but the town also boasts the oldest Chinese temple in Malaya. It lies at the end of a street full of coffin shops, where one can buy great ornate Chinese coffins and paper and cardboard replicas of one's most valued possessions – televisions, stereos, fridges and motor cars – to go with one to the next life. We reached Kuala Lumpur, aimed for the area of cheap hotels, and got lost in the narrow streets, becoming more and more confused by the convoluted twistings of one particular one – Jalan-al-Salah. It seemed to run from north to south and east to west, sometimes even parallel to itself, following a meandering course and not even appearing on our map. Eventually it dawned – Kuala Lumpur is full of one way streets and Jalan-al-Salah means just that. We found a Chinese hotel – a long high-ceilinged hall with ten foot high, beautifully carved, partition walls of darkened wood where the charm of the physical surroundings made up for the noise which travelled over them and under the swinging doors from the adjoining rooms and central corridor. Effectively designed to ensure

Due for restoration – old British bikes in Malaysia

maximam air circulation we expected to, and did indeed, see unwelcome visitors come over the walls that night but they were smaller than we envisaged and stole only the bread and biscuits we'd left with our empty tea cups. Our ride to Kuala Lumpa that day had been through the cool, green regimented forests of rubber, a small mosque sat in every kampong and churches and temples lined the road. We passed by the rapidly-developing port of Kalang which local newspapers were boasting would become the second Rotterdam by the year 2000. The government was actively encouraging larger families, seriously intent on more than quadrupling the present population of thirteen and a half million. The country was full of the young: teenage boys affected Michael Jackson hairstyles, and pirate compilations of the American grammy-winning songs blasted out from almost every cafe and market stall. On white sandy beaches on the other side of the peninsula, east coast Malays lived a relaxed, more traditional life. We rode there, over the central hills camping the night in the damp, misty rain forest, and then settled for several days in a thatched hut on stilts in a village by the sea. Sharing the kampong with several large extended families and a half dozen other western tourists, mainly young Australians, we all dined on freshly-caught fish and freshly-picked fruits, families and travellers together. It was the sort of quiet tourism I appreciated. On our second morning there was a commotion in one of the huts. A young Malay woman had scalded her breast with boiling water and to ease the pain had smeared it with the only cream to hand – toothpaste. Through the persistence of an Australian nurse in the village the woman was persuaded to wipe off the paste, bathe the breast with water and leave it to heal itself.

Giant leather-backed turtles were starting to arrive on these eastern beaches and, under security of darkness, to lay their eggs in the sand. It was a magical night when we set out, armed with a torch, in search of one. The thin sliver of a crescent moon rose over the water and tiny particles of phosphorescence glittered blue in the sand. We walked for three hours without success until, returning to the village, we heard a shout from a hundred yards down the beach. The magnificent creature had already laid and buried her eighty-three eggs and was now, surrounded by a small group of encouraging tourists and locals, digging a decoy hole. Grunting hard and clearly exhausted, it took her over an hour to dig the hole and then slowly drag herself back down to the waters edge. With buoyancy came relief and exertions over, and to the cheers of the crowd, she glided effortlessly out to sea. The eggs, soft shelled and slightly larger than table tennis balls, are eaten as a delicacy by the Malays. The government enforces a closed season for egg collecting which lasts two months and ensures the survival of the species but that time had not yet arrived. Before the turtle had reached the sea a local egg collector arrived and began his search. Prodding in the sand with a wire rod he soon found the batch and dug it up – he would get a good price in the market. It seemed that nature, endowing the turtles with the instinct to dig a decoy hole, had not anticipated man.

We had now been on and off the road for the better part of two years and although we met other travellers, mostly Europeans and Australians travelling on public transport, none, apart from a couple in Sri Lanka, had embarked on a journey of quite the magnitude of ours. Through curiosity and interest we sought out fellow overlanders, be they travelling by bicycle, van or motorbike. There had been Martin on his bicycle in Syria; Will on his 250 Honda in Abu Dhabi; Jack and Jo in their van in Amritsar; Charles Batham and Veronique on their Honda Gold Wing, towing a miniaturised container behind them, in Sri Lanka. Our meetings had sometimes been brief, sometimes delightfully protracted, but for the great majority of our time we had only each other with whom to share the common experience. In Kota Bahru, a little further up the coast, we met Keith and Tanya. They had arrived in the small town on the same day as us and we soon heard of each others' presence. Through an intermediary we arranged to meet outside a hotel with the endearing name of Ah Choo, and there, over many cups of tea and plates of fried noodles, we compared notes. Riding a Honda CX500 two up, they had set off on a similar journey around the world from the Isle of Anglesey a year after us. They had attached the same model of Squire sidecar but by Germany had become so disenchanted with it that they swapped it for some panniers and discarding some of their luggage, took to solo motorcycling. Among the things they left in Germany was Keith's hang-glider – he was sorry to have to sacrifice his romantic intention of practising his sport around the world, but without the sidecar space was at a premium. Having lost their extra carrying capacity they rode as far as Pakistan with a spare tyre around Keith's waist. For our part we continued to welcome the luxury the extra space of the sidecar afforded us. An outfit was probably more tiring to ride but I enjoyed its unusual characteristics and we accepted the extra wear it put on tyres, spokes, chains and engine as a necessary compromise. Although we left it on the streets at night, its contents firmly locked inside the box, it had never been broken into, nor had we found evidence of attempts to do so. The foam had begun to disintegrate within the saddle, which made our riding extremely uncomfortable after a couple of hours. We tried various methods of relief, stuffing towels and clothes beneath the sheepskin cover, eventually trying the collapsible bag from inside an Australian wine carton as a water seat, until it burst.

A road from east to west had recently been built through the forested hills at the northern end of Malaya. The most direct route to Penang, we rode it with Keith and Tanya. The considerable cost and effort involved in building the road had not prevented sections of it disappearing down the hillsides or being buried from above by landslides during the rains. The road was kept open by bulldozing into the slopes, thus further destabilising them – it was unsettling to ride around a corner and find nothing but a gaping hole. As the remnants of a communist guerilla force was still active in the area and Thai bandits occasionally wandered over the border, the army patrolled between the camps that guarded the bridges and the road. Heads would pop up from behind the sandbagged machine gun emplacements, soon followed by smiles and waves as we passed by.

It was eighty miles from Penang to the Thai border. We stopped in Hat Yai

At the Sri Tak Sin Hotel, Hat Yai

– a brash commercial frontier town with neon lights, clubs, bars and cheap consumer goods – a Malay sin city just into Thailand. At the Sri Tak Sin hotel the manager insisted we bring the motorcycle into the restaurant.

"No good outside," he said firmly when we told him it was securely locked. "No locks in Thailand. All locks finished."

On the landing between rooms were numerous signs and notices, some were bus and train timetables, others warned visitors "not to take the wrong girl" but told nevertheless exactly where to find her, still more asked guests not to "piss in the shower" or "bathe in the mandi". The mandi, in this instance, was an old oil drum from which we scooped water to wash ourselves. It was as well that these signs were written in English and German for the Thai language was as incomprehensible as any we had met. We had experienced surprisingly little difficulty with language since Hungary, relying on a few words of French, Turkish, Arabic and Hindi, and as English was usually compulsory for schoolchildren, we used a very basic version of it to people to whom it was often long forgotten. Talking to each other at the end these days of halting communication and sign language, we found we still used the oversimplified version. "You come eat?" I would ask Mopsa. "No. First I wash. Then, you and me, we go restaurant. We eat." At the crowded restaurant we went to that evening we sat opposite an English teacher who gave us an introductory lesson in Thai, teaching us the courtesy words and how to ask for a cup of tea. These Mopsa wrote phonetically in her notebook, and the next day we tried them out. Riding north up the eastern side of the isthmus towards Bangkok, we stopped

97

outside Nakhon Si Thammarat at a roadside hut for lunch. Old metal tables and chairs were randomly placed outside and in front of the hut stood a long bench holding a row of six large galvanised pots, each containing a different brilliantly-coloured dish. To the two women behind the bench I clearly enunciated a request for two cups of tea as we had been taught the previous night. As all I got were looks of total incomprehension and bafflement I tried again. The reaction this time was no less encouraging for they dissolved into fits of giggles. What they thought I had said I had no idea but they sat us down and brought us a bottle of Coca-Cola to share. Thai is a tonal language so what might seem to be one word can in fact have many different meanings depending on the tone in which it is said. It would have been impossible for us to even begin to grasp the subtle nuances and complexities of a language such as this in a few short weeks and so, although very few Thais outside of the main tourist areas spoke English, we reverted to the sparse version of our native tongue heavily embellished with exaggerated gesture.

The ride north was through wide paddy fields, bounded by ditches of water in which small boys enthusiastically splashed and into which men cast weighted fishing nets. In the coastal towns fleets of fishing boats, painted in shades of blue, green and vermillion, clustered around the rickety jetties. Along the quays fish and squid were laid out to dry on large mesh screens tilted towards the sun. The nearer we got to Bangkok the busier the road became, and by the outskirts we were embroiled in the frantic rush of traffic heading for the centre. The city authorities had, a month previously, introduced a new traffic flow system in an attempt to ease the appalling congestion. It had not, it seemed, been a success, only adding further confusion and they were considering reversing it. The oppressive humidity and suffocating pollution of the city was exhausting. Returning to our guest house on the days we were brave enough to venture out on the bike, we needed a thorough wash for our faces, hair, arms and clothes were covered in a oily film of dirt. Bangkok was, nonetheless, a fascinating place but a week was enough. The shipping agents told us there was the possibility of a ship from Singapore to Japan in a month, so we fled back into the countryside and further north.

It was over two hundred miles across the flat southern plain before we reached the hill country. The tree-lined road was banked above the surrounding paddy and fields of corn. Water lillies and ducks filled the ditches and the men and women now fished with a twelve foot square net, suspended from a bamboo frame and a long pole. After Tak we climbed into the folds of the forested hills where showers left the road steaming and the jungle glistening in the strong returning sunlight. With the monsoon approaching the showers became more frequent as we slid around on the muddy roads in the far north of the country around Chiang Rai, visiting tribal villages that nestled in the higher hills. At one of the more touristed of these, very close to Chiang Rai, we were taken in hand by a thin, determined local who accompanied us through the craft stalls of the one main street, leading us encouragingly on to a small hut on a hillside at the end of the village.

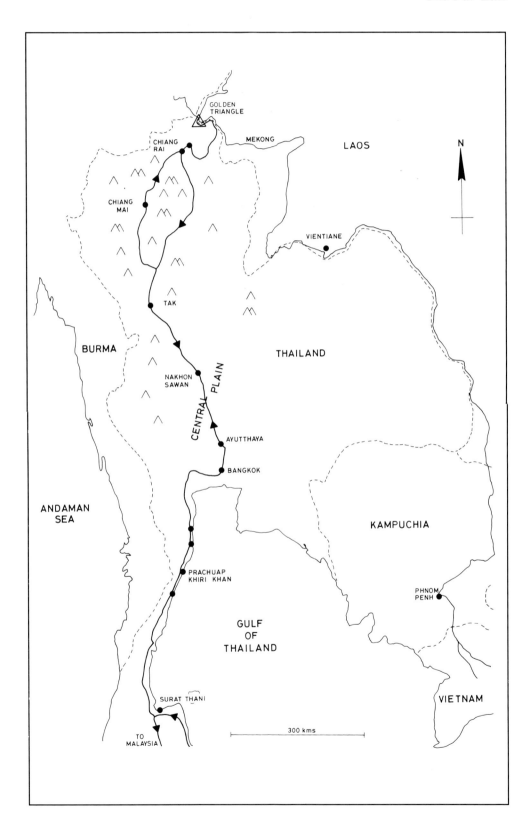

"Come, come. I show you, I show you." He repeated insistently and pushing me into the darkened hut whispered harshly "You want to smoke opium?" The windowless and mud floored hut was bare except for a pair of bunks against opposite walls. From one a shadowy form grunted and raising his head stared at us vacantly for a few moments.

"I think not," I said firmly but the man was undeterred.

"Opium very good for the stomach."

"But he has to drive the motorcycle," said Mopsa uneasily from the doorway.

"No problem. Very good for the head. Opium number one." I thanked him for the offer and we returned through the village to where the bike was parked, leaving him by the hut looking disappointedly after us.

Once we reached the Golden Triangle and, in rain more insistent than we were used to, gazed across the chocolate coloured Mekong to Laos and Burma, we could go no further.

We learnt, through telephoning Bangkok from Chiang Rai, that a boat leaving Singapore in ten days could take the motorcycle to Japan. It departed on a Monday and we were asked to report to the agents in Singapore on the Friday. This left us seven days for the two thousand mile return journey. It was a long hard ride and the rains were now well established. We rode almost continually through the available hours of daylight, slowed by the many security checks in southern Thailand. A determined effort by the government to bring the bandit problem under control had soldiers riding shotgun on top of the trucks and buses and an increase in road blocks. The rain, torrential at times, was at least warm, so it was only tiredness and not exposure that we had to deal with. The border crossings were simple, the officials recognised us from our northward journey, and each night we hung up our soaking clothes to steam through the night to an almost dry state. This was our second forced march and was more enjoyable than the one across Saudi Arabia, despite the rain. Meal and tea stops developed into games of who could finish soonest and the saturated air absorbed our loud singing as we cajoled the bike ever onward, collapsing exhausted at the end of the day. Arriving back in Singapore we returned to our Chinese hotel, and at the port ran into trouble.

The bike, was, to our pleasure, to be loaded onto the *Strathfife*, the same boat which had carried the three of us from Dubai to Karachi a year and a half earlier. Over coffee in his cabin Captain Seddon expressed his regret that he couldn't take us too this time, due to restrictions at the port of Yokohama in Japan. The agent told us that all was arranged, and as soon as we had paid the loading fee, the bike could be winched aboard. The loading fee was five hundred Singapore dollars, payable in all cases where uncontainerised cargo was loaded – the rationale being that this would discourage the shipment of such cargo and help the port, the world's second largest, to run more smoothly. Five hundred dollars was more than a hundred and fifty pounds, money we could ill afford, so we asked whether, as the bike was so very small, and would after all be loaded by *Strathfife's* shipboard crane, the charge might be waived. Mr Loh had never

With a hill tribe family in northern Thailand

heard of this being done but agreed to appeal on our behalf to the Singapore Port Authority. Much to his surprise, they agreed. We saw the bike loaded and without time to catch our breath took a bus to the station where we boarded a train for a forty-eight hour journey back to Bangkok, where we could find a considerably cheaper flight to Tokyo than was available in Singapore, in time to meet it.

The train was also cheap but had little else to recommend it. Economy demanded that we travel third class, which was spartan, though not crowded, and all went well until the train was halted by a derailment just south of the Thai border. A bus would come soon we were told to take us to the frontier but from there we would have to make our own way to Hat Yai to pick up a connection. Some hours later, no bus had appeared, but an express train pulled in and we were allowed to travel on it as far as Hat Yai. It had no third class compartment so we sat in second, only to be ordered to pay a fine for so misbehaving. When we finally boarded the Bangkok train at Hat Yai, there were no free seats and we spent the night and half the next day in a small, damp space beneath a wash basin, being offered strong Thai whisky by one of our companions, until a security guard handed us a note, printed in three languages, warning us to accept neither food nor drink from stangers as it might be drugged – how we missed the motorcycle.

★　★　★

The first thing I saw when I woke was the sky – darkly overcast and threatening rain, which would break the week of glorious sunshine through which we'd made our return ride from Japan's most northerly isle, Hokkaido. I guessed it had been light for about half an hour. The previous evening we had been frustrated in our search for a suitable camping spot and finally, in darkness pulled up a sidetrack, on the edge of a built up area about thirty miles from Tokyo. The night had been clear so we did no more than pull out our sleeping bags and slept beside the motorcycle. Sitting up, I now saw where we had camped. To our right was a small copse of Japanese spruce and to the left a large vegetable allotment, beyond which stood a row of houses. Among the vegetables a middle-aged man, dressed only in long underwear, was pulling onions. Seeing I was awake, he trotted over.

"Hotto? Hotto?" he nodded quizically, rubbing his hands together. I blinked incomprehension and he motioned for me to follow. Struggling out of my sleeping bag and into my trousers, he took me to the front door of his house and disappeared inside. There followed a loud conversation punctuated with a series of exclamatory "aahs" before he returned to thrust into my arms a jug of hot water, a jar of coffee, two small, new, individually-wrapped towels, a block of soap, two packets of cigarettes, a bar of chocolate, packets of sugar, a disposable razor and two ice apples. I bowed my thanks deeply and he bowed an appreciative grin in return. Back at the motorcycle Mopsa was awake and beginning to wonder where I might be.

We were on the road by seven and after winding up out of a wide river valley and over the final mountain pass before the drop down into the vast metropolis of Tokyo, we rounded a sharp corner and there displayed in a layby, in a profusion of primary colours, were fifty or so "sports" motorcycles. The

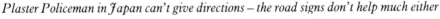

Plaster Policeman in Japan can't give directions – the road signs don't help much either

young riders, some in racing leathers, others who couldn't afford them in one-piece brand name overalls, were smoking and chatting and watching their cohorts scrape knees and footpegs on the tight bends of the mountain pass. Some had been up all night, others at least from the early hours of the morning, and many would be returning within the hour to their jobs in the city. Many of the bikes were fast accelerating two-strokes but not one was over 400 cc. Japan has strict laws regulating the motorcycle industry. The manufacturers may not market any motorcycle over 750 cc within the country and any enthusiast wanting a larger capacity bike of Japanese make must re-import an export model from abroad. There is a four-tier licensing system, related to engine size, which becomes progressively more expensive and more difficult, with the result that only two per cent of motorcyclists are entitled to ride bikes above 400 cc. Style is very important to the Japanese rider – whether one rides a sports or off-the-road model one can not be seen out on it without the appropriate clothes. Honda had recently introduced a 250 cc single four stroke with classic British styling, and these were often being ridden by men dressed in black leathers, white turtle neck sweaters and sporting silver pudding-basin helmets. Perhaps most extaordinary of all is a group of Harley-Davidson riders who trim their machines as exact replicas of Southern Californian police bikes and at weekends, dressed in the requisite costume right down to the sleeve patches, and with POLICE emblazoned across their helmets, ride two abreast along the city streets and overpasses. It was so very different to the functional role of the motorcycle in the rest of Asia but there is a functional aspect in Japan too. Ninety per cent of Honda's domestic sales of 1.3 million units annually is made up of bikes under 50 cc – glossy little step-thru's for the housewife or high-school girl, with names like "Love", "Spacy", "Racy" and "Tact"; and the Honda Cub, of course, with its Yamaha and Suzuki counterparts. Used as delivery vehicles around the cities, often with a curious cantilevered attachment behind, which carries a decorative lacquer tray set with a take-away meal – bowls of soup, rice, raw fish, whatever – not a drop of which is spilt as the rider skilfully weaves his way through the city traffic to make delivery to an office or shop.

As we reached the outskirts of Tokyo the rain began to fall in sheets. We were heading for the centre and the British Embassy compound. The British Ambassador, an old friend of Mopsa's family, had invited us to stay at the official residence within the compound. We were due to arrive at eleven o'clock and as we pulled up on the gravel drive outside the mansion the butler, footman and two maids appeared to welcome us. They had been warned not to expect a limousine, and although their expressions revealed nothing, we felt they were a little surprised to see two wet, bedraggled figures in muddy boots and Barbours stepping off an equally wet, muddy and greasy motorcycle. We dutifully followed as they processed through the main hall and up the stairway to our room, carrying at arms length our dripping helmets, gloves, rucksack and tank bag. At least on this occasion we were not required to bring the motorcycle up the steps and into the hall for safety.

★　★　★

A finely restored early Kawasaki, based on the BSA A10

We had arrived in Japan two months earlier on an Air India flight from Hong Kong. The bike was unloaded at the port of Yokohama and we spent some days entwined in a strict and complicated bureaucracy with regard to its temporary importation. We were required to have the carnet authenticated by the Japan Automobile Federation, insurance had to be obtained and the paperwork was meticulously made out by an official who constantly referred to a huge book of regulations. Japan is not a place where people usually temporarily import a vehicle – there is nowhere else to take it except out again and shipping costs from another continent are naturally high. The document we received from the customs at Yokohama was numbered 00006. Was ours only the sixth vehicle ever to be temporarily imported through that port?

We were short of money again and spent our first six weeks pursuing additional sponsorship and contacting magazines and newspapers with a view to selling them our story. On our return to Tokyo from Hokkaido we were invited to appear on a housewives' morning chat show on television. It was a very brief appearance, we were asked just two questions to which we gave monosylabic replies while the compere rattled on in Japanese about us and our trip. The show was live and we were asked to ride the bike onto the studio floor. As we waited off camera I started the engine, as arranged, about a minute before we were due on. Technicians immediately leapt into action, two of them dashing over to ask me if I could turn down the volume of the engine.

Before our tour to the north we were asked to Osaka by a potential sponsor and had friends of a brother-in-law to visit there. The heat and humidity that settled over Tokyo during July and August was enervating in the extreme so we were looking forward to leaving its slow, congested and heavily regulated streets. We decided to go via Mount Fuji which was, as is often the case, hidden in mist, and then take the coast road to Osaka. Unwilling to ride the expressways, which have prohibitive tolls, we found the alternative road passed through an almost continuous strip of ribbon development stretching from Tokyo over 160 miles to Nagoya. The traffic was as slow and congested as in the city we had left. Four-fifths of Japan is steep sided mountains – effectively uninhabitable. This leaves an area of about 30,000 square miles for a population of over 120 million, so it is not surprising that the coastal areas are so built up. As we were making such slow progress we took to the Expressway, despite the cost, but at the first toll station the collector obstinately refused to let us pass. Stepping vigorously out of his booth he became extremely agitated, gesturing towards Mopsa and the sidecar box, and began to shout. We had little Japanese and no idea what he was saying and sat bemused while his outburst became louder and angrier. Eventually, exhausted by his failure to communicate, he took our money and, shrugging in despair at our stupidity, let us continue. We later learnt that the carrying of pillion passengers is illegal on expressways. The poor man had been trying to explain to us that Mopsa would have to sit on top of the sidecar box before he could allow us to proceed.

We returned to Tokyo via the quiet and tidy simplicity of the temples and shrines at Kyoto and the inland road through the mountains. After the initial shock and thrill of arriving in a modern high-tech city we were now a little perplexed by the apparent contradictions within Japanese society. Their homes are cramped but pleasingly uncluttered and perfectly arranged. The exteriors of the modern buildings, however, are often ugly concrete, of no real design, around which are spread pipes, air-conditioning units and haphazard wires that then spread themselves out across the sky. In the rapid re-building that has taken place since the war, it seems that the Japanese have simply ignored the uglier aspects of development. The mountains are beautiful but it was difficult to take a scenic photograph that did not include electricity pylons or some other manifestation of technology. A paranoia of earthquakes, of which Japan has a long history, has resulted in their engineers and road builders encasing the steep slopes by the sides of the roads in concrete and wire. It felt as though they were attempting to cover the whole country in a hairnet of concrete and steel. To appreciate the country we had look as though through Japanese eyes and concentrate on the the beauty that is there – in the temples, the shrines, inside people's houses, in shop window displays, in gardens and in flower shops. Travelling by motorcycle we viewed all that was around us. The Japanese, in aesthetics at least, seemed more concerned with the individual item. There are two images of Tokyo which remain very clearly in my mind: the city fishermen who, in their lunch hour, would dangle their rods into concrete pools of water, stocked with carp, surrounded by modern buildings and within yards of a busy flyover; and the evening golfers, who on multi-storeyed platforms, and under floodlights, relentlessly drove their balls into a huge net placed no more than a hundred yards away. Both of these pastimes reflect the Japanese city dwellers' longing to escape: on crowded commuter trains business men are seen snatching a few minutes' sleep in which to dream of rural scenes. They have a name for it. They call it "rowing one's boat".

Our ride north to Hokkaido along the central mountain spine of Honshu brought fresh air and showed another side of Japanese life – one of quiet back roads, rural villages, forested hills, and lonely shrines. Leaving Tokyo on an August public holiday we joined an unbroken stream of traffic heading for the hills – families bound for the inland holiday resorts. On a much-favoured road which winds up to the beautiful and sacred lake of Chuzenji, we were jammed in solid traffic across two lanes for more than two hours. Every few minutes the line of cars moved a few feet forward and then stopped again. The drivers and passsengers took it in their stride, were patient and unperturbed – it was no different to what they were used to in the cities – and if their engines began to overheat they would pull into one of the crowded lay-bys, open their bonnets and sit admiring the view.

The further north we travelled the emptier the roads became and we camped by pebbly river beds or next to flat, silent volcanic lakes. A four-hour ferry ride carried us to Hokkaido, where we found the tourist buses and followed them through the fishing villages where seaweed and fish lay drying in the sun, filling the air with a salty tang. The Japanese love their northern island and the wide open space it offers: during the summer they visit in their millions, so we joined the ranks of camera-toting tourists at every scenic spot, and were often asked to join in with the ritual of the snapshot, either by posing or snapping. In Sapporo we were interviewed by the island's main newspaper and our photograph appeared in the following day's issue. The Japanese are inveterate newspaper readers and since almost every person on the island read this particular one we were constantly being recognised. After a night beside an isolated lake in the north of the island we were quietly enjoying breakfast when a minibus full of tourists passed by. The sharp-eyed guide spotted us and stopped. The passengers piled out of it and walked over.

"Photo okay?" asked the guide, with a quick bow. "Photo okay" Mopsa nodded resignedly, so they lined up in front of the bike, obscuring both it and us, while the guide took a quick photograph with each of the cameras that lay in a pile at his feet.

Our time in Japan was unco-ordinated, without rhythm, we had no sense of travelling onward, rather we went out on several side trips from Tokyo, and on returning were each time hit with a barrage of sensory overload, from the crowds, the sounds and lights of the electronic devices which controlled the traffic, the pedestrians and the public transport system with an iron hand. We had met many people and made many friends, had been welcomed into their homes, taken on outings, fed and cosseted with a warm politeness that made our life both interesting and comfortable. We met a wide cross section of Japanese society. There had been our motorcycling friends who belonged to Transcyclist International, a Japan-based fraternity of riders interested in foreign touring. Then there was the Sidecar Community who took us out to festivals and rallies, and business men to whom we'd applied for sponsorship. There were sailor-suited schoolgirls who giggled at us when we stood in for a German friend's English lesson. There was Doctor Sato who ran his own psychiatric

Mopsa could always find me in a crowd – with a group of motorcycle enthusiasts in Hokkaido, Japan

hospital in northern Honshu and who gave us an insight into more traditional Japanese ways, leaving Mopsa rather put out when she was firmly left out of the conversation until I made specific attempts to include her, while Dr Sato's wife hovered between kitchen and table waiting on but not joining us for the meal she had cooked. In a small town on the northern coast a middle-aged woman invited us in to her home because, as she was later to tell us, she had a heavy heart – she had been asked for directions by a touring motorcyclist, which she gave, but hadn't thought to ask him in to shelter from the rain. As atonement for her thoughtlessness she decided to invite the next motorcyclists she saw, who happened to be us. We were with a young student at the time who spoke some English and could translate. Our hostess told us she was deeply honoured to have two people who had come so far to lift the weight from her heart. As we entered her house she knelt down in front of me, touching her nose to the ground in traditional respect and welcome. Tea was ceremonially prepared and served. "You have come all the way from England by motorcycle," she sighed through our interpreter. "You must be very tired."

★　★　★

"Of course, Mr English, there is no problem in taking your motorcycle to South Korea. If the customs office at the ferry port agree then we agree." This was a somewhat reticent consular official at the South Korean embassy speaking. We had received the same response from the customs vis-a-vis the consulate. There was a problem: namely a regulation which stated that no two- or three- wheeled vehicles be allowed to enter the country, even temporarily, by ferry from Japan. This regulation was designed to prevent their home market being swamped by cheap second hand Japanese motorcycles and to protect their own fledgling motorcycle industry that was producing Honda and Suzuki bikes under license. No-one wanted to be the one to turn down our application for a dispensation so we were passed back and forth between consulate, embassy, tourist development office and customs. Finally we appealed to one of the Korean motorcycle manufacturers and they offered us the use of two of the largest bikes they were then producing, a Honda designed 125 cc Daelim model, for the duration of our stay in the country.

An overnight ferry from Shiminoseki in southern Honshu took us to Pusan, Korea's main port on the south eastern tip of the peninsula then a taxi-ride from the docks to the Daelim dealers where we picked up the bikes. Riding out of the city that afternoon was a wobbly experience – we were unused to solo riding and sections of the main streets had been torn up and covered in two-inch steel plate

Korea's largest stone Buddha at Kwanch'ok-Sa

– an underground rail system was being built for the 1988 Olympics. Korea is developing fast but had not yet reached the stage where the roads were ordered and smooth – we were back to Asian conditions with a vengeance. Long wheelbase bicycles with vast loads and bundles wavered between the speeding traffic with dusty, diesel fuming buses veering to sudden halts whenever potential passengers beckoned. We coughed and spluttered our way over the hills which surround the port, passing slow-moving but highly polluting buses and trucks and then as the late afternoon sun cast long shadows over the golden rice paddy and the field workers began to walk home via track and verge, we stopped to savour the moment. It was mid-September, and all over Korea the rice was being harvested, mostly by hand, by groups of workers or families who sloshed around up to their knees in mud. The countryside was green and golden. Willow, beech, and poplar trees lined the narrow country roads, which carried the slowly plodding ox-cart or the small multi-purpose rotavators. A change of wheel converts these into a tractor which can be used on the road, in the field or the paddy, as well as for ploughing. They are fast replacing the ox and beginning to revolutionise farming all over Eastern Asia. It was a landscape of flat bottomed and tapering cultivated valleys, and gentle forested hills; the houses of small farming communities cluster together to protect themselves from the bitter winter winds which rush in from the Siberian plain. The houses are stongly built and courtyarded, with blue glazed tile roofs and underfloor heating. We stayed in places such as these, small cheap country inns where the bikes would be propped against the huge stone wash stands which stood in the centre of the courtyards, and slept on thin mattresses on the floor. Eating was easy, our staple was "Pekpan" – a bowl of rice, a bowl of soup, and a choice from up to fifteen different side dishes of fish, meat and vegetables in sauces or spicily pickled. Language was again a difficulty but as the Koreans were unreservedly open and friendly it never became a problem and once again a few words, with lots of smiles and gestures, went a long way – we certainly never felt isolated. To the villagers the road is their own, so they stride or saunter across in front of the traffic, stating a right of abode. There was a definite need to be wary here: we had become accustomed to the Japanese way, where school children collect a yellow flag at one side of a crossing, wave it as they cross, and then deposit it in a bucket on the other side.

Riding these uncluttered roads we visited small shrines, brightly coloured and set back from the road with carved dragons' heads to protect them from evil, and great working temples high in the hills. A highway runs diagonally across the country and most of the heavy traffic runs on this, leaving the minor roads to local vehicles and to motorcycles which are not allowed on the freeway. In a warm autumn sun we stopped to admire the ruins of past Korean kingdoms as we made our way northward to Seoul. The capital is a cauldron of development: a rapidly expanding city which was badly damaged during the Korean war in the fifties so now has the advantage of being planned. But, as in Pusan, the wide streets were in a state of upheaval with the construction of two more subway lines causing disruption to an already tangled traffic system. It was a challenge

Mopsa enjoying a traditional Korean meal

and a pleasure to slip amongst the trucks, buses and cars on our 125s, so much nimbler and more mobile than the outfit. Our two weeks in South Korea became a holiday, a break from the greater journey. The rich colours of the countryside, bathed in a warm autumnal sun, and the optimism and open friendliness of the people masked the darker side. The numerous military road blocks in the north, the beaches on the east coast fenced off with barbed wire and mine warning signs showed a nation divided and the heavy hand of a dictatorial government curbed freedoms in the interest of security. First by ship, then by train and then by motorcycle we returned to Tokyo, to start our preparations for finally leaving Asia.

Chapter Seven

North America

IT WAS a real scorcher of a day. One hundred and ten degrees, perspiring people muttered to us during our frequent roadside stops for iced tea and to let the engine of the Triumph cool a little. We were in the Columbia Gorge, on the Washington/Oregon border, heading towards Portland and the Pacific coast of the United States. Hot winds from the interior pursued us as we slowly snaked our way westward. I had been nursing the motorcycle all the way from Chicago, determined to make it back to Los Angeles, where a workshop and spare parts awaited us for the major overhaul we were planning before we crossed the border into Mexico and continued on to South America. During the last few months the bike had suffered from two major tantrums and a series of subsequent grumblings which had begun seriously to undermine our confidence in its ability to get us back to England. Before we arrived in North America it had, like ourselves, been temperamental at times, but always got us to our destination without major delay. Now clouds of doubt were casting shadows over the whole enterprise. The original intention had been to arrive in Alaska from Japan and to journey south down the full length of the Americas. Our timing was disrupted, however, and with winter closing in we flew instead to Los Angeles. Once there we reluctantly decided to ride an eighteen thousand mile loop around the North American continent. While snow covered the north and midwest we travelled across the south, then with the spring we headed north and were now, in the summer, returning to Los Angeles.

Four miles on from Lyle, a small town with a population of three hundred the familiar sound of the engine changed abruptly and was followed by a loud, resounding crack. The engine seized as I grabbed the clutch lever and we coasted silently to a halt.

"Something's bloody snapped," I shouted, turning to see a rather strained expression on Mopsa's face. As our eyes met a mounting tension that had been building up between us on this too hot, too dusty day dissolved. We both grinned stupidly for a few moments.

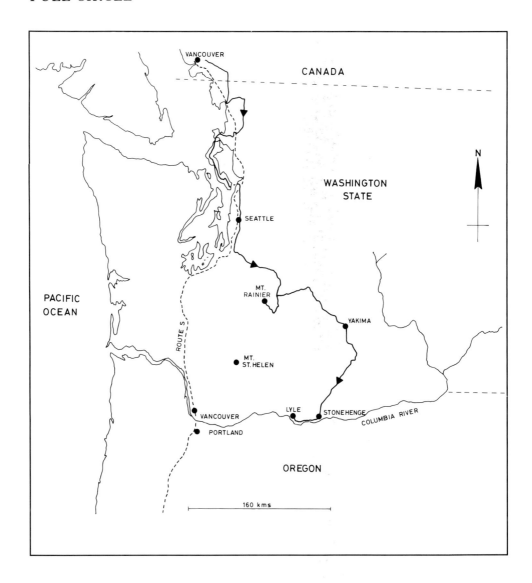

"Well, nothing like yet another breakdown to add some sparkle to a hot and boring day's ride," declared Mopsa as we pushed the outfit fifty yards down the road to a lay-by. I began to lay out the tools when a Dodge pickup drew alongside.

"Having problems?" the driver asked, introducing himself as Jack Bryan, the local Fire Chief, from Lyle. We explained. His friend ambled to the back of the truck and pulled out some cold beer.

"I think you'll be needin' one of these."

★   ★   ★

Eight months previously we had arrived in LA, tired and gummy-eyed from a long flight across the Pacific. After the high-tech congestion of Tokyo the city looked spacious and unhurried and full of a seaside light similar to Sydney which had us, in our disorientated state, imagining we were back there. The only cloud in a blue sky tinged with smog was the usual fiscal one. We soon found, however, that things, as they always seemed to, fell into place.

Four days after our arrival we collected the outfit from the docks. In return for free nights of accommodation at the youth hostel we spent our mornings cleaning and painting and doing general chores. In the afternoons we started to make contact with the Los Angeles motorcycling and sidecar fraternities. Here in a city where the automobile is king exists a sizeable cult dedicated to the alternatives of two and three wheeled travel. Embraced by the United Sidecar Association, the Velocette Owners Club and disparate British biking enthusiasts we were then invited in to the warmly chaotic household of the Krautz family where we stayed until our departure. Weekend rallies up canyons and along craggy mountain ridges led to massive all-you-can-eat brunches and endless cups of watery black coffee. Mopsa found work with a telephone answering service and I was in demand as a casual carpenter and house painter. The weeks slid by. Indira Ghandi was shot and America re-elected its President with a detached indifference. Thanksgiving was soon followed by Christmas and I prepared the bike in the Supertwins workshop of Chris Scott, an archetypal blond-haired Californian whose all-consuming passions were for motorcycles and surfing. The magazine *Cycle World* took us on board as peripatetic contributors and we were donated a lifetime's supply of spark plugs by NGK. By the end of January we were ready to move. Escaping the urban sprawl of Los Angeles, with its MacDonalds, its Taco Bells and convenience stores on every corner, and with the sun setting over the sea and a cold wind biting at our faces, we rode over the Anza Borrego mountains, to see the desert spreading out before us to the east.

Leaving the protected coast of Southern California we were assailed by a continental cold front that had swept down from the north. Our first night in the open had the temperatures dropping to well below freezing and the morning greeted us with driving sleet. Outside of Yuma row upon row of motorcaravans were spread out across the stony desert like a huge encamped army. It seemed that the whole of retired America was on the move. Snowbirds we heard them called and they became our constant companions as we toured the southern states. An elderly couple from Illinois presented us with their card. "Hello, we are the Mosers. General delivery, USA South in winter. North in summer. No job – not looking. Our social security tax at work. No phone, no schedule, no worries."

Across the southern Arizona desert along a wide black strip of freeway, we raced to Tucson with the rattling and snaking body of a Southern Pacific freight train, over a mile long with its four massive engines and sixty-five carriages. We detoured to find snow on the surrounding hills around Tombstone, the legendary town that now welcomed tourists, not gunfighters. Across the state line and into New Mexico, proudly declaring itself the home of Miss USA 1984. Back on the Interstate the miles rolled by with a regular monotony. Lordsbury, a pale, dusty and run-down town boasted four campsites, ten motels, eleven restaurants and seventeen modern gas stations on consecutive roadside billboards, but there was little reason to stop. Derring, city motto "Pure water and fast ducks", was home to the fastest duck race in the west. We pushed on through Las Cruces to camp below a mountain ridge overlooking the White Sands Missile Base, huddling against the cold around a blazing fire and gazing with awe at the myriad stars in the clear night sky.

It was a curious life we now led. Not journeying on and homeward but round and back. The country was at times tedious, at others dazzlingly fresh. One could travel the length and breadth of the United States staying in standardised motels, eating in fast food chains and being waited on by young men and women wearing the same uniforms. The accent might change but the service didn't. It was so easy as we travelled on, over the Sacramento mountains through a world of white, white snow, where fresh-faced families careered on skis, snowmobiles and rubber inner tubes down the monochrome slopes. Then the chimerical wonder of the Carlsberg limestone caverns, in stark contrast to the tackily painted town of Whites City at the entrance. "Old-time" plywood facades fronted overpriced curio shops and in an attached coffee bar we observed an embarrassed father, closely watched by his two young sons, test his quick draw technique against a plaster cowboy.

Across Texas and the countryside began to change. A richer soil covered the ground with green pastures and stands of oak, elm and pecan trees. Oil wells ground on like foraging birds in a seemingly perpetual motion, dipping and

Sidecarring American Style

rising, dipping and rising, and white picket fences enclosed them, the cattle and the stud. We stopped at a campsite in Gonzales on the alternative Route 90 and stepped tentatively into the attached bar. Country and western blared from the juke box and in one corner Mexicans were playing pool.

"Well, howdy! My name's Wylie Watson," the creased and sunburnt face of the man behind the counter exclaimed, thrusting forward an equally creased and sunburnt hand. "I'm the concessionaire. Now, you're not to worry about paying for this campsite. I shall take this five dollar bill of yours and when you're all settled in you can come on over and spend it on beer."

When we returned the Lone Star Lites had already been taken from the icebox and stood warming on the bar. They knew how the English drank their beer. Denny Thibodaux, a watery-eyed cajun was enraptured by Mopsa's voice.

"We ain't never had nobody from England visit us here."

"Yeah, ain't their's the cutest accent," added Jeannie fluttering her eyelids forcefully at me.

"I ain't never seen a good lookin' man," put in Herman, Jeannie's six foot seven inch husband, thrusting another Lone Star Lite into my hand.

"Hey – how come y'all can say those places like Whoost'n and San Antoneioh? My, if I ever was to go to England, I'll bet I couldn't even say London." Denny Thibodaux was getting a little drunk.

"Say, do y'all have niggers in England?" . . . "You do?" . . . "Yeah, well we don't go in for all that integration stuff around here. I say a nigger's a nigger whether he's black or white."

Ricky, the weigher at the local cattle auction arrived and invited us along to view the action the following morning. Then he asked confidentially if it was true that we ate horsemeat in England.

"Oh y'all do now! Ask anybody round here. All our old horses go to England for meat. Them they don't eat in New York that is." He went on to describe to us the local casseroles made of squirrel and dove. Next morning his girlfriend Patsy showed us into the auction. It was pure Texas with corn-coloured stetsons, checked shirts and a deep drawl over the intercom. Behind us sat a row of stolid Mennonites in their nineteenth century clothes of baggy blue denim jackets and trousers and flat, black felt hats, each one sporting a long wispy beard. Heifers were being sold at the rate of four a minute while over the loudspeakers we listened to the auctioneer's extraordinary morse code-like patter ". . . . . de dum de dum de dum 65 65 de da de da de da 66 66 de da de dum got two folks from England here visiting by way of Japan on a motorbike. Yeah. De dum de dum 66 66 67 67 67 Sold. Now move him on out o'here. Next . . . 58 58 . . ."

We continued on to Louisiana, trying to guard against a creeping complacency which would have us taking the softest option, the straightest road or the most available campsite. Adventure and interest had to be sought out, they didn't just exist as they had through most of our travelling. The roadside services increased as we travelled east. At the Louisiana border the tourist office dispensed a free plastic glass of orange juice to each new arrival and was of Greek revival design, as were the picnic shelters and the pet's rest area. Through the bayoux the forests of cypress floated in a grey water that reflected the sky with a grey weedy lichen, called Spanish moss, tumbling from the branches. It rained incessantly as we splashed along secondary roads first through Cajun country and then past the large leafy gardens of old, rambling plantation homes. We crossed the wide waters of the misty Mississippi on a small ferry which plied its way back and forth, captained by a former aircraft pilot from the Isle of Man. He invited us to the bridge thus conferring on us a great honour, for he had known Geoff Duke and remembered with nostalgia those glorious years of British motorcycling.

The motorcycle had been running well all the way from Los Angeles, but now as we crossed the pan handle of Florida towards Daytona on the Atlantic coast it started to display symptoms I knew were warnings of trouble ahead. It was a strange relationship that I, and in a different way Mopsa, had with this machine that had grown over the miles. To make oneself so totally dependent on a machine to realise a dream that involved several years of one's life was an unusual condition to find oneself in. On the one hand the journey was a personal one involving the people, the countries and the landscape through which we travelled. On the other hand it was often an obsessive exercise involving a stubborn determination to complete an around the world trip on our chosen vehicle whatever the cost. The engine, due to its several rebuilds of which some had taken place in less than ideal circumstances, was now prone to breakdown. Daily I checked the oil level and the condition of the spark plugs. We found a campsite in the Ocala Forest, about thirty miles from Daytona where we planned to join the tens of thousands of other motorcyclists who had travelled from the four corners of North America on the annual pilgrimage to the racetrack for Bike Week. It was full of serried ranks of large and luxurious caravans, the permanent homes of elderly Americans from the north who had retired to the sunshine state. The bike had been losing power that day and was tending to get unduly hot, so early the following morning I undertook a thorough check but finding nothing amiss we set out for the coast. We managed ten miles before the motorcycle spluttered to a halt. The engine was extremely hot, lacked compression and I feared a partial seizure. Our disappointment was extreme and an intense frustration at the audacity of this stupid lump of moving metal to break down on us once again brought Mopsa to tears and sent me into an uncharacteristic rage. I sat by the side of the road for a few minutes to let the feelings of resignation take a hold while Mopsa tried to flag down a passing vehicle. Eventually one stopped and towed us back to the campsite where with the help of a one-armed Vietnam veteran the engine was dismantled, and the cause of the seizure found – the head gasket had been blown away between the two cylinders. The seized pistons and scored barrels were salvaged by Rotten Ron, a freewheelin' Triumph mechanic in Gainsborough and we rode in for the final three days of racing at Daytona. Outside the stadium the spectacle of so many motorcycles of such varying types, ridden by such varied people, from portly conservatives on full dress Honda Gold Wings to the more radical chain

An extra engine would have suited us well

and leather set on their chopperised Harley-Davidsons, more than compensated for the upsets of the last few days. Cruising on the hard packed sand of the legendary beach on which the races had once been run we saw an uglier side of American life. It was the weekend when the bikers left and the students arrived, cramming into hotels ten to a room, for a spring break from the eastern colleges that involved getting drunk and getting laid. The mixture was a volatile one. Two pink faced youths in a souped-up truck took exception to the cruising antics of a large black Harley rider and started hurling abuse. A vicious argument ensued, knifes and handguns pulled and shots fired into the air, before the arrival of the law. We rode away shaken by the experience. It was not the violent argument I found upsetting but the natural way both antagonists had resorted to their respective weapons. On occasions people, and Americans in particular, would ask if we travelled with a gun. Both Mopsa and I have an aversion to any form of aggressive self-defence and a firm belief in the self-deprecating smile as the way to forestall potentially dangerous situations had worked well in our travels to date, although we hadn't been threatened or violently robbed as yet. What could you do if two or three surly bandits were to approach with knives and guns demanding money – try and shoot them? I would rather hand over the money. I did, however, when feeling a little vulnerable when, for instance, we were camped by the side of road, making sure that the small hammer we travelled with was within easy reach.

From Daytona we rode on through the alligator-filled marshes of the Everglades and out across a hundred miles of turquoise sea on a causeway to Key West. On 19th March we reached the most southerly point of the continental

United States, albeit on an island, and with a sigh of regret, for we would have preferred to continue south, we turned our backs on the sun and rode towards New York.

After a further 650 miles the bike started panting again. We had arrived in Talahassee on the doorstep of some friends of Chris Scott from LA. Jon Bergland was a genial mechanic who had only recently sold his Triumph dealership and the remains of his stock of parts and bikes were stored below his wood-panelled house. Together we battled for three days with the idiosyncrasies of our ailing machine which had again begun to blow a gasket. The cylinder head was showing signs of warpage and the apparent reason for our troubles, so the barrels were milled and the engine carefully reassembled. Even then the bike refused to run well and it was only after much tinkering, two false starts and the retarding of the timing that we felt confident enough to continue.

We travelled with the spring through Georgia, our first in three years. Pretty white weather-boarded houses, rose-covered fences, pink azaleas and flowering dogwood lined the road. The towns with their fine colonial courthouses and elegant church towers exude more solidity, community and history than those in the west. The Smoky Mountains, misty and ethereal, were followed by the joys of the Blue Ridge Parkway. Scenic roads of such beauty, catering solely to the motorised tourist, exist in very few parts of the world and it seems apposite that a country with such a love for the automobile should build them to entice its drivers. We swept from bend to bend as panoramic views flicked by on left and right and raced with the clouds until a fierce blizzard engulfed us and we descended, freezing and wind-blown to face the broken up

Young sidecar adventurers at a British Bike Rally in Washington State

and pot-holed roads of inner city Washington DC. American inner-city decay and urban blight were never so forcefully revealed to us as here, where they surround the prestigious avenues, monuments, museums and government buildings of the richest and most powerful nation on earth.

The towering skyline of Manhattan revealed itself as we approached from the pedestrian greyness of New Jersey. It sparkled through the thickening dusk, like some great medieval citadel. We coursed towards it over elevated highways, swept along by the rushing traffic, dropping into the dank darkness of the Holland Tunnel before emerging into the colourful chaos of Chinatown. We worked our way uptown, through the drizzle, to the St. Moritz Hotel on Central Park, where we'd been booked in by CBS Television who were due to interview us on the morning news the next day. Tramping through the foyer in our riding gear we felt like gauche backwoods children, visiting the big city for the first time. In the lift fur coats and expensive suits were held carefully away from our dripping barbours. Our room, although not as extravagant as we had hoped or anticipated, considering the hotel's facade and foyer, was warm and comfortable and overlooked the Park. We had lately been surviving on an economical diet based on pasta, potatoes and porridge, so our eyes were drawn to the room service menu which we studied greedily until we saw the prices. Our thirty dollar per person expense allowance would not go very far here, with tea for two from CBS running at twelve dollars. Determined, however, to enjoy our one night of relative luxury we went out to an Indian restaurant nearby eating hugely and cheaply, and without french fries. We had spent the previous two weeks in the open, camping on hard, cold earth so on returning to the hotel we immediately sank with deep sighs into the comfort of hot baths and thick towels, soft beds and crisp sheets. An uninterrupted night's sleep, however, was too much to ask. At eleven o'clock the studio telephoned. They wanted a map of our route. At two o'clock they telephoned again. This time they wanted details of our home life. At four o'clock they rang a third time. They had just received some exciting film from space – we had been "bumped" and were no longer going out live. At nine the limousine arrived to take us to the studio. What would have taken ten minutes to walk took a full half hour as we crawled through Manhattan's impenetrable traffic. Collected by the programme's producer, a woman who seemed as disinterested as she was aloof, we were bustled into make-up before being shepherded into the studio. A former Miss America more renowned for her looks than her journalistic expertise, was talking to a bespectacled academic about beetles. As he left we took his place, and the cameras rolled. Within five minutes it was all over. They wanted to get home.

"When do you think you'll be showing it?" Mopsa asked.

"Oh, it could go out anytime. You're generic now."

We stayed more than two weeks in New York, with friends both in the city and on Long Island. We spent much of our time just walking, enjoying every street, avenue and edifice made so familiar by movies and television shows. It is a vibrant and exciting city, populated by people from such diverse ethnic origins and where as blond haired, fair skinned people we felt part of a small minority.

The city moved rapidly about us, we planned trips to shows, to museums, but found stimulation enough in shop windows and menus, street dancing and buskers. But there was another side to New York life, one that we could only guess at. The disparity between rich and poor was never more glaring than in the dishevelled dropouts who openly begged in the street and in the number of homeless, estimated to be over ten thousand. The effort required to keep a city of such vitality and contrast functioning must be enormous. For ourselves money was also short so we looked around for a suitable way in which to raise some. Interest came from a glossy "you can have it all: stunning figure, successful career, healthy sex life, loving partner" woman's magazine called *Self*. They were intrigued that our relationship had survived nearly three years of constant companionship and asked to interview us for their "Real Love Stories of the Eighties" series. The piece was entitled "One couple's round the world recipe for feeding love and marriage". Flinching a little at the mawkishness of their approach we nevertheless put our credibility on the line for they offered to pay us handsomely for the interview, and we spent a day careering around the city's sights being photographed. On the Staten Island Ferry the shots were of us eating extravagant ice cream sundaes wearing New York Yankees' baseball hats, but not until we were passing through Times Square at the peak of the afternoon rush hour did the photographer, draped in a selection of cameras and hanging from the back of a jeep, suddenly yell "Stop! There's the shot I want." We brought traffic to a standstill for over ten minutes while trying to follow her inaudible and wild gesticulations, clambering all over the bike and sidecar, deafened by the noise of the protesting horns and the haranguing of New York's legendary cabbies, while she emptied three cameras in rapid succession until we had achieved the pose she most wanted. When we told the editor how much a year of travel actually cost us her mouth dropped open in disbelief. She earned more than that in a month. It was a different world.

Once out of the city we slipped back into a travelling routine that in the States involved country roads and nights in isolated forests and State Park campsites. The freedom to take each day as it came, of not knowing where we would be at the end of it, was tempered by a need for structure, for an overall plan that would see us in eighteen months or so, back in England with our wanderings complete. In four months the three years we had originally envisaged for the trip would be up. In New York we had come as close as we ever would, both practically and emotionally, to packing it in and returning to England. Our finances were at a low ebb, the motorcycle was behaving erratically and letters came from Mopsa's father suggesting that we had been away long enough and nobody would begrudge us our achievement of having been around the world if we came home now. One-way air tickets to London were being advertised at only $125. Homesickness affected us in waves, and was usually dependent on how interesting a time we were having or on how well we were getting on. It was more the attractions of the landscape that held our interest in the States, rather than a culture which, as people from England, we could quickly assimilate despite its many anomalies and puzzling contradictions.

There was landscape in North America that we still longed to see but it lay to the west whence we had come. We also knew that in South America and Africa we would find the adventure we still craved.

New England had a settled air of quiet tradition and respectability. There was little of the brashness of other parts of the United States. At Plymouth the rock on which the Pilgrim Fathers had landed was surprisingly small and a weather-beaten replica of the Mayflower floated forlornly nearby, patiently waiting for the mass of tourists who would trample her decks once the season began. On a hill overlooking the harbour lay the cemetery and it was here that one was able to feel, rather than be spoon-fed, the history of the town. Grey tombstones with simple engravings dating back to the seventeenth century are clustered together under spreading trees. Of the first one hundred and two who arrived in 1620 only fifty survived the first harsh winter. Soon after the first settlement had been established ninety per cent of the Indian population of the area was wiped out by a smallpox epidemic brought in by the settlers. On leaving the rugged Atlantic coast we rode through forests of silver birch and beech, towards Quebec. There had been no conscious decision made between Mopsa and I as to whether we were to continue after our thoughts, only half discussed in New York, had raised the possibility of our returning to England. Our journey was predetermined, an amalgam of each others dreams and wishes, and had a momentum of its own. Now it seemed inconceivable that we would not be able to travel through the continents we had planned.

A few miles before the Canadian border we stopped for breakfast at a roadside cafe, on the edge of the small town of Stratton in the forested hills of upper Maine. It was a Sunday and inside the cramped cafe the proprietor's unruly family of six was busily serving up a huge breakfast to another family, which also numbered six. Our arrival created an imbalance between opposing forces and sent the place into noisy chaos. When order had been re-established and we were tucking into our bacon, lettuce and tomato sandwiches the owner sat down with us.

"Nice day for it," he said, nodding in the direction of the window through which the sunlight streamed. Quite what it was a nice day for I had no idea.

"Yes, it's a great day for it," I replied.

"Where you headin', Canada? Best watch out for them moose." With this he stood up and shuffled his way back to the kitchen.

It was their first real day of spring as we crossed into Quebec. The contrasts between countries were immediate and refreshingly tangible. People were filled with a joie de vivre as a result of a warm sun and the sudden change in the temperature. They walked or rode bicycles between villages and around towns, quite unlike the Americans who seemed obsessively dependent on the automobile. Motorcyclists had opened their garages and sheds, serviced their bikes and were now enjoying their first ride of the year. As they zipped by on sports models or glided smoothly past on Honda Gold Wings they all raised a hand to us in acknowledgement of their own particular rite of spring. After a month's inactivity we had to think again about speaking a language that was not our own. We assumed that all French Canadians would be bilingual, but in this part of Quebec that was the exception rather than the rule. Despite the many visual similarities between the two countries, it still felt very foreign and this temporarily revived our travelling spirits which had been blunted a little by the American urge to standardise. When we arrived in Ottawa we were met with a curious mix of British, French and American influences. The Victorian neo-gothic grandeur of the Houses of Parliament dominated the town but was being increasingly surrounded by more modern buildings and Marks and Spencers vied with American chainstores on the high street.

Before leaving Canada we decided to visit Niagara Falls. We had been in touch with the Canadian Sidecar Club's president, Osie Shanks, who lived in Hamilton, some fifty miles distant. He soon organised a group of sidecarists from the area to escort us there. It was an unusual honour. When we arrived to meet them they were pacing restlessly, dressed in full leather riding suits, each the owner of a gleaming large capacity Japanese motorcycle, in contrast to our own travel stained appearance – we were forty five minutes late. After formal introductions we set off, three outfits and three solo motorcycles on the road to Niagara. They kept their speed respectfully slow to accommodate our overloaded Triumph. I prayed the bike would behave itself. We were about half way there and passing through Grimsby when there was a sudden phutting noise from behind and smoke began to pour from one of our exhausts. We all pulled over. A cursory check revealed almost no compression in the offending cylinder. Our escorts stood uncomfortable silent while I worked, no doubt wondering how the hell we had managed to ride the motorcycle this far around the world. I knew we were beaten yet again and would have to pull apart the engine but there was no anger this time, just a practical determination to get the bike fixed as quickly and as efficiently as possible. Conveniently, we were no more than a hundred yards from a motorcycle workshop so we all pushed the bike there, and within twenty minutes the fault had been found – a cracked piston – but the remedy took a little longer – two days in fact. Two of our escort volunteered to ride into the United States to pick up new pistons from a Triumph stockist in Buffalo. Rick, the mechanic at the shop, undertook to effect the repair free of charge. He knew Triumphs well having for several years prepared them for short-track racing. The *Hamilton Spectator* was called in to write a feature on the event. "Travellers get lucky break(down)" they titled the piece, continuing: "After 54,000 miles on the road, Richard and Mopsa English are beginning to think that luck travels with them." Well, it might have been luck, or maybe just the law of averages. Travelling involves a measure of vulnerability that makes one very dependent, when things go wrong, on the people whose land one is travelling through. All societies recognise this vulnerability. In some of the nomadic cultures it has been refined into a code of conduct that requires one to offer hospitality to the traveller whoever they might be. The west has developed its services to such an extent that there is no longer a need for the individual to take responsibility for the succour of the traveller in need. The sentiment remains, however, and throughout our travels the offers of hospitality and help were never far away. Coming from a society that teaches individual self-reliance we had tried to make ourselves as self-sufficient as possible. On occasions it served us well, but we were still dependent on the goodwill of people. In Canada and the United States people readily identified with what we were doing. The motorcycle, here, was the modern equivalent of the horse. It was a license to roam. They transferred to us, through friendly hospitality, their own fleeting desires to take to the road.

We returned to the States by way of Detroit then paused awhile in Illinois. From on top of the Sears Tower, the world's highest building, we gazed out across the sprawling city of Chicago, enmeshed on three sides by a linear network of roads that stretched out as far as our eyes could see. Immediately below us, neatly parked but insignificantly small, stood the motorcycle. The city centre is dynamically modern, a statement of intent for the twenty-first century. In the paved enclosures between the soaring structures of steel, concrete and glass stand the giant Picasso sculpture, the Calder stabile and the mosaic by Chagall. From 1350 feet we were able to choose the route we would take through the city streets. It reminded me of when we had first opened out the map of the world and tentatively pointed to the places through which we would like to ride.

Ninety miles north of Chicago, just across the Illinois/Wisconsin state border on the shores of Lake Michigan, lies Milwaukee – home to famous lager breweries such as Miller and Schlitz. It is also Mecca for the true American motorcyclist – home to the legendary Harley-Davidson Motor Company. It was in Japan that we'd first experienced a real cult-following for the all-American Harley-Davidson dream. There those who could afford the hardware chose a more disciplined and uniform aspect of the cult, more in keeping with their own traditions, decking and dressing themselves and their bikes in all the formal paraphernalia of the Californian police force. In the United States the freedom cult of the sixties had adopted the motorcycle, and in particular the Harley which was made famous by such films as Easy Rider and infamous through the media's portrait of the Hell's Angels. The resulting uniform white tee-shirts, blue denims, leather waistcoats all emblazoned with American eagles, badges and other symbols, made the followers of the cult as indistinguishable from each other as their Japanese counterparts. Harley-Davidson had survived the economic onslaught of the Japanese motorcycle industry by harnessing – and successfully marketing to – the patriotism and style identification of a not inconsiderable section of the American motorcycling public. And we met many a Harley rider who was as zealous to his cause as any Iranian fundamentalist.

Through Doug Bingham, a sidecar-owning friend from LA we had an introduction to Ron Plender who worked at the factory. We phoned him from Chicago.

"Com'on over tomorrow and I'll fix for someone to show you round."

So we duly arrived and were escorted around the big old brick factory by members of the marketing and customer relations sections. As we moved between offices, watching the newest designs shift in exploded views across the computer screens where theoretical tests were made on metal tension and fatigue and life expectancy for the present and future generations of Harley's, we were the butt of a stream of friendly anti-British biking jokes:

"Do you know why you British drink warm beer?" asked one.

"Because you keep it in Lucas refrigerators."

"Triumph still sloggin' away with that chain drive?" asked another. "Outdated technology, man, they wanna try using belts."

"You know Ron, we oughta give them a new Harley in exchange for that ol' Triumph for the rest of their trip," ventured another.

I was most interested in seeing their research and development building but we were politely refused. Their latest Sportster model was due out the following month and they didn't want us leaking any information to the motorcycling press. One of these bikes stood outside, carefully hidden under a huge wrap. As we were leaving one of our hosts handed us a selection of mementos – Harley badges, hats, maps and literature.

"Well, do you want to take one of our Harleys instead of that Triumph," he asked, nodding towards our outfit. I couldn't quite tell if he was serious or not, but we had put our trust in the Triumph and it would have been an act of treachery to discard it so casually.

"Thanks for the offer," I smiled. "But no thanks. It's managed it this far and with a bit of luck should get us home."

Returning to Chicago from visiting the Harley-Davidson factory in Milwaukee later that week we stopped at traffic lights in the blighted area just outside the centre. We were unsure as to exactly where we were, but my sense of direction had been developed by months of constant travel and I knew our way lay straight ahead. Mopsa didn't have such a firm belief in my directional ability, for I had at times blithely carried us several miles off track, refusing to countenance her protestations. Neither did she have much faith in her own navigational skills, having had no relevant experience before our departure, but she had rapidly achieved an efficiency which far outstripped mine. My faith in her skill became the cause of one of our very few continuing frictions. She would quietly seethe as I demanded, again and again, on arriving in unknown towns "Which way do we go?". Only my eternal obsession with repacking the sidecar and reducing our load matched this irritation in Mopsa's eyes. Both these continued for the full fifty-two months of our trip. Not that she didn't irritate me too. I never really managed to accept her slow moving lethargy in the mornings, nor her habit of demanding that I change my clothes so that she might wash them. But on the whole our relationship was equable, and we rarely held grudges. Indeed on one day when I had annoyed Mopsa so much that she emptied a very sticky American fast food super-sized chocolate milkshake over my head, by the time we came to writing our journal that evening neither of us could remember what the argument had been about.

A large truck pulled up alongside and the driver, with pink face, heavy jowls and the hint of a middle European accent, asked us where we were heading.

"Straight on" I said firmly.

"I wouldn't advise that, sir," he replied. "You won't ever come out alive." Chicago's reputation was such that we took him at his word, and turned right instead, regretting a little that we hadn't the courage to see what lay down that particular road.

After a week among the sidecaring fraternity of Northern Illinois, guests of honour at Pow Wows and rallies where disparate individuals from the motorcycling tribes of the area gathered to jaw, kick tyres and play foolish games now that summer had arrived, we spent a further fortnight in Union, (just outside Hope) where I worked, cash in hand, for an all but cowboy building outfit. It was June, hot and dry, and although well looked after and our days filled, we still came to resent the fact that we had chosen so long a journey around North America. The knowledge that this time might have been better used earning the money required to get us through South America and Africa added to the frustrations brought on by a misbehaving bike.

The ride across Iowa and South Dakota rolled by in slowly undulating fields of corn and soya, clusters of cottonwood and elm, straight roads, wide, sluggish rivers, and nights spent amid vast panoramas of a midsummer sky. When we reached the Badlands the weather started to behave erratically. One hundred and five degrees of heat in the morning was followed by electrical storms and high winds in the afternoon – this dry land of grotesque erosions lived up to its name. Escaping temporarily from a hard and penetrating rain we revived ourselves on expensive coffee at Wall. In the 1930s Wall had been no more than a store owned by an enterprising family who advertised and sold iced water to thirsty travellers heading west by automobile. In true American fashion it had grown into a town dedicated to persuading the people who passed through to buy what they had no real need for. Apart from the bars, the fast food restaurants and the rows of one-arm-bandits, there were acres of shop space given over to selling cheap tourist mementoes at not so cheap prices.

That evening we passed through Rapid City and entered the Black Hills, to camp in the Custer State Park. We trekked several miles away from the road attempting to find the walk-in campsite, carrying water, food, tent and sleeping bags. Our navigational skills through open countryside on foot didn't match our abilities on the road and after an hour we decided to bed down in an open area of long grass without erecting the tent. At dawn we woke to a terrific rumbling – it wasn't thunder for the sky was an unbroken blue. Sitting up for a clear view the reason for the noise was immediately apparent. We watched amazed as a herd of perhaps one hundred and fifty bison thundered towards the woods immediately to our left. Had we camped a little further on we might have been more rudely awakened – a full grown adult bison can weigh as much as a small car, and can run as fast as a horse.

We visited Mount Rushmore that day to view the stern, stony faces of America's four greatest Presidents, massively carved into a granite cliff. Returning to the bike we found a rather radical-looking biker, dressed in tatty leathers, inspecting it. After introducing himself and his equally radical looking old Triumph Tiger 100, he questioned us on motorcycle touring in Europe.

"I was in England once," he sighed. "In Portsmouth with the Navy."

"Oh yes," I replied. "That's where I was born."

"Got myself a tattoo there. Wanna see?" He thrust his head a little closer and curled back his lower lip, proudly revealing his hidden tattoo. "Rock On" it read.

Across Wyoming we lugged the motorcycle up over the Big Horn mountains on a road that rose to 10,000 feet. The inefficiency of our badly-worn engine made it a strain to haul both sidecar and passengers at such heights as we slowed to a walking pace. I now knew that the engine would need new pistons before we could attempt to cross the Andes in South America. High up in the mountain meadows grew a profusion of alpine flowers, among which Mopsa wandered, only a fairly romantic figure in her heavy waterproofs, singing to the edelweiss. As we crossed the intervening plain between the mountain ranges of the Big Horn and the Rockies and turned towards Yellowstone National Park, the weather changed. Darkly banking clouds loomed, and from out of the growing mists, a motorcycle gained on us from behind. The rider gave us a friendly wave, familiar yet not American, and stayed a short distance behind us for some minutes before overtaking and disappearing into the gloom. A few minutes later the skies opened and hailstones the size of maltesers poured down. It was impossible to continue and I quickly pulled over, yelling with pain as the hail tore into my unprotected face. We both wore open-faced helmets, and I preferred sun glasses or goggles rather than an attached visor. This choice had proved to be perfectly adequate in warmer countries, but I did have a tendency to lose, break or sit on the cheap sun-glasses we were continually buying. The

With Tetsuyo in Montana

longest I managed to keep of a pair was six months, the shortest just half an hour. Mopsa wears glasses to counter her short sight and is more experienced in keeping hers intact, but she still crushed two pairs and had one set swept from her face by pre-monsoon turbulence when swimming in the Indian ocean.

The hail storm lasted five minutes and we continued into Cody. Inside the Portacabin used as a tourist office we met the motorcyclist who had passed us. Tetsuyo was a short Japanese fellow, and was having trouble understanding the rich accent of the information officer. With our skills at broken English, and with an opportunity to repay some of the hospitality we had received in Japan, we helped him out. We were heading in the same direction and Tetsuyo announced emphatically that he would travel with us. On a month's holiday from Japan, he had ridden across Canada from Vancouver to Toronto on his 400 cc Suzuki and was now returning via the States. He had the endearing habit of starting every sentence with "Oh, sorry", as though apologising for his strange appearance in this foreign land. We explained that we travelled on a very tight budget, preparing our own food and even avoiding fee paying campsites except where absolutely necessary.

"Oh, sorry. I very interested in cheap travel," he exclaimed with some glee. "You teach me." He had been using commercial campsites that charged as much as ten dollars a night and was eating out each day at the first restaurant he found. He was running very short of money. At the end of the day he tallied up his expenses.

"Oh, very cheap day!" he exclaimed with delight at the end of our first day together. "Record cheap day."

When we entered Yellowstone there had been an overnight fall of six inches of snow and visibility was severely reduced. It was unusual weather for the time of year, even at these heights, so we hired a small one-roomed wooden cabin for the night and with a little of the money that Tetsuyo had saved, he bought a bottle of gin. Huddled around an inadequate fire the drink warmed our spirits and we soon emptied the litre contents. Once Mopsa was asleep Tetsuyo's conversation immediately turned to the subject that seems to fascinate Japanese men most when in the company of westerners – a comparison of each races' sexual behaviour. I was assailed by a barrage of questions relating to how much, how many, when, where, how and with whom. The following day the weather, if not our heads, had cleared and we moved on into Montana. We camped that night in a forest with bear warnings prominently displayed. Both Mopsa and I had, of necessity, learnt to put aside all thoughts of possible danger when camping out, in the interest of getting a good night's sleep. Here we took the required precautions and removed all our food from the tent and sidecar and hung it from the branch of a tree. Next morning as I prepared breakfast Tetsuyo gingerly emerged from his tent, looking a little pale.

"Oh, sorry!" he blurted, aware of the knife he was still holding and with which he had slept. "I hear noises. Not good sleeping."

At Kalispell Tetsuyo left us, he had some hard riding to arrive back in Vancouver in time for his flight to Tokyo. Our own ride took on a dreamlike quality as we climbed the narrow road through Glacier National Park, the landscape violently etched by scouring ice with precipitous cliffs, razor-sharp ridges and walls of ice. We re-entered Canada, crossed the Calgary plain and left the bike for three days of walking in the grandeur of the Canadian Rockies. With endless evenings, deep turquoise lakes and snow capped peaks, the sun shone perfectly on what was an idyll of relaxation. We became slow-moving ourselves, walking about fifteen miles each day, up and down gentle slopes, crossing ice-cold streams, coming face to face with porcupine, deer and mountain goats in the gold pink stillness of the mountain air. When we arrived in Seattle after winding our way down through British Columbia and the islands and ferries of north western Washington State, we were both relaxed and happy. We spent a week there with Mark Bocek, a playwright friend of Mopsa's sister, who had no interest in motorcycles but a healthy one in the comparative merits of the many small breweries in the area, which produced beers more palatable to British tastes than the watery lager to which we were becoming accustomed. He took us to a bar called Arthur's Pub, which he assured us was one of the better, and we were entertained by a group of middle-aged Americans dressed in lederhosen singing "When Irish eyes are smiling". We dipped inland past Mount Rainier, to Yakima to visit Mark's family, before our planned return to the coast via the Columbia Gorge. It was hot and dry as we picnicked in the shade of a full-size mock up of Stonehenge, built as a war memorial by a Quaker pacifist earlier in the century. Then we began the long ride down the gorge.

★　★　★

Hajime and Teiko, Japanese sidecarists, contemplate the unusual combination of British bike and American ingenuity – an early Triumph with a flexible-mounted sidecar at a rally in California

With Tetsuyo in the Yellowstone National Park ▶

▼ *The Canadian Rockies*

◄ *Fishing in Florida*

Gas Station, Georgia ▼

▲ *A turn around the Square in San Antonio de las Aguas Calientes in Guatemala*

Christmas in Mexico City ▶

◄ *Trilby seller in Otavalo, Ecuador*

▼*Barge across the swollen waters of Lake Titic*

Lake Titicaca in flood ▲

Food market at Chinchero, Peru ▶

Sunset over the Chobe River, Botswana

On the Makgadikgadi Salt Pan, Botswana

Loading the Mwongozo on Lake Tanganyika ▶

With the Masai in Kenya ▼

◄ Masai flocks at a watering place, Kenya

▼ At the Pyramids, Egypt

Jack Bryan towed us back to his clean, white weather-boarded house in Lyle. We stopped on the way at a grubby shack where a hidden hi-fi sent the lilting sounds of a Grateful Dead song echoing around the oily frames of half-dismantled bikes. Several figures, lounging in the shade of the veranda, slowly rose to hear of our problem, but were not able, through the wafting clouds of marijuana smoke, to give much help. Jack Bryan assured us we were better off without them anyway. The alternative lifestyle of the biker, as opposed to the motorcyclist, is tolerated if still not accepted by the majority of God-fearing Americans. The motorcyclist, on the other hand, became infinitely more respectable with the advent of the Honda Gold Wing. Solid and traditional middle-aged men are able to relive the dreams of their youth and take to the road on two wheels with comfort and reliability assured. The Japanese have produced the bikes that all America can ride and so motorcycling has become a highly marketable leisure activity. For many touring motorcyclists the comfort accessories, the latest digital controls, the in-built speakers and the overall visual effect of their mighty steeds, bedecked in chrome and lights, are as important as the ride itself. Our plain and practical rig brought no more than a cursory interest from many of the riders we met and I often felt that they viewed us as no more than a quaint, historical curiosity. How different it was to our reception in the less technologically developed world, where motorcycles were big if they were over 200 cc, utilitarian, and only within the reach of the wealthier classes.

As I began to strip the engine on Jack's lawn, Dolores, his wife, brought us lemonade and hovered, alarmed at the thought of pools of oil on her beautifully mown grass. While I struggled to lift off the cylinder head, she told us with an assurance that all would be sorted out in no time at all, and we should soon be on the way to our appointment that evening in Portland. Her confidence, however, was badly misplaced, because as the barrels came off, one of the pistons came too, and fell accusingly to the ground. It was a shock to see the snapped connecting rod, the broken barrels, and then the crack in the crank case.

"Not too serious, is it now?" Dolores asked complacently. "You'll be away in no time now." Surprisingly we were, but not on the bike. We organised a complicated scheme which involved detaching the bike from the sidecar, loading it onto Jack's pickup and driving to North Bonneville, half way to Portland, where we had arranged a rendezvous with Debbie Trousdale, a potter friend of the family we had stayed with in LA, with whom we'd planned to stay that night. Debbie, for her part, had driven east in her Volkswagen minibus, and by torchlight we moved the machine from one vehicle to the other. It was a tight fit for our broken motorcycle in the back of the VW, finally effected only by letting air out of both tyres, and by midnight we were tucking into tea and toast and freshly made raspberry jam in Debbie's kitchen. The events of the day had been traumatic and our tour of North America brought to a premature end, but we quickly adjusted to our new circumstances. We put aside all thoughts of repairing the motorcycle in Portland and the following morning hired, at huge cost, a three ton truck. We loaded the bike and returned to Lyle to collect the sidecar. Dolores was as comforting as ever.

The ignominy of trucking the bike back to Los Angeles

"Back on your way are you now?" she asked. "Didn't take you a minute to get fixed up, did it now?" We accepted the indignity of driving the last thousand miles back to Los Angeles with the outfit in the back of a truck. I tried to create an enthusiasm for the magnificent countryside we were travelling through, but somehow it just wasn't the same. The summer heat continued while we sat sweating and shackled to our enclosed cab, watching enviously as the touring motorcyclists rolled by, and listening to our tape of Ella Fitzgerald singing Cole Porter songs – "I want to ride to the ridge where the west commences, gaze at the moon till I lose my senses, I can't stand hobbles and I can't stand fences – don't fence me in."

Chapter Eight

Central and South America

ARRIVING BACK in Los Angeles we deposited our broken motorcycle at Chris Scott's workshop in North Hollywood and again presumed upon the hospitality of the Krautz family. While Mopsa returned to the company for which she had previously answered telephones, I began the slow process of rebuilding the engine. I had ordered new cylinder barrels and pistons to be sent from England and JRC Engineering, who had been the West Coast importers of Triumphs before the factory's demise, donated or sold at cost the other parts needed. The crack in the crankcase was expertly re-welded but when we came to fit the cylinder barrels we found that they were the wrong size. The motorcycle dealer from whom I had ordered them had milled down a set of 750 cc barrels for our 650 cc engine but too much had been taken off. The pistons, when the barrels were fitted, poked up by about a quarter of an inch. It was another month before a replacement set arrived from England.

During the evenings we both struggled with Spanish from some borrowed tapes, contorting our mouths and tongues into odd unpractised shapes, learning to ask if Gonzales was in his oficina or if Maria was casada. Then, as the date of our departure neared, the old feelings of nervousness returned. They were fuelled by the Americans' concerned delight in telling us of all the terrible dangers that lay in wait across the Mexican border. We were not to go near a Mexican hospital, since we would surely get hepatitis, and we were all too likely to be robbed, or shot, or at the very least run off the road. Small warning incidents developed into a rationale that begged us not to go. On Hallowe'en, returning from a friend's house on a borrowed bike, we almost took a tumble when we hit a bottle on the freeway. Arriving home we found a hole in the exhaust, and wedged between it and the engine a playing card – the ace of spades. In the lift going to the Panamanian consul we fell into conversation with the only other occupant.

"Every time I go near this office it gives me the creeps," he said, nodding at the Panamanian's nameplate.

"I rode down on a motorcycle, back in '81. In Panama I was run down by a truck. Broke both my legs!"

I told him our plans.

"What bike you on?" he asked.

"A Triumph."

"I took a Triumph," he said, shaking his head. "It blew up in Mexico on account of the bad fuel. Oh boy! My advice to you is not to go."

We paid an exorbitant fee to have painful gamma-globulin jabs against hepatitis but refused to contemplate paying over $60 each for a course of malarial tablets. These, along with booster jabs against cholera, typhoid and tetanus would have to wait until we reached Mexico, where we were sure they would be considerably cheaper. Despite our nervousness and the warnings of our friends we were desperate to leave the comfort and safety of LA and to begin our return journey to England. Every time we switched on the radio, it seemed, Willie Nelson was singing "On the road again". We had to go.

On 11th November we slipped out of the United States and into Mexico at Mexicali. The town was full of advertisements for cheap dentists and young, dusty boys loitered on street corners. We were waved through barriers without being asked for papers or passports and it was only by insisting that we were directed to officials who put them in order. Across the Sonoita desert the wind blew hard, there was little habitation, and only short green cactus and low shrubs. The following day it rained all the way down the sparse Pacific coast from Guaymas to Cualican. The Mexicans were polite but shy and we felt we were viewed no differently from the many North American gringos who travelled the coast in their camper vans. In Cualican we camped in an expensive trailer park between rows of huge American recreational vehicles while throughout the night armed guards and their dogs patrolled the perimeter fence. South of Tropic of Capricorn lies the seaside resort of Mazatlan – full of tourists, holiday condominiums, boutiques, restaurants and open, white buggies that operate as taxis along the beach front. We pulled into the dirtiest, most run-down caravan park we could find, assuming it would be the cheapest but it was closed, having been recently sold to developers for over a million dollars. The attendant let us stay there anyway – the plans were for a luxury hotel to be built on the site. This was not the Mexico we had anticipated.

Climbing away from the Pacific coast, up to the lofty heights of the Sierra Madre Occidental, brought a fresher air as the countryside changed to green forests and pastures. In a cheap hotel on the outskirts of Guadalajara we chatted with a talkative taxi driver who slept there between shifts, alternating occupation of the room with his partner. He spoke some English.

"Where you from?" he asked. "Ah, from England. Land of the Beatless, yes?"

From Zamora to Zacapa, Patscuaro, Malinalco and Taxco – old colonial towns with whitewashed buildings, red tiled roofs and delightful squares enclosing gardens and wrought iron bandstands where every evening middle class families dressed in their best came to parade. The markets were all colour, the great variety of produce carried in on the short, strong backs of the peasant farmers. Within the old, colonial churches we found gory depictions of Christ only recently descended from the cross. The Mexicans, it seems, are not averse to presenting suffering with graphic detail. In the newspapers, murder victims are shown, naked, with their wounds revealed for all to see. In the countryside we wound along beautiful mountain roads, braving the "curvas peligrosas" and the reckless driving of the thankfully fairly scant traffic. The petrol was so bad away from the touristed coastal routes that we were forced to top up our tank with copious amounts of the local fuel additive called Bardahl to avoid the permanent accompaniment of a pinking Triumph. When we stopped to fill up, young boys rushed forward, dragging damp and dirty rags from their pockets, offering to wash the bike. Horses and mules clattered down the roads and the creased, stoic faces of the peasant farmers attested to a calm, if severe rhythm to their daily lives. The fields were mainly of maize or pasture and on the higher slopes wild flowers grew in magnificent abundance. The drab, single-storey houses of the villagers were brightened by the profusion of flowers that tumbled out of the rows of hanging and rusty tin cans.

Late on a misty Sunday afternoon, we climbed slowly up to a high pass and gazed down upon a carpet of smog spread over the sprawling mass of Mexico City. It was dull, grey and dirty in contrast to the clear green countryside through which we had just passed. Descending more than three thousand feet onto the enclosed plain within which the city stands we followed the multi-laned highway, thankful that the weekend traffic was light and that we didn't have to make snap decisions about our route. Towards the heart of the city we began to see depressing evidence of the earthquake which had devastated the centre just six weeks previously. We decided on the Monte Carlo Hotel, quite simply

Demolition in Mexico City after the earthquake

because our guide book said that D. H. Lawrence once stayed there – small enough reason, but we had no other criterion by which to choose from the almost endless list. It was central, easily found, and of badly decayed grandeur: its foyer high and wide, its concierge charming, its hot water system non-functioning and its plasterwork crumbling. On asking the concierge where we could park the motorcycle, he pointed to a cavernous black hole at the far end of the central corridor. I rode the outfit up over two steps, then through the tall carved wooden doors and disappeared into the depths of the hotel, to park the bike among the dust sheets and broken-legged gilt chairs of the long disused ballroom, a rubble-strewn grand piano at its side. We booked, despite attempts by the concierge to send us to more comfortable lodgings, into a cheap room on the sixth floor – a suite of rooms, rather, with lobby, dressing room and bathroom in addition to the bedroom, decorated in striped maroon wallpaper and lime green satin furnishings, old and faded despite still being covered by protective plastic sheeting. What it lacked in comfort it made up for in floor space, and at less than a pound a night, and with us as the only guests, we wondered how they managed to stay open. A newly built multi-storey carpark next door had collapsed like a house of cards, and the cracks in the pavement and the tilting edifices made us very aware that this damaged city stood on a thick layer of mud where once a lake had been. Many buildings and offices were closed until further notice and dust filled the air from those that were being bulldozed or slowly hacked to pieces by pick and drill.

We had intended to stay no more than a week and after eight days we recovered the outfit from the ballroom where it had been covered in a layer of thickening dust. Having exchanged a friendly farewell with the concierge we found not only a flat battery but also that enthusiastic push starts were to no avail: the engine refused to run. A closer look revealed a burnt out alternator, and while I stayed with the bike, Mopsa set off with the damaged part to find someone who could repair it. Again, to no avail, but we did, at least, discover that Lucas had an office in Mexico City. Sheepishly we returned to the Monte Carlo, some four hours after booking out, only to find its massive doors locked, and a sign posted: closed for refurbishment.

We contacted Lucas and through them managed, after a several telexes and telephone calls, to have a new one sent down from Los Angeles. We had to rely, however, on the Mexican postal system. By airmail the part would take no more than four days, or so we were told. The next sixteen days we spent shuttling between the airport, the central post office and the international sorting office desperately seeking our missing part. On one such outing as we walked down a main road just outside the city centre two young lads came at us from out of a narrow alley. One pulled a gun, while the other went for the front pocket of my trousers where I kept my wallet. I instinctively pushed him away, turned, and ran. I had fled no more than five yards when I realised I had left Mopsa behind. Turning back I saw her screaming indignantly at our assailants in vitriolic English. The two young men stared at her for a few moments in stunned disbelief, then hurriedly retreated back down the alley.

As we waited impatiently for the alternator to arrive, we were bustled around the city streets in a festive pre-Christmas turmoil. The noise was cacophonous as vendors of all ages sold everything from combs to peanut brittle to woolly ear muffs to pumice stones. Each declared their goods to be of a most superior quality, reliability and value, their shouts in syncopation with busking accordionists, church bells, P.A. systems, traffic horns, police whistles, screeching children, the whine of the two-stroke Carabella motorcycles and the occasional off-key brass band. Along the sides of the Almeida, the city's main park, rows of drunken Santa Clauses, in multicoloured beards and wigs continually tinkled small bells vying for the attention of the parents of bewildered and distressed children, who were scooped up and placed within the gaudy displays of disney-like sleighs and animals to have their photographs taken.

Throughout our stay in Mexico City we ate almost exclusively at a popular restaurant near the main square. It opened for breakfast and closed at 11pm. We developed a relationship with several of its many waiters and waitresses and were continually drawn back by its cheap and filling food. It was reliable to the extent that if one got what one ordered it was invariably cold, and if one didn't it was at least warm. One of the waitresses, a woman of stern countenance and bulky stature, softened her tone a little when she heard that we came from England.

"Ah, ha!" she exploded with great relish. "Senora Thatcher!" and clenching her fist bent her pudgy arm fiercely at the elbow.

By the sixteenth day we were near to giving up, and I was about to ask Lucas to send another by air courier. I rang the Lucas office in Mexico City one last time. They had some good news. The parcel had arrived. On our last morning we went to the restaurant for a final breakfast. Mopsa was determined that the meal should be perfect but her eggs were not only undercooked, they were also cold. She complained to the waitress. With a look of utter disdain, the woman placed her hand onto the eggs.

"These eggs are hot," she replied curtly and walked away.

The chilly pass between the snow-capped peaks of Popocatepetl and Ixaccihuatl was the one through which Cortez had marched on his first visit to Montezuma's fabled city. Further west at Cholula a Spanish church stands atop the grassed over ruins of a mighty pyramid. The town was pastel bright and surrounded by fields of commercially grown flowers, a custom that predated the conquistadors. In Oaxaca young boys patrolled the restaurants and cafes with large hollow radishes, a candle burning within, which they traditionally sold at this time of the year for fake money. Outside the cathedral fried pig skin doused in an oily sauce was being served in small rough pottery bowls. When the meal was finished the bowls were thrown high into the air to smash upon the flagstones. We left the Oaxaca valley and descended through a landscape scattered with organ pipe cacti to the coast on the Gulf of Tehuantepec. Here ferocious winds tore across the narrow isthmus that separates the Pacific Ocean and the Gulf of Mexico. Climbing into the mountains again, towards Guatemala and Christmas, we got locked in a shallow gap between a warm earth and the

135

cold clouds which hung damply above our heads, occasionally drifting to give us swirling glimpses of the sunlit plain far below. Groups of Indians walked the road, or remained seated on the verge, tempting us with roasted sweetcorn and tangerines. The men wore bright ponchos, striped in embroidered pinks and oranges, and fastened at the sides with garish tassels, from which hung a coloured pompom. We spent our last night in Mexico at Comitan. The hotel had only recently opened and they had not yet bought blankets for the beds. Needless to say it was bitterly cold that night.

In the morning I shaved in honour of the border and we both attempted to smarten up. It was sometimes difficult to keep our clothes clean for if we washed them in the evening, they were unlikely to dry in the cold night air and be ready to wear the next morning. I was always a little on edge before a border crossing, envisaging confiscations, extra costs and at worst a refused entry. It was a time when we felt very vulnerable and at the complete mercy of officialdom. It was a little different once inside a country for then we could rely on the honourable intentions of the majority of the country's people. Many border officials were both charming and courteous but it is the men who were either obstinate or on the make that one remembers most.

That day's crossing was relatively smooth. One of the Mexican officials was concerned – he felt sure that we had entered Mexico in a car and were now exiting on a motorcycle. At the Guatemalan customs and immigration huts the man in charge of vehicle entry wanted numbers for the two spare Avon tyres we were carrying, strapped to the top of the sidecar box. Eventually, after a long animated discussion with his assistant, 4×18 was carefully written into a large leather-bound book. Our final stop was the fumigation hut. As we drew up a small unshaven and unkempt man staggered out, blinking furiously at the bright early morning sun. He motioned to a youth sitting under a tree, who, with a small hand pump proceeded to wet our tyres with disinfectant. Then the first man, grinning toothlessly and breathing alcoholic fumes into my face, demanded payment. My request for a receipt was immediately met as he handed over a small scrap of grubby paper, duly signed and stamped and with our payment firmly in his grip he weaved his way towards the nearby bar.

The mountains of the Sierra Madre extend into Guatemala on its eastern side and form the backbone of the country. It is here that the majority of the Indian population lives. Guatemala is the one country in Central America where the majority of the descendants of the pre-conquest inhabitants have maintained a distinct regional culture. These people refer to themselves as Indigenas. Ladinos are people of European or mixed race, or those indians who have adopted the European-based culture.

We took the country's one main potholed but serviceable North/South road – the Pan-American Highway through the glorious mountain countryside. Maize is the main crop on the steep terraced slopes which are scattered with low whitewashed houses, with thatched or red-tiled roofs. Along the sides of the roads family groups of Indians were bent double under huge bundles of firewood, maize or Christmas greenery and small nativity creches and cornstalk ornaments were sold by young children. Our first night was in Quezaltenango and on the morning of Christmas Eve, while we ate what had by now become a regular breakfast of huevos rancheros, eggs fried in a spicy tomato and pepper sauce, and dusty tortillas, fir needles were spread around the floor of the small restaurant by the old Indian woman who had served us.

"Para navidad," she smiled. "For Christmas."

We continued on to Chichicastenango, an Indian town which boasts one of the most colourful markets in Guatemala and so is very popular with tourists but there were few about at this time of the year. The Christmas Eve service in the church that night was an extraordinary mixture of the incantations of a European catholic mass and local pagan traditions. The congregation, mostly women, sat on the flagstoned floor. Incense smoke thickened the air, flowers and candles were moved around in complicated ways and the Lord's Prayer was sung in Quiche to a marimba band accompaniment of the music of Paul Simon's Sounds of Silence. At midnight the town erupted to the deafening noise of a thousand firecrackers, many placed into cans and dustbins by the local youths.

We knew that an English woman called Jenny Taylor had lived in the town for many years working as a nurse. Some young boys, who were more intent on taking us to a hotel, eventually directed us to her house. It was one of a modern set of bungalows on an estate on the edge of the town. Jenny was old and rambling and apt to repeat herself and we spent several hours with her as she told us of her adopted daughter, born premature, whom she had managed to save and who had been presented to her by the family. She gave us two large pieces of

◀ *Pig Market at Chichicastenango in Guatemala*

Festive dancer, Chichicastenango ▼

Christmas breakfast in Chichicastenango, Guatemala

cake left over from her adopted grandson's first birthday. It tasted strongly of mildew.

In Guatemala we found that we were not the only foreign motorcyclists heading south. In the old colonial town of Antigua, we met a tall Frenchman on his way to Tierra Del Fuego, a young Swede on a Kawasaki and later two more Frenchmen on BMWs, also on their way to that fiery land of ice. Our own destination in South America was less ambitious. In a small village nearby I delighted the local children by piling them onto our sidecar and driving them around and around the central square.

"Where are we going?" they cried.

"To Brazil!"

"To Brazil! To Brazil!" they chorused. When we finally stopped and they all tumbled off, they gazed around their tiny square:

"Is this Brazil?" they asked, ready to continue their imaginary adventure.

We stayed in Antigua whose full title, received in 1566, was the Muy Noble v Muy Leal Cuidad de Santiago de los Caballeros de Guatemala, The Most Noble and Loyal City of St. James of the Knights of Guatemala, on and off for three more weeks. The city was ravaged by a series of earthquakes in 1773 and the remains of its many churches, convents, mansions and palaces are magnificently wedged between buildings of a later period. We left the motorcycle for a week and flew into the jungles of the Peten in Western Guatemala to visit the Mayan ruins at Tikal, returning to meet up with Mopsa's parents who had quite independently decided to visit Guatemala for a holiday.

The only really viable route south from Guatemala was through Honduras. The civil war in El Salvador made overland travel both extremely dangerous and inadvisable. We left the cool mountains of the Sierra Madre, and took the dirt road to Honduran border at Copan. It was now more than two months since we had left Los Angeles and although our progress had been stalled by two lengthy waits, we didn't feel we were travelling too slowly. On the contrary, I often felt frustrated by the fact that as soon as we had begun to understand and feel comfortable in the country we were visiting, it was time to move on. Travel might broaden the mind but it also begs more questions than answers. Our Spanish had improved sufficiently for us to hold tolerably intelligent conversations but it was still very basic. In Guatemala the Indians have been oppressed for centuries but have retained the dignity of their own culture. Honduran society was more mixed and it was the contrasts between rich and poor that focused one's attention rather than the contrasts between cultures. On our second day in Honduras we stopped for a meal on the edge of the town of Santa Maria. Newly built bungalows with green, water-sprinkled lawns lay next to tumble-down adobe shacks. We were joined by a stocky young army sergeant dressed in fatigues. As in many other places in the world Great Britain, or England, was known as a name alone. Was it a democracy? Was it attached to the United States? We explained. On other occasions England had been variously placed in Portugal, in North America, or had never been heard of at all.

"England? What is that?" an elderly hat seller had asked us in Guatemala. His grandson had hastily informed him that it was the same as Great Britain, but this hadn't helped. In one small village in India we had even been asked whether we weren't really Japanese.

In Tegucigalpa, the Honduran capital, the contrasts continued. Outside the pink Presidential palace ornamental soldiers stood guard, like characters from a children's picture book while across the river that snaked through the town and served as an open sewer, the crowded slums hummed with activity. Among these streets lay the city's main market. In the restaurant attached to our hotel we met Robert Millar, a sad, worn-out Englishman and ex-honorary consul, convinced that a grand communist conspiracy was at work within Central America. The hotel was situated next to the police station and throughout the day, long queues of people patiently waited for the references that every employer required from the police before they could be employed. Continuing towards Nicaragua we stopped briefly at Choluteca to visit a Welshman who ran a successful and expensive hotel. The lobby was full of North American evangelists on a weekend convention and hard, muscular Hispanics in Rambo T-shirts and khaki trousers waiting, no doubt, for the next Contra offensive. We were granted a fifteen minute audience with the owner who spent the time bemoaning the fact that Britain had gone to the dogs ever since the class system had begun to break down and how a loss of genteelness on British Rail was symptomatic of the decline.

To reach Panama, where we hoped to either fly or ship ourselves to the South American continent, we had first to pass through Nicaragua and Costa Rica – two very different countries. The Nicaraguan people had been very poor under the Somozan regime and now under the Sandinistas were desperately trying to achieve a more equable distribution of their resources in the face of considerable pressure from the US-backed Contra rebels. Costa Rica has a longer democratic history, and is proud that its relative prosperity and stability are maintained without a standing army.

We arrived at the Nicaraguan border on Sunday afternoon. Before we were given entry visas we each had to exchange $120 at the official government exchange rate of 28 cordovas to the dollar. The bank rate was 750 and one could get as much as 1100 on the black market. We were then directed to an adjoining caravan to arrange for the temporary importation of the motorcycle. A disembodied voice from behind a wiremesh grille asked us for forty more dollars.

"How much?" we gasped in unison. We were unused to paying such large amounts at customs posts.

"Forty dollars for road tax on weekends. Twenty dollars on weekdays."

Rather rashly, and without thinking things through, I asked if it would be possible for us to camp at the border that night, and then pay the twenty dollars in the morning. The faceless official agreed.

Around the border post a small village had sprung up and from a small shack of a stall I bought cigarettes, some biscuits and a cold drink, so dispensing with $15 worth of cordovas. Working on the basis of 28 to the dollar things were

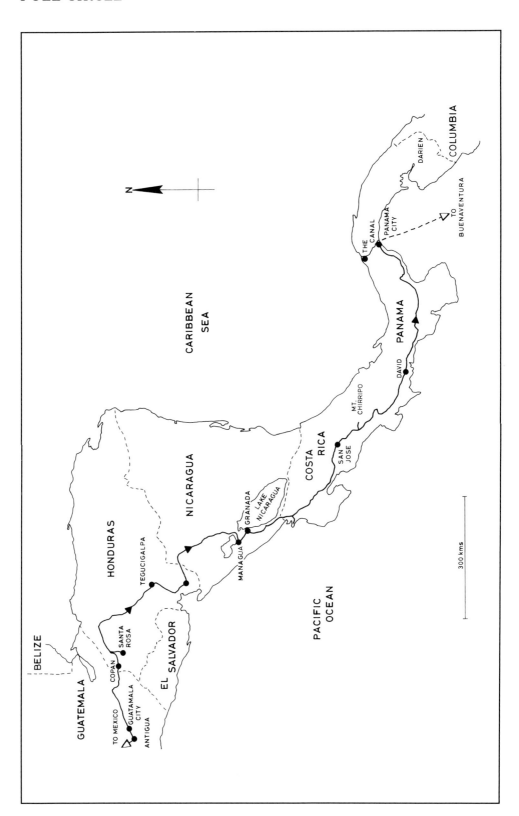

ridiculously expensive – on the basis of 1100 to the dollar ridiculously cheap. After a group of the village boys had enthusiastically helped us with the tent, two border guards wandered over for a chat:

"What will you do," one of them asked, nodding at our flimsy tent "when the Contras attack?"

"They won't will they?"

"For sure. They come once a month. On Sundays," the other added jokingly.

Mopsa expressed a hope that they would protect us. They reassured us that all was tranquillo here – for the moment. There was a full moon that night, and a pleasantly cool breeze, and only a couple of rounds of automatic gunfire from the nearby hills.

The main road to Managua was full of high-clearance troop trucks and small MZ motorcycles, some with sidecars. All the bridges were heavily guarded and due to a lack of public transport, hitch hikers, both military and civilian, lined the road. Several times we stopped to offer lifts to anyone game enough to ride with us and twice we carried our own personal armed bodyguard, perched on top of the two spare tyres. The centre of Managua has yet to be rebuilt after the twin destructions of the 1974 earthquake and the Somozan bombing during the revolution. The Intercontinental Hotel was where the foreigners, be they journalists or visitors, eventually gravitated. It was the one place where one was guaranteed a telephone line. They also served a sumptuous all you could eat buffet for only 1000 cordovas – it was the best meal in town. We stayed in rather cheaper lodgings for $2 a night.

After two days in the city we retired to the more attractive old colonial town of Granada on the shores of the lake from which the country takes its name. From the leafy central square, two main avenues led down to the lake shore and the terraced rows of two storey houses that lined them had front rooms that opened directly onto the pavements so giving a brief glimpse into the private lives of the population. Cane rocking chairs filled the town – large, more elaborate ones for the adults, smaller ones for the children, and during the late afternoons and cooler evenings these were brought out onto the streets for neighbourly conversation while the children played their games on the cobblestones.

On our first morning in Granada we both awoke in some discomfort. Mopsa had been badly bitten by the mosquitoes that bred in profusion in the grimy waters of the lake's edge. I had not escaped, but the aggravated itching was far outweighed by a toothache which had been growing for some days. We sought out the nearest dentist and by mid-morning I was ushered into his surprisingly well-equipped surgery.

"Tengo dolor," I mumbled pointing at my mouth. The dentist was delighted to be able to exercise his limited grasp of the English language.

"Ah!" he exclaimed with great glee. "Pain!" and after some strenuous activity on his part the tooth was pulled and the pain alleviated.

My decayed tooth was not the only memento we left in Granada. Returning

At the Equator, Ecuador

Antigua Guatemala ▲

There are even traffic jams and ▶
contraflows high in the Andes – this one
was the result of a landslide in Ecuador

to the bike we were approached by a young man who had been inspecting our spare tyres the previous night. He owned a 250cc Honda, whose rear tyre was completely bald – the baldest I had ever seen – and due to the great scarcity of foreign goods he was unable to find a replacement. Could he, he ventured, buy one of ours? A simple request, but one that was almost impossible to negotiate. It was no use him paying us in cordovas for we were leaving the country in two days and would be unable to change our excess local currency back into dollars, of which he had none. Also our tyres had been listed on our temporary importation documents and we would have to pay duty if they were not re-exported. We managed, however, to reach a compromise. We swapped our almost worn out rear tyre for his bald one, putting a new one on the Triumph and carrying his bald one as our spare. A tyre that would only have only lasted us a couple more weeks at our rate of mileage, would last him considerably longer. He was well pleased to be able to ride again.

Costa Rica was in the throes of a Presidential election when we arrived, the people jubilantly celebrating their democratic process with parades, flags and partisan T-shirts and hats. The bars and drinking houses, however, remained firmly closed for a full three days, sealed and bonded with official tape by the authorities until after the result was declared. From San Jose we climbed up over the dramatic central divide, where at 10,000 feet the chill mists of the cloud forest swirled through the mountain pines. Once we had begun the descent I switched off the engine and engaged neutral and we were left with only the sound of the wind as we freewheeled down for over twenty-five miles. Before leaving Costa Rica we detoured to Canaan, a small village in a high valley at the foot of Mount Chirripo and at the end of a very wet and very muddy dirt road. We managed to ride the motorcycle to within a mile of the end of that road before we slid to a stop on the slippery surface of one of its steepest sections. Undeterred we walked on. The few locals we met were happy to engage in conversation and we remarked to them how beautiful we found their valley.

"Yes, we think so too," they smiled. I still remember it as the most beautiful place we visited.

It was a Sunday morning when we wheeled into Panama. The reception we received from the Panamanians was disconcerting. Small boys and girls ran from their homes with large buckets and launched water at us as we rushed by. We stopped at Santiago to fill up with petrol and the young attendant turned the water hose on us. Drenched and confused we continued on to David, where outside a small cafe was massed a good-sized assembly of large motorbikes. There were Harley-Davidsons, Gold Wings, Shadows and Viragos. Such a collection of motorcycle hardware we hadn't seen since leaving Los Angeles – the Road Knights Motorcycle Club from Panama City were out on a weekend ride. A disparate group of US servicemen and Panamanian citizens, they enlightened us on the reason for the drenchings. It was part of Panama's pre-lent festival. They led us to the town square where a vast crowd of near naked people jived to music from live bands while tankers blocked the entrances and played millions of gallons of water over the spirited gathering. Our new-found hosts escorted us in style to Panama City and housed us in the relative quiet and comfort of their clubhouse on one of the US airforce bases. Here Mopsa took full advantage of the facilities by going down with a bout of malaria, contracted, we felt certain, back in Granada.

We were three weeks in Panama City arranging our onward passage to the South American continent. The grandiose idea of linking Central and South America via the Pan-American highway is a dream that is bogged down by the jungles and swamps of the Darien Gap. The massive amount of investment and technical expertise required to initiate such a project is at present well beyond the resources of both the Panamanian and Colombian governments. The overland traveller is left with only two choices – to ship or to fly. Richard Goodwin, a British ex-pat who worked for Lykes Lines, arranged for our motorcycle to shipped to Buenaventura on the Pacific coast of Colombia – we would have to fly. While staying at the Road Knights clubhouse we met Ed Culberson, retired from the American Air Force, who now worked as a motorcycle safety officer in Florida. He had previously been stationed in Panama and during that time made two abortive attempts to become the first person to cross the impenetrable Darien by motorcycle. Now he was back for a final try. After helping him a little with his preparations, we bade him farewell as he left on his spartan BMW which he had christened Amigo, trusting that we might meet up again once we had all arrived in South America. Before our own departure, we met Dave and Verena, a British/Austrian couple from Kenya who were also travelling the world but in a more spacious and comfortable VW van. As our vehicles were being shipped together we decided to accompany each other to and through a lawless Colombia, on the principal that there was more safety, if less anonymity, in numbers.

★ ★ ★

Buenaventura is a seedy, steamy, tropical port town of dubious reputation. We found an hotel amongst the bars, pool halls and eating houses in the run-down and ramshackle confusion of the downtown area where at night the prostitutes lingered in doorways cooing quietly at Dave and myself despite our accompanying wives. Although the ship had docked we had to wait until after the weekend before we could begin to process the vehicles through a tedious and corrupt bureaucracy. Lykes' agents supplied us with an unemployed crane-operator who knew the ropes and how much to pay which official. Much to his surprise the vehicles were released after only two days – something of a record it seemed. The costs he considered quite reasonable too, which with his cut amounted to $60 for the motorcycle and $100 for the van. Municipal elections were held that weekend and although the alcohol was once more firmly locked away there was some jubilation on the streets on the Saturday night until the troop trucks rolled in and sent everyone home to bed.

As we left the tropical coast and rode up into the folded slopes of the Central Cordillera, the tattered wood and palm leaf huts of the lowland blacks gave way to more solid structures. As we neared Cali, the prosperous-looking estancias and weekend retreats of the rich became more numerous. The country's lawless reputation had made us less than confident, but rather than trouble what we got was the concerned attention of shopkeepers, hoteliers and bystanders who, with a mysterious scratching of their faces or with a pulling down of their lower eyelids, constantly warned us to take extra care for fear of thieves and bandits. We passed through Cali in pouring rain, the streets awash, and then climbed high on a crumpled road into the crumpled Andes towards Ecuador. Landslides threatened to engulf us, the damp steep-sided slopes occasionally loosening a rock to scud down and bounce across the road as we passed by. In Japan the road engineers had seemingly wrecked the landscape by enclosing the sides of their mountains in great hairnets of concrete and wire. Here the unchecked erosion of the slopes, caused by the careless cutting of roads, was resulting in a far greater ecological damage. We stopped at a high vantage point, with sheer cliff above and below, to find that a craggy protruding rock had become a shrine to the memory of past accidents and their victims. A small statue of the Virgin Mary was surrounded with the remains of disembodied headlamps, bumpers and licence plates.

We left our temporary companions when we entered Ecuador and pushed on towards Quito. The landscape was green and lush, a patchwork panorama of fields extending to distant peaks, the highest sprinkled with snow. Crossing the Equator we returned to the southern hemisphere after an absence of more than two years. After the contrasting sections of a sprawling modern and then cramped colonial Quito, we rode to Banos: a grimy, faded health resort which boasted medicinal hot springs and had the air of a run-down, out-of-season English spa town, but high in the splendour of the Andes. Ancient photographers, protected from the incessant drizzle by tattered umbrellas, stood endlessly waiting in the square, their old wooden box cameras wrapped in polythene, while outside the many candy shops, long wads of sticky brown toffee were thrown and stretched and thrown again to and from high wooden pegs for hour upon hour by patient men, before being cut into blocks and stacked ready to sell to the tourists when they finally arrived. The thermal springs at Banos are fed into a series of outdoor concrete baths built at the bottom of a small, steep valley and next to an icy stream. We spent an afternoon there, bathing with a group of young western tourists, some middle-aged Ladinos, and a large extended Indian family. The Indian women wore home-made costumes to bathe, which failed to contain their pendulous breasts. But more extraordinary was the sheer quantity of clothes they wore in normal life. Mopsa and I watched fascinated as layer upon layer upon layer of blouses and underskirts were added until their tiny frames had been transformed into tubby little pyramids to be topped by the ubiquitous Ecuadorian trilby.

Although our route through to Brazil did not allow us any contact with the Amazon itself, we felt compelled to make at least a gesture toward it, and so set off eastwards from Banos on a rain-soaked morning, to the west of territory long disputed between Ecuador and Brazil. The stony, descending road had rivulets crossing at every turn. As the Quito government looked on this area as politically sensitive a special permit was required, obtainable at the point of entry, and so we were as usual questioned as to the contents of the sidecar: had we a corpse inside? they suggested, or perhaps just marijuana? or cocaine? The road opened out after this, and we could see below us the roof of the jungle stretching toward Brazil. It rained all day, and as we sat in a cafe in Puyo, drying out over a plate of rice and beans, a small television high on the wall fuzzily announced Prince Andrew's engagement. So far from home and yet so near.

To reach the Peruvian border we had to return to the coast – steaming hot and lined by acres and acres of bananas. In the town of Tumbes just across the border on the Peruvian side we shared breakfast with a parched-looking North American whose burnt and craggy face, bleached hair and dusty clothes made him the personification of the dry coastal desert of Northern Peru, through which he had just walked. Two years before he had driven the same route through Central America as us but in a car, and had shipped it from Panama to Buenaventura. There he become so frustrated with the bureaucracy of importation that he simply walked away, and was walking still, living the life of a hobo, in a country far from home.

Our first hundred miles in Peru were not encouraging. In January 1983 fierce waters had tumbled down from the mountains in a rare display of wrath, to sweep away bridges and sections of road laid upon the loose sandy surface of this coastal strip. It was slow and tiring riding as we ploughed through the soft sand or bumped along on the partially re-made sections. Signposting was all but non-existent and confusing bifurcations led far out into the desert oil fields.

Toward the end of the day, and running short of fuel, we inadvertently took a detour and were only much later rescued, hopelessly lost, by a passing oil company truck, the driver of whom supplied us with the petrol we needed and the directions we sought. With the worst of the coastal road behind us we shot out, along well laid tar, across the shifting sands of the Sechura Desert. As the afternoon's passing lengthened the bikes's familiar shadow at our side, I heard a familiar drone and turned to see Ed Culberson aboard Amigo riding alongside. His ambition had been achieved, and he was riding on the elation of that success. It had taken him, with the help of six hired Indians, two weeks to get through the Darien. Over the eighty kilometres with neither road nor track, he had put just thirty on his odometer, for the rest they had dismantled the bike and carried, hauled and winched it, hacking away the jungle as they went, building rafts to cross rivers and breaking a pulley with a one ton weight capacity in the process. We briefly shared in his delight, and then he pulled away aiming to be in Lima within three days to keep an appointment with the BMW agent.

We followed more slowly. Our journey was picking up momentum again but as always there was a balance to be achieved between covering distance, which had its own particular satisfaction, and seeing more of the country we rode through than its dead flies on our visors. The two were usually incompatible.

The 800 miles from Tumbes to Lima, is all desert apart from the blessed greenery that surrounds the oasis towns which cluster around the half dozen or so rivers that bring them their only water from the Andes – it hardly ever rains

3000 year old cartoons at Sechin, Peru   *Coastal Road in Peru*

on the coastal plain. For a mile or so sugar cane and bananas and corn would abundantly and luxuriantly grow, then again we'd be out in the wilderness with only a few isolated chicken farms, smelling terribly of the fishmeal on which the chickens are fed, to break the monotony. Peruvian eggs invariably tasted of fish.

In Lima the Maoist group, Sendero Luminoso, had been active and at night tanks and troops rolled out from their protective barracks to guard the main public buildings and intersections. A curfew meant we had to be off the streets by midnight. We spent the days trying to sort out our onward journey. Our route through to Brazil was far from certain. There had been extensive flooding on the Peruvian and Bolivian altiplano and the road through to La Paz was reported closed. From Bolivia the only road eastwards into Paraguay was often impassable in the wet. The alternative was to go south into Argentina but consistently they had been refusing visas to British tourists following the war in the South Atlantic. We had applied in Mexico and Panama and were again refused by the Argentine consul in Lima. So we carried on in hope southwards through six hundred and fifty more miles of desert. The sound of the pounding surf was a constant rumble on our right and to our left the prevailing wind relentlessly blew yet more sand into the dunes that for centuries had been piling up the slopes of the brown crinkled foothills of the sierra. Our faces were raw and red, abrased by the flying grit, and the front of the bike and sidecar were stripped of paintwork by the sandblasting. The coastline became more wild and desolate and after passing through a deserted and ruined fishing village we rode along a high cliff where two vast, majestic condors swooped by within a few feet of us. Seabirds crowded the eroded cliffs and stacks and with flashes of red and black the rare and shy Inca terns darted though the spray. Early one afternoon in the fishing town of Chala, we checked into a cell-like room in a yellow-washed hotel on the edge of a sandy cliff. We knew it was our last night on the Pacific coast. Through the bars of the tall narrow window of our bedroom we watched the sun dip over a seascape fringed by a perfect crescent bay, and next morning we turned eastwards again.

Arequipa stands at over seven and a half thousand feet, a fine colonial town whose older buildings are made from the pale volcanic stone of the area. It was April and almost six months since we had left LA. The initial apprehension over our intent to ride through Central and South America had long gone and our travelling life again developed its own rythms and rituals. To travel on endlessly each and every day was exhausting and we were glad that almost every sizeable town though which we passed provided ample reason to stay for more than one night. In Arequipa the bike was left in the courtyard of a friendly hotel, and we took the train up to Cuzco and the famed Incaic city of Machu Picchu. On our return we approached the Argentinians one last time. The rules had suddenly changed and within twenty four hours we were off again, clutching our passports with those valuable visas stamped inside.

The climb over the cordillera and across the wide altiplano was painfully muddy and slow. I had thoroughly serviced the bike in Arequipa and fitted a smaller carburettor jet to help with the petrol mix once we were over ten

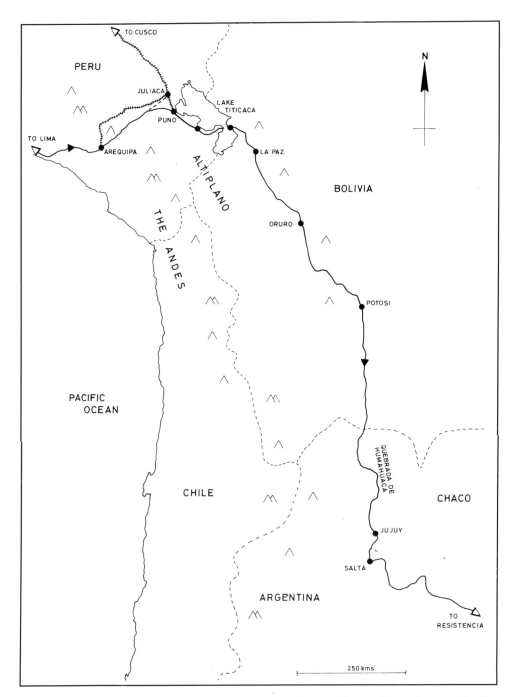

thousand feet. The rains had eased but the road was still appalling. An erratically
twisting loose gravel road took us over the first pass and onto a high plain with
the most beautiful of scenes. A bright mid-morning light shone out across the
wide expanse of an aquamarine lake in which hundreds of flamingos fed. Llamas
grazed on the tufted grass, coloured identification tassels hanging from either
ear. By mid-day the frozen road turned to mud and a falling drizzle to hail and

then to snow. The way ahead had been churned up with furrows up to two feet deep so following the example of others who had passed that way we headed out across the soggy open moor. We also had the rivers to negotiate. With mud up to the wheel spindles or water over the silencers, I slipped both outfit and clutch, Mopsa pushing from behind to free us from bogs or from the slippery pebble-strewn beds of swollen streams while the icy waters poured into our boots. While immersed in these waters the engine never stalled although it suffered terribly at these heady heights from a drastic loss of power. On the steeper sections I would half ride and half run alongside, furiously pushing and working both throttle and clutch until the summit was reached and I would collapse, lungs screaming and head pounding from a lack of oxygen. Then I would wait for Mopsa who would trudge wearily behind muttering rebelliously to herself. It always seemed possible that the Triumph would not be powerful enough to lug us and the loaded sidecar over the Andes, so it was greatly satisfying, despite the pain, when we got the outfit across these knee-deep rivers and up the next slippery stretch. At dusk we reached the Juliaca turn off. Although we had seen none since a few miles outside Arequipa, most vehicles proceeded there rather than taking the more direct route to Puno. We decided on the less used but shorter route and camped out at over 15,000 feet, alone on the bleak moorland apart from a silvery fox who, with warning barks, slowly circled us in the dead of night. The Andes had loomed large as a major and unavoidable obstacle in our journey, but now it seemed the worst was behind us, and after a morning of further mud and flooded plain we arrived at the swollen waters of Lake Titicaca. We had averaged a mere 15 mph during our two day ride to Puno. The streets of the town along the lakeside were cracked and muddied in the aftermath of the inundation of the farming land around. The inhabitants poled their reed boats to their half-submerged houses and farms, which seemed to be slowly dissolving into the clear waters. Makeshift villages of canvas and corrugated iron housed the homeless, and the Indians continued on their daily grind with a grim reserve ingrained by centuries of harsh climate and subsistence living. A lone freight train ploughed arduously across land that had now become lake, passenger trains were still not running and the road connection to Juliaca had only just been restored by the raising of causeways across the flooded land. We were told on arrival in Puno that we were the first vehicle through on the more direct route since the rains had eased.

Two bitterly cold nights in Puno, a day spent hanging and laying the entire contents of the sidecar out to dry, then we followed the lake's edge to Bolivia and La Paz. Our first view of the city was extaordinary, for peering over its canyon rim from nearly a thousand feet above, it sprawled longitudinally, toy-like and crowded, hemmed in by the steep slopes on either side. We booked into a hotel for ten million pesos a night, while outside on the main street the money-changers loitered: a large bag of pesos in one hand, a fat wad of dollars in the other – the peoples' hedge against a rampant inflation which in 1985 had reached an incredible 23,000%. It was the first major city we had visited in South America where those of Indian descent outnumbered the Ladinos – the women

Boy with football, Lima, Peru   *The Peruvian Desert*

wore bowlers precariously balanced atop a long black braid, the men a traditional knitted hat with earflaps or the less traditional baseball cap proclaiming the Mexico City World Cup or "I Love LA".

The road south to Argentina was open – we checked before leaving with the Highways Department in La Paz. It was a long two-day ride to Potosi through the barren, dull brown hills of the underpopulated Bolivian altiplano. Small children ran from isolated farm shacks, hats in hands, begging imploringly, and a lone stocky Indian stood patiently waiting at a junction, holding out the hind quarters of a sheep, trying to sell it to one of the handful of vehicles which would pass by that day. Potosi is a town dominated by a huge hill which for centuries had been mined for its store of silver. Now it supplies mostly tin, but is still the lifeblood and major reason for the town's continued existence. The miners descend from the chilly mountain side to work, near-naked, in the sweltering depths and some only last ten years before they are forced to retire, their lungs ravaged by silicosis. Looking back only stark images remain from this, the poorest nation in the Americas.

As British nationals we were a little apprehensive as to our reception on entering Argentina – our countries had been at war just four years before. Before crossing the frontier I removed the Union Jacks stuck to the front and rear of the bike and covered our GB plate. At the border we were left in no doubt about official feelings on the matter for huge signs still lined the road declaring "Los Malvinas son Argentinas". We descended through the dramatic gorge of the

Quebrada de Humahuaca with its fantastic erosions in shades of dusty reds and arrived in Jujuy (pronounced Hoohooee), a town of European feel and relative affluence so very different from the harsh Bolivian altiplano. In the tourist office the woman behind the desk politely asked where we were from.

"From Britain," Mopsa answered emphatically.

"Oh! Well we shan't mention Margaret Thatcher then, shall we?" came the reply. As elsewhere politeness, assistance and concern were what we got and any blame for the war was placed deftly and squarely upon the shoulders of our leader.

So with the mountains finally behind us we rode on welcomed pavement across the flat expansive marshy and grassland terrain of the Northern Argentinian Chaco in a straight line east south east, stopping only to admire the abundant and varied birdlife and to replace worn-out bearings in both the front and sidecar wheels. At Resistencia we turned north and entered Paraguay through the city of Ascuncion, possibly one of the most provincial capitals in the world. The authorities considered the country a peaceful haven of stability in a violent continent. "The land of peace and sunshine" the government tourist brochures proudly proclaimed. Everything was muito tranquillo said one of the city's inhabitants who, having appointed himself as our official guide, took us to eat a great steaming bowl of fish-head soup in the local market. The Botanical Gardens on the outskirts of the town had a campsite and it was to there that we retired before Mopsa, through an inspired piece of deduction from reading one of our newly-acquired banknotes, discovered that tomorrow was Independence Day. Back into town we went for we rightly surmised that everything would

Replacing the front wheel bearings in Jujuy, Northern Argentina

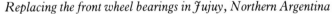

close for the day. Outside the cathedral young conscripts with hair shaved at the sides and thick on top were sweeping a long red carpet in preparation for the President's visit. Mopsa was determined to catch the scene on film but as soon as she raised her camera a strutting Lieutenant tore out of the doors demanding that she desist.

"But why?" she countered. "It's quite a harmless scene."

"It is forbidden to take a photograph of the army on duty," was his angry reply. She didn't persist. The civil rights record of the Stroessner regime, the world's longest surviving dictatorship, has not been particularily good.

We continued on through the rolling green cattle country to the south, exploring the ruins of former Jesuit settlements but the air of pastoral tranquility was rudely shattered one night when a passing gaucho took exception to our camping out on his route home and let loose with two shots from his pistol. After a few moments weighing up the pros and cons, I gingerly stuck my head out of the tent, only to see our assailant galloping off into the enveloping darkness. We assured each other that we had only heard the crack of his whip, and went back to sleep but in the morning we found a neat hole in the sidecar, and a slug fell out of my Guatemalan straw hat. While we were packing up the tent an old Guarani peasant pushing an antiquated bicycle stopped and with faltering Spanish engaged us in conversation. He had never heard of England and was puzzled by our desire to sleep by the side of the road, rather than in a house. Why indeed?

The Iguacu Falls were a fine introduction to Brazil. Despite the holiday crowds from the industrial cities it was sheer splendour to see so extensive a series of waterfalls set in such luxuriant jungle with colourful birds swooping through the spray and the near perfect rainbows. The mists which surrounded the falls merged with the heavy rains which came and went over the next few days as we rode to the Atlantic coast and on up to Rio. We had now spent eight months in Latin America. Brazil is an enormous country – the world's fifth largest, only slightly smaller than the United States, and slightly larger than Australia. If we travelled through it as extensively as we had those other two, we would never get home. We decided to try to ship from Rio de Janeiro to Africa. Our original plan, to be away from England for some three years had long since fallen by the wayside, but we had promised our families that it would not be more than four, and that was fast approaching. So we made our way up the Atlantic seaboard, bathing from sandy beaches and on one night were engulfed by a torrential rainstorm. Mopsa cooked dinner inside the tent, trying desperately to keep our belongings away from its walls, while I dug trenches to avert the flow from a broken banked river. A cracking flash of lightening illuminated the scene. In my haste to stem the flow I had climbed out of the tent naked and now a sheet of silvery water was rushing towards us, some eighteen inches deep. I shouted to Mopsa to abandon tent and to move things to the higher ground on which I had parked the bike. As she crawled out of the tent it rushed away from us. We both scrambled after it, abandoning all attempts to keep anything dry, and then standing up to our knees in water tried to field our belongings as they swept past our outstretched arms. After an hour the waters subsided and we then had the unpleasant task of removing the leeches from each other's feet and legs by candlelight, using burning cigarettes to force them to release their grip and finally, wrapped in everything dry we could find in the sidecar, we curled up for a squelchy night's sleep. In the morning we picked clothing, cooking equipment, watches and even the bike keys out of the sand and bushes, hanging everything up to dry under a brilliant sun.

We reached Rio in time for the opening matches of the World Cup taking place in Mexico City. Brazil thought, as they apparently always do, that they had a pretty fair chance of winning. Football is a national pastime, small boys play in time honoured ways with tin cans in dusty lanes or fields, each one hoping to be the next Pele or Socrates. League games draw huge crowds and for important occasions, such as the World Cup, national holidays are decreed. Giant screens were set up in city squares, portable black and whites taken into those offices which could not close. On match days an unnatural silence hung over the Rio afternoon, broken by firecrackers and whistles and hoots of delight as goals were scored. Not, perhaps, the best time to embark on the time consuming task of finding a ship and re-exporting our machine, but we had no choice. We found a reasonably-priced passage for the bike on a Japanese container ship bound for Durban, but were forced to book ourselves onto a costly flight to Johannesberg on South African Airways. I had no particular desire to go to South Africa, rather the contrary, but our options were limited to there or Nigeria, and we knew that the bureaucracy involved in getting the bike in or out of Nigeria would make Karachi and Buenaventura look like a vicarage tea party. Here in Rio, although the form was complicated and rigid, the officials were helpful, and we spent an afternoon in the office of the Chief of the Port Customs as he typed our letter to him in Portuguese, asking for his permission to export our temporarily-imported machine. The shipping agents informed us that we could pay freight charges on the motorcycle in Brazilian cruzados and we subsequently changed the requisite amount on the semi-official black market, so saving ourselves eighty dollars. The Bank of Brazil, however, then insisted we pay the charge in dollars. We were so short of money that we took our case to the Head of Foreign Exchange Controls at the Central Bank. He listened politely to our pleas then quietly informed us that as foreign visitors we were required to pay in foreign currency and that only foreign residents of more than three years standing were otherwise entitled. He was very sorry but these were the rules. Then as we were leaving his office he called us back and, taking our papers, scribbled hurriedly on each form. Smiling, he handed them back and shrugged his shoulders.

"What the hell," he laughed. "With a foreign debt of over a hundred billion dollars, what difference can eighty make."

Chapter Nine

Africa

THE RED dirt road, pot-holed and corrugated, was beginning to rattle my nerves, the sidecar to slip on the fixing clamps. It was nearing mid-day, the sun almost directly overhead. We were at latitude 33 degrees east, longitude 9 degrees south in Northern Zamia on the road from Chipitu to Nakonde. As we crashed into another pot-hole I swore.

"God damn this road!" But before either of us had time to readjust our positions the sidecar slammed into a protruding rock, which sent us into the air, and launched the spare fuel can from its bracket. As we landed, all at different times, the sidecar started to weave – a puncture. I stopped the bike without pulling over. As far as we were aware we were the only vehicle on the road that morning. Mopsa recovering her composure, wiped the dust from her glasses and then from her watch face. It was Saturday, 20th September, and back in England my brother was getting married.

"They should be taking their vows now." Mopsa was always the romantic. We raised an imaginary glass and then settled down to the repair. We were outside a small village, surrounded by dry scrubby bush and the drought had not yet broken in this part of Africa. A local woman passed by, a colourful bundle on her head and a child strapped to her erect back. She joined her hands in a single silent clap and mouthed a gentle Jambo in traditional greeting towards Mopsa. Two scrawny lads, clad only in ragged shorts, soon joined us and squatted in the dust, fascinated by our labours. Within an hour we were moving again, and soon arrived at Nakonde on the Tanzanian border. Our most direct route north was through that country but we had been refused entry visas. We needed petrol but none was available.

"Hey mister, wanna change money?" We declined the smiling youth but asked him if he would cross the border with our jerry can and have it filled on the Tanzanian side. He could, but said there was no petrol there until after the weekend. It was a hundred and thirty-four miles, directly west, on a scarcely-used track to Mbala and Lake Tanganyika where, we had been assured, we could board a steamer to Burundi in Central Africa, thereby skirting an unwelcoming Tanzania. We had about 9 litres in the tank – enough to get us there. The road was no better than the one we had been travelling that morning. The surrounding bush was flatter and there was more sand on the track, but it cooled a little as the huge yellow African sun began its slow descent to the wide horizon. By four o'clock the jarring road was inflicting some damage and we were forced to stop and improvise temporary lashings to the top box which had broken three of its four welds. Then as darkness fell we spluttered to a stop, out of fuel just twelve miles from our destination. Rather than camp out until the morning we started pushing and within a mile arrived at the main road – it was tarred. Mopsa immediately perked up.

"They'll be dressing up ready for the evening reception now."

A group of young boys emerged from the darkness. They gathered around babbling inquisitively then helped to push the outfit up a mile of incline.

"Now downhill right to the town," the tallest enthusiastically informed us and they cheered us on our way. After a further two hours of alternate free-wheeling and pushing through the silent pitch black night we saw lights in the distance. When we arrived we found an electricity sub-station. I was beginning to feel a little nervous. Over the last few months the Zambian security forces had arrested several white Europeans travelling through their country and interrogated them, none too gently it was alleged, on the grounds of their being possible South African spies. Following cross border raids by South African forces against the ANC camps in Zimbabwe, Zambia and Botswana, the situation had grown tense. The Zambian government had been reacting in a particularly zealous way, keen to divert public attention from a battered economy that had already resulted in strikes and food riots in several towns. Not only had we been to South Africa, but we were silently and surrepticiously pushing our motorcycle through the northern border country at night.

"Do we risk asking them where we can get fuel?" I asked Mopsa. She nodded dubiously and together we approached the gates.

★ ★ ★

Eleven weeks previously we flew across the South Atlantic from Brazil to Johannesburg. The South African Airways stewardess had frowned when we asked her to wake us when we passed over the Greenwich Meridian, so technically completing our circumnavigation. She, no doubt, had been flying around the world for years and saw our request as merely irksome. She never did wake us. On landing we took the airport bus to the main rail station in the city centre. The change from a lively Rio to a dour Johannesburg immediately depressed me. The streets of the city centre were modern, clean, uncrowded and orderly and a bright sun shone down on them from a clear and cloudless sky. A strange hush sat on the centre which only briefly came to life at rush hour when people took public transport and privately run mini-buses back to their segregated living areas.

At the station we enquired about tickets at the whites only booth. The motorcycle was due in Durban in two days and we wanted to be there to meet it.

The gruff middle-aged Afrikaner behind the counter warmed a little when he heard we were from England.

"Your Mrs Thatcher, she's the only one who's for us now." Despite her condemnation of the Apartheid system, Mrs Thatcher's consistent refusal to impose sanctions seemed to have only endeared her to those wishing to maintain the status quo. He then told us that the trains for the next two days were booked solid, but if we turned up half an hour before the overnight train was due to leave we might get a cancellation. It was a long wait as we shifted between the restaurant, where tennis from Wimbledon was on the television, and the whites only waiting room where three drunken semi-derelicts were singing Irish songs.

The scene on the platform when we arrived was pandemonium. A crowd of people, all trying for cancellations, were hounding the guard, while a full regimental piped band played in front of one of the carriages before boarding the train. We were taken in hand by some young soldiers just back from "the border". Their seats had been booked by the army but they were short on numbers. We were both assigned unpronounceable Afrikaans names and the ranks of corporal and told to keep our mouths shut when the conductor came. These youthful conscripts with whom we shared the carriage were all of British descent and were intent on becoming as drunk and as rowdy as possible, a necessary release it seemed after the stresses of the border patrols. As the drink took hold, a boisterous vocalisation of their resentments became louder and more vitriolic and was directed not only at black people in general but also at the authority of the Afrikaner. It was only through the timely intervention of a senior officer that a nasty scene involving knives and a machete was avoided. When we arrived in Durban the following morning, tired and exhausted after a sleepless night, the young men were transformed. Very spruce and pink faced, shaved and tidied up, they were embraced by their waiting parents as heroes back from the war.

In Durban we stayed at a guest house overlooking the city, where the guests were naturally all white and the waiters, kitchen staff and cleaners all black. After collecting the outfit from the port we hurried back, via the black homeland of Kwazulu and across the white rolling farmland of the Transvaal, to Johannesburg. In a workshop above a Kawasaki bike showroom on Main Street I overhauled the motorcycle again, fitting new piston rings and valve guides. We had come the 14,000 miles from Los Angeles without mechanical incident, apart from the burnt-out stator in Mexico City and it seemed that our run of bad luck in the States was not to be repeated. Our route north through Africa, however, was far from certain. Having visited South Africa we were unlikely to be allowed to pass through Tanzania. The south of Sudan was closed by the civil war so an overland route up the eastern side of Africa was out. The alternative was a long haul through the jungles of Zaire to Chad before crossing the western Sahara to Algiers. Our last continent looked fraught with difficulties but as before we could only start out, take one country at a time and see what transpired.

We crossed from South Africa into Botswana. For the first time on our journey we had to list the value of the foodstuffs we were carrying on the customs declaration form. Before we were allowed past the barrier a smartly uniformed sergeant asked us to open the sidecar.

"I shall be very quick but very diligent," he declared with a glint in his eye. After five minutes of delving and opening and inspecting he gave up, overwhelmed by the mass of carefully packed articles and particularly by the many stubs of candle we kept in various places – just in case. After a series of army roadblocks we reached Gabarone, even smaller and more provincial than Ascuncion in Paraguay. Parking outside the British High Commission, Mopsa went to change money at the bank while I stayed with the motorcycle. A barefoot boy cheerfully swinging a bucket and rag asked if he could wash the bike.

"I'm sorry but there's no point in washing it," I replied. "We're only going back out into the dust." He slowly circled the outfit, studying it intently as our conversation continued. I told him where I was from.

"What do you want most in the world?"

"Most? I don't really know." I answered, a little flummoxed by his directness. His eyes widened in disbelief.

"You don't know?"

"Well," I countered, to hide my embarrassment, "What do you want most?"

"I want to work." he declared emphatically.

Botswana is a huge and for the most part parched extending plain, home to three of the world's more unusual physical features: the Kalahari desert, the swamps and inland delta of the Okavango river which flows from Angola, and the vast salt flats of the Makgadikgadi Pan. Once across the border we shook off

Brief encounter on the road to Maun – John had cycled from England

our discontent with South Africa and enjoyed the warm weather and the dusty landscape. As we rode, first to Francistown and then out on a long and dusty road to the Okavango swamps at Maun, the sun, the dust, the light, the sounds, the sky and the smiles of Africa took hold. We passed by the clusters of enclosed villages, circular mud huts with thatched rooves, cattle and goats in among the thorny bushes – the African drought still had the country very firmly in its grip. At the point where the road crossed a thin finger of the Makgadikgadi pan, a dried up salt lake which stretched to far distant horizons, Mopsa set our compass at 240 degrees and we sped across its crusty surface like a speedboat with a white powdery dust as our wake. Fifteen miles out we camped beneath brilliant stars, their light reflected back into the cool night air by the flat white pan, and in the early morning after breakfasting under the steady gaze of a trio of ostrich we sped back, astonishing a group of boys herding their goats among the scrubby grassland at the pan's edge. Once at the Okavango delta we hired the services of Two-boy, a local fisherman, who in his dugout poled us around the swamps, gliding us through the papyrus while we sweated and burnt under a harsh sun, listening to the sounds of the water life. Two-boy fished as the sun set, then smoked his catch overnight over fires we built on the small islands on which we slept, sharing some of it with us in return for coffee and sugar. The rest he bartered for tobacco or for mealie, a stodgy and unappetising maize meal that is one of the staples for the vast majority of sub-Saharan Africans, with the families who lived by the water. The bird and wild life was extensive but it was hippo we really wanted to see and when we eventually found some Two-boy refused to pole the precarious dugout any nearer than was absolutely necessary.

We soon discovered that there was a disadvantage to motorcycle travel in Africa. We were unable to enter the game parks, motorcycles deemed too vulnerable to the predatory nature of lions and the unpredictable behaviour of elephants and rhinos. So we made do with the wildlife we saw from the road: mostly various species of deer, impala and wildebeest, giraffes, also ostrich and one huge and rotting elephant carcass – poached for its ivory.

Entering Zimbabwe at Victoria Falls, we met at the town's campsite the first batch of overlanders who had left Northern Europe the previous autumn, each expecting to be lone travellers in a vast continent but finding they were part of a steady stream of four-wheel drive vehicles, Land Rovers and motorbikes all heading south, on the same roads. Their route through Algeria, Niger, Chad, the Central African Republic, Zaire, Uganda and on to Kenya, was called the Main Road. It is a difficult route involving the sands of the Sahara and the mud roads of Zaire and would possibly be our only viable route home. We camped alongside Kevin and Charlotte and their BMW bikes and were later joined by Rob in an ailing Land Rover. Their experiences had been varied and in somecases extreme. Kevin had broken his collarbone in the Sahara while showing Charlotte how to ride up sand dunes. Rob's original companion had been set alight while transferring fuel from a jerry can to the tank. In the fierce dry heat of the desert the fumes ignited and he was very badly burnt, his life saved by the prompt action of his insurance company who directed an air

With fellow overlanders and their machines at the campsite at Victoria Falls in Zimbabwe

ambulance to fly from Paris direct. Within 25 hours of the accident he was in a burns unit in England, the grateful recipient of one of the fastest air evacuations to have taken place from the middle of the Sahara desert.

The road from Victoria Falls to Bulawayo was considered notorious for ambushes by rebel bandits still opposed to the government of Robert Mugabe. We were advised not to stop along the 243 mile route except at Hwange, Gwai River and Halfway House. The possibility of a puncture or a break down made us very vulnerable but we had learnt to put such fears aside. This vulnerability was brought forcefully home when we read several months later in an English newspaper of a German couple who were also travelling through Africa with a sidecar and were ambushed and shot on this same stretch of road. Incidents such as these often do disservice to the reputation of a country. We found Zimbabweans, without exception, to be friendly and hospitable, although we were clearly lucky who we met.

As soon as we arrived in Harare we tried, unsuccessfully, to persuade the Tanzanian High Commission to give us visitors visas despite our visit to South Africa. The consul was sympathetic and promised to refer our case to Dar-es-Salam but each time we returned we were told to come back the next day. After two weeks we gave up, realising that what they really meant was no. Rather than ride from the bottom to the top of Zambia we decided to take the shortest route north to Malawi which involved crossing with a convoy accompanied by the Zimbabwean army through the Tete province of war-torn Mozambique. At the border town of Nyamapanda we camped behind the freight companies' caravans and woke to the sound of truck engines warming up for the trip ahead. As the small border town stirred a uniformed sergeant guided us into

Mopsa and local boys among the boulders at Mutoko, Zimbabwe

Advertisements in Blantyre, Malawi

a Red Cross hut for what he said was a routine medical examination. Unshouldering his automatic rifle, he slipped on a white coat and proceeded with the inspection. On the other side of the curtain his female assistant explained to Mopsa that there was a particularly virulent outbreak of VD in the area, which they were attempting to contain. Doctoring done – we were last – the sergeant ushered us out and climbed aboard one of the Armoured Personnel

Carriers which were to escort us through as far as the town of Tete where we would meet up with the convoy coming from the Malawian border. We then sat for two hours, patiently waiting in line until told the reason for the delay – the convoy heading south from Malawi would not be moving that day because there was a shortage of diesel for the army vehicles. As well as the forty or so trucks there were, besides us, two private cars. One of these carried four pentecostal preachers due to address a meeting in Blantyre the following evening. They were determined to cross that day and persuaded the officer in charge to allow the private vehicles to accompany the three armed personel carriers about to drive to the garrison at Tete to replace the diesel that was being sent up to the Malawian border.

"Is your motorcycle strong?" the officer asked pointedly. "It won't break down?"

"Oh no," I replied "it's very strong."

So we set off, tagging along behind the lead vehicle which kept a close eye out for possible landmines hidden in the pot-holes and broken tar or for Renamo rebels waiting in ambush among the skeletal remains of scrubby bushes. The dry, barren countryside had been depopulated, the villagers forced to move to safer areas by the rebel's brutal harassment and indiscriminate killing. As we descended towards the Tete river basin it began to get uncomfortably hot and our faces, arms and bodies to furiously itch. I suspected the sides of the road had been sprayed with a chemical defoliant. We were about two thirds of the way when I felt the motorcycle begin a familiar weave. We slid to a stop, a puncture in the rear tyre. One of the APC's pulled alongside, while the rest of our tiny convoy passed on. Once they saw we had the means to repair the tyre they continued on, leaving us to spend a nervous half hour alone with our rear wheel detached before speeding on to catch them up.

Eleven miles the other side of Tete we found the other vehicles parked outside a modern church building next to a tumble down school. The Zimbabwean army were nowhere to be seen. The preachers thought they would go it alone but we were not about to take such risks. A large group of wide-eyed children gathered solemnly around us. They were dressed in aid clothes – old T-shirts, cut-down dresses, silk blouses and one young boy in padded skiing dungarees. All seemed to be suffering from the effects of a meagre diet – distended stomachs, ring-worm, scabs on their arms and legs. It seemed pointless to hang around so we left the preachers and returned to the Zimbabwe army garrison in Tete. There the duty sergeant introduced himself with a warm, firm handshake as Trevor. I told him that the preachers were still wanting to go on that day

"I cannot allow that," he replied indignantly. "If they try I will capture and detain them. And the same goes for you." He then issued us with some army rations and a packet of cigarettes. Later that evening, over large cups of black and steaming tea he told us what his life was like here in the war zone. As a professional soldier he disparaged the ragged barefoot army they were here to help.

"Without us they would lose control." His sympathies lay with the women and children whom, he said, lived very desperate lives.

At mid-day the following morning we joined the convoy of trucks we had left in Nyamapanda and rode with them to Malawi, arriving in Blantyre after dark. By taking out temporary membership for the Blantyre Sports Club, we were allowed to camp on a piece of grass overlooking the cricket pitch and to use their shower facilities, restaurant and bar. The club was one of those bastions of a colonial past, kept alive by the rich, the influential and the visiting British ex-patriate worker. The majority of its clientele was white. Malawi had a strained relationship with the rest of black Africa. It is ruled with a firm and dictatorial hand by the President for life, Dr Hastings Banda – once a general practitioner in Willesden. Under the Ngwazi's (which means peerless one) "wise and dynamic" leadership political dissent has been effectively suppressed and Malawi's friendly relationship with South Africa has not endeared the Ngwazi to other black leaders. On our second day in Blantyre we witnessed the preparations for the welcoming of Robert Mugabe, Kenneth Kaunda and Samora Machel who were on a reported goodwill visit to Banda, although the unofficial story was that they were coming to put pressure on him to distance himself from the Pretoria regime. Truck loads of women were brought into the city to line the approach road from the airport. Each wore a kanga on which was printed the large, smiling face of their fatherly leader.

Malawi takes its name from Africa's third largest lake, a corruption of the word maravi, the local tribal word for bright haze. Before the second Bantu migrations from West Africa in the sixteenth century, there still lived around the lake a dwindling band of original pygmy inhabitants called the Amaravi. Bantu folklore recalls their complex about being small and how on first meeting an Amaravi, he would always ask when you had first seen him. The correct reply, to prevent a trust from his poisoned spear, was "I saw you from a long way off." At this he would jump up and down in glee crying "You see, I am big after all."

Along the lake's western bank and up the high escarpment to the mountains beyond is contained some of the continent's most beautiful scenery. We rode from Blantyre to the Zomba plateau on whose slopes the gentle spring tones of the African msasa tree ranged from pink to red to faded orange and coppery brown, and then up the dry scrubby rift valley where primitive looking baobob trees, some dating from the time of the Amaravi, dotted the horizon. Climbing on twisting road up the escarpment, we passed young boys who offered for sale models of motorcars, buses and trucks fashioned from lengths of wire. There was even the motorcycle and I wondered whether in a few weeks time a sidecar might be added. It would have been an unusual honour.

From the small modern capital Lilongwe we continued along the plateau until stopped by a roadblock outside of Kuzungu, close to where the Ngwazi was born. He was visiting the town and no traffic was to be allowed through until after his departure by helicopter.

"How long must we wait?" I asked.

The soldier shrugged. "One hour, two hours."

Mopsa and onlookers above Lake Malawi

Town Children in Karonga, Northern Malawi

"All day?"

"Maybe."

We parked the bike and walked over to where the huge celebration was taking place, having our cameras and a box of matches temporarily confiscated by the guards. A large dais was crowded with dignitaries and surrounded by a contingent of the army, and a bright red carpet led to a helicopter nearby. In front were massed several thousand dancers, the majority women, divided into groups of around a hundred. The groups of women wore the same kangas we'd seen in Blantyre, but each had a different coloured background for Dr. Banda's face. The event was a tightly choreographed succession of dances by each group and the Ngwazi would from time to time descend from the podium to shuffle briefly amongst his people. It was a colourful display but it lacked the natural and spontaneous exuberance we had become accustomed to since leaving South Africa.

On the road again and high above the lake, overlooking its misty blue waters, a sidecar suddenly appeared. It was a BMW, and well equipped for both desert and rough road. Its riders were astonished to see us.

"But we thought we were the only people travelling through Africa on a sidecar," the owner, a German, exclaimed. We were less surprised, by now being well used to the unexpected. We spent an hour squatting by the side of the road comparing adventures, while a small crowd of children and youths gathered round. As elsewhere they were fascinated by the bikes. The more forward of these groups who so often gathered, would peer into the instrument panel, into the very soul of the machine, and then turn to gaze at us in awe.

"Is this your Honda?" they would ask and soon the magic words 150 rustled through the assembled. If I told them that our low compression, overloaded, and worn-out Triumph could scarcely manage 60 mph on the flat, then clearly I was a great god being far too humble. Big motorcycles go fast and that was the end of it.

The next day we passed through Karonga, the last port of call on the lake's western shore, pausing awhile to have one of the exhaust pipes fixed in the only welding shop in town, which also served as a cold drinks bar and discotheque. In the afternoon we rode to Chipita on the Zambian border. The next day, in England, my brother was to be married.

★ ★ ★

After rattling the padlocked gates of the perimeter fence that surrounded the sub-station for several minutes the nightwatchman eventually appeared. He didn't seem unduly perturbed to see us there, wearing motorcycling gear and carrying helmets, and he was pleased to tell us that we were now only about a mile and a half from the town. We pushed on. By the time we reached the outskirts of Mbala we were exhausted, both from the long and hard day's ride and from pushing the outfit for over two hours. While summoning the strength for the final incline a car stopped and the rather drunk and noisy occupants asked if we needed help. It was the first vehicle we had seen all day and we gratefully accepted a tow for the final half mile to the Grasshopper Inn. The security forces overzealous treatment of some visiting Europeans arrested as suspected South African spies had been reported in the newspapers both in Zambia and abroad. The driver invited us to join them later for drinks at the bar, adding that when we got back to London, we should "tell them that not all Zambians are bad men."

The hotel was not cheap but in the circumstances we welcomed the comfort of hot baths and a roast beef dinner. There was some shortage of goods in Zambia, especially in the more isolated areas, but as with most other like places you could invariably get what you wanted if you were prepared to pay the price. Here in Africa, where we stayed at night was usually dependent on the general security situation and on the relative cheapness of hotel accomodation. Until Zambia we had camped out almost exclusively, in established campsites or by the side of the road. Although more time consuming, camping was what we both preferred. Cheap hotel rooms were often depressing places consisting of no more than two beds with thin uncomfortable mattresses, a single unshaded bulb, dirty-whitewashed walls and the added possibility of bed bugs, cockroaches, mosquitoes or rats. I enjoyed living constantly in the open, be it on the motorcycle or sleeping under the stars. In this way I felt very much more a part of the world rather than one travelling through it and then retiring from it each night. Mopsa enjoyed the camping as well. Her interest in and enjoyment of cooking and food, she adapted accordingly. Sometimes in Africa all she could find in the markets were potatoes, onions and a very gritty rice, apart from mealie, of course, to which we never did take. Before leaving Durban she had stocked up on Indian spices and she now prepared delicious curries from the limited produce available. She became very adept at creating these on our small Optimus stove.

It was from Mpulungu, on the very southern tip of Lake Tanganyika, that we hoped to catch one of the ferries that steamed north to Burundi. We found on arrival at the port that we would have to wait four days. What at first seemed like yet another frustrating delay became in fact a pleasant rest. We camped at Nkupi Lodge, a collection of half-finished rondavals which the owners, Kathy and Dinish planned to rent out to tourists looking for quiet vacations in this isolated corner of Zambia. Kathy was a winsome girl from Norfolk who had married Dinish, a Zimbabwean of Asian origin, and together they had decided on Mpulungu as their place to settle. Within their half acre of land Kathy had planted, and nurtured through constant sprinkling, a whole variety of local trees, some of which had disappeared from the surrounding countryside. With an increase in the population of the area through improved fishing of the lake, the majority of burnable trees had been cut down for firewood. Their garden was an oasis in the dry surrounding bush. Dinish was following in his family's footsteps and had recently opened a dry goods and haberdashery store in town. We spent lazy days with them and their young son Joe, fishing by the lakeside and chatting over long extended meals.

Once we had cleared customs and all the other passengers had embarked, we watched nervously as an old and tired crane swung the outfit across to the decks of the tired and dishevelled Mwongozo, while a Danish aid worker at our side remarked on how they had dropped a car into the waters of the harbour a month previously. On boarding we found that our very small, very bare and grubby first class cabin had been re-assigned to a Tanzanian District Commissioner who would be boarding the boat further up the lake shore. We argued resolutely with the steward who eventually acceded to our demands and arranged another cabin for the VIP. Once settled in and a few hours out we heard a blast of the ship's horn and the Danish aid worker, popping his head around the door, suggested we go on deck to view the impending scene. From out of the darkness a flotilla of small lights emerged, perhaps thirty to forty small wooden boats, a few with motors but the majority being furiously paddled, and loaded down with people, bundles, chickens and goats, sacks of cassava root, sugar and mealie, all converging on the ferry. In the choppy waters the boat men clamoured and scrambled for a place alongside in order to off-load their cargo and passengers whilst less sturdy boats started to fill with water and near naked men baled frantically to keep their vessels afloat. The foredeck was soon piled high with mounds of baggage and the motorcycle disappeared beneath a mountain of sacks, and rolls of coarse tobacco. The scene was often repeated as we chugged our way 420 miles up the Tanzanian lake shore to Bujumbura. As more and then less people joined the boat the toilets became flooded and unusable, awash with a mixture of shower water and human excrement.

A family of hippo wallowed in the waters alongside the wharf in Bujumbura. We waited patiently in line in the warm morning sun to clear immigration. The countryside had changed, it was lusher with palm trees in amongst the buildings that dotted the hillsides, parts of which lay shrouded in a thin and delicate mist. In Malawi we had heard through the travellers grapevine, often a dubious and exaggerated source of information, that the Immigration Department there issued visas on behalf of the Burundi and Ugandan governments who had no representation in the country. We had subsequently obtained them in Lilongwe, at a cost of five kwacha each. When our turn came I handed our passports, opened at the relevent page, to the Burundi official. After studying them intently for a few seconds he turned to ask us what they were.

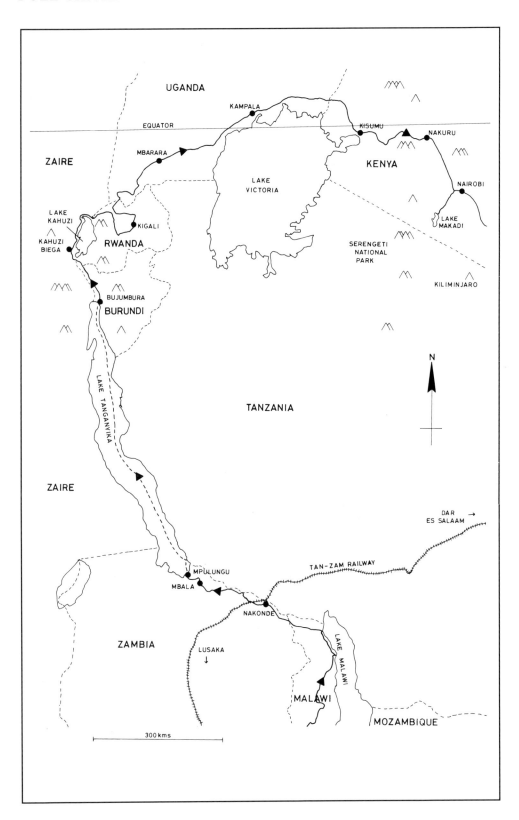

"They're our visas, issued by the Malawi government," Mopsa replied confidently.

"I can't accept these," he said. "The Malawi government has no authority to issue visas for other countries." I groaned inwardly, imagining that we would now be sent back to Zambia and Lusaka to obtain the necessary visas there.

"You must go immediately to the Chief of Immigration in the city. You must be regularised," he added.

Prior to independence, Burundi was a Belgian colony, so French is the European language most used. Despite having not been regularised we were allowed to proceed with the temporary importation of the bike and then rode on a rutted road into the city. The thirties style Art Deco buildings of the centre were peeling and decayed and unkempt bougainvillea tumbled over walls and fences. As we stopped outside the immigration building a smartly dressed young man approached, and as invariably happened at entry ports we were asked if we wanted to change money. We declined.

"How do you find Bujumbura?" he then asked. "Tres chic, non?"

The following morning our regularisation was officially complete and then within forty-eight hours we had obtained visas for both Zaire and Rwanda. Travellers often bemoaned the length of time it took to obtain visas for onward travel in Africa but this time we found no such problem. We had an introduction to a family of American missionaries in Bujumbura and as we arrived at the Vugizo Mission we were welcomed by the Rev. Carl Johnson, his thick white hair swept back from his gentle face.

"Rocky's somewhat confused," he shouted over the noise of the bike's engine as his large black dog scrambled eagerly at our wheels. "My son has a sidecar and he can't understand why you're not him." Within a few minutes Ken arrived riding a 1953 BMW with a small bullet-nosed sidecar attached. There were only two sidecars in the country, he told us proudly, and both belonged to him.

Leaving Burundi we crossed a short 23 mile slice of Rwanda to enter Zaire at Bukavu. We had planned a detour around the Zairian side of Lake Kivu, rather than take the more direct route through Rwanda to Uganda, to visit the wild gorillas in the Kahuzi-Biega National Park. It was a short detour through Zaire, no more than 125 miles, and the extra distance on a very rocky road, was more than compensated, not only by seeing the gorillas but also by the pleasures of the ride. High in the rain forests of the National Park we were taken by a guide and two trackers who hacked a path through the dense, dank and soggy jungle to come face to face with Mahesh, a fully grown 550 pound silver back gorilla and the dominant male of his group, gently feeding on bamboo shoots and eying us curiously as we squatted just ten feet distant. It was an extraordinary experience to meet a wild gorilla face to face. Rationally I knew that they were gentle creatures who didn't attack, but when first in his presence more primitive instincts took hold and as the adrenaline flowed so the heart beat very quickly. Twice, when wanting to move to more succulent shoots, he mock charged to within two feet of our small band and while the experienced trackers stood their

With a guide and trackers at the Kahuzi Biega ▲
Forest, Zaire

◄ *Mahesh in the Kahuzi Biega Forest, Zaire*

ground both Mopsa and I fell over backwards in fright into the muddy undergrowth. We later met an English anthropologist who had been studying the gorillas in Rwanda. One day when out watching a group he got caught in a torrential downpour and while attempting to shelter under some foliage one of the gorillas came and crouched over him from behind and with her huge arms kept the rain from falling on his head.

"The Zairians are an exuberant people. "Un drole d'histoire, Un drole d'histoire," the officer at the border kept chuckling as we told him of our journey. Despite the exuberance, life was slow – it took us all of a morning to change a travellers cheque at the bank in Bukavu, due, so they told us, to the death of a teller. Huge two-handed waves and loud cheering from the children greeted us as we rode around the lake. Older men slowly raised a hand to their hats, the women, often loaded down with produce, water or wood, mouthing a silent greeting as we passed. When we stopped in villages, small children gathered round in a hectic bubble of activity demanding gifts, be they sweets, biros, our helmets or gloves, or whatever they saw as reasonably small and detachable. It was only our cameras they feared and from those they scattered in panic. So we rose and fell on the rocky and sometimes steep and muddy road, through the cultivated patchwork of banana, corn, sugar cane and coffee fields, with Lake Kivu, silver and placid, below. The motorcycle was again taking a severe hammering. The spokes I had fitted in Los Angeles had held firm but cracks had begun to appear in the wheel rim and I prayed that they would remain as small as they were, for we had long discarded the spare rim with which we had left England. By late afternoon the outfit's handling had become strange and erratic and on stopping I found that one of the holding bolts had snapped and the rear of the sidecar had sagged to within an inch of the road, having been disarmingly crashing against the irregularities of the road. Again we had left

England with spares but had already used them up. We solved the problem by jamming in two smaller bolts where previously there had been only one but it was getting dark and I was loathe to continue on to the border on this road at night. We eventually found a flat spot by the water's edge on which to camp and by the time a welcome dinner had been cooked we saw a group of men approach.

"Bon soir. You are tourists?" the tallest who was in uniform asked. We told our story and he importantly informed us that he was the local Chief of Police and that he would give us permission to sleep there that night. With beer on their breath they bade us goodnight and continued on their four mile walk to the next village, five drunken men and a goat.

The mountain roads of Rwanda were paved, then as we entered Uganda the land flattened and paled. Long horned cattle grazed the bush, passively watched over by tall, emaciated herdsmen. The country was in a sad state of disrepair, ravaged since 1971 by tribal rivalry fuelled by the disastrous mismanagement and brutal policies of Idi Amin. Things were now a little calmer after a year of relative stability under a government of national unity but the legacy remained and large tracts of land in the north were still not controlled by the central government. Given the atmosphere of tenuous stability we decided not to camp out and at Kabale inquired at the police station for the best place to stay. We were offered a spot to pitch our tent next to the cells but they suggested we might be more comfortable in the All Saints Church Hostel next door. We spent the evening there chatting to the vicar who had studied theology at Oxford and to a travelling telephone technician who remarked that one effect of the colonial carve up of Africa was that in order to phone Kigali, the capital of Rwanda just sixty-two miles away, you have to go via London and then Brussels. Typewriting and office procedure courses were held at the hostel and as well as the usual signs forbidding people to drink, swear or spit was the following : "At the end of each course a test will be held, and if any person is found not to be fit, the office will think what to do."

Petrol was in short supply in Uganda and the road system a disaster. We were delayed overnight in Mbarara and only through the friendly generosity of the Ugandans who were waiting at the pumps next morning were we allowed to jump the queue and continue on our way. I spent two days constantly swinging the outfit from one side of the road to the other trying to avoid huge gaping pot holes into which a car, let alone our bike, could quite easily disappear. Occasionally we passed the burnt-out shell of a wrecked army vehicle and in towns bullet holes still pockmarked the facades. The roadblocks were manned by a ragged and ill-equipped security force, young boys, watched over by dour elder men, rummaged through our belongings asking for presents. Finding none they waved us on with cheeky smiles. We crossed the equator, and re-entered the northern hemisphere in the rain, stopping only long enough to take a photograph. We hadn't the energy or the inclination to do more than pass quickly through this troubled land. Our impulse was to get to Nairobi as soon as possible for then a decision would have to made as to how we would get home. For months now we had both been quietly hoping that we would be back in 169

At the Equator, Uganda

England in time for a Christmas re-union with our families. It was now the middle of October and it still seemed possible. Neither of us had any regrets about where we'd been or the time it had taken, but now that the end was in sight, our attention and our emotions were directed firmly towards home. We were both tired, physically and mentally sapped by the demands of a year of almost constant travel through two of the world's more difficult continents.

So we skirted the northern edge of Lake Victoria, passed through Kampala and on into the African Highlands of a more ordered Kenya. Groups of small whitewashed coolie cottages contrasted with the vivid green of the tea bushes and the splendour of the views over the Rift Valley refreshed our spirits before the descent to Nairobi. The motorcycle over the last couple of days had begun to show the by now quite familiar signs that its engine was in need of attention. Intermittent firing and an increase in oil consumption was followed during our ride into Nairobi by the engine completely missing on one cylinder and blowing smoke from the other exhaust. The clutch cable snapped, quickly followed by our only spare, one that had already seen many miles of service. We rode the last twenty miles crashing through the gears and desperately trying not to stop at such unfamiliar things as traffic lights and roundabouts as we crawled through the city's outskirts. We had arrived none too soon. The heat, the dust and the dubious petrol of the last year had taken their toll and in the campsite, or rather the suburban garden of an enterprising Polish lady who ran a guest house and garden for overland travellers, I pulled apart the engine for what we sincerely hoped was the last time. Once the barrels had been rebored I put in the set of oversize pistons we had carried from Los Angeles, and to run the engine in we set off on a weekend ride with Paul and Vic, two Londoners who were riding BMWs through Africa from south to north. We descended deep into the Rift valley to the salt lake of Magadi, whose mineral content and shallow waters made it glow silver and pink and grey in the evening's sloping sunlight. Flamingos grouped together, then took flight at the sound of our three rumbling engines. On the far side of the lake, which we crossed by causeway, Paul was all for seeing what was on the other side of the escarpment which blocked our way: the steep track did not, however, seem a sensible route for our new pistons, so we all took a longer, but equally rocky route around the obstacle. By mid-day both the air temperature and our newly overhauled engine were so hot that the stops were frequent and long. Mopsa and Vic revelled in each other's company, both here and at the Nairobi campsite, for Vic was a chef and shared Mopsa's priorities about life on the road: it didn't matter if the road was long and bumpy, the bed hard, the water cold, or the clothes dirty – so long as the food was plentiful and good. Mopsa has four sisters and missed the type of relationship which I, try though I might, could never adequately supply. We were in a strongly Masai area and in the villages the tribal people maintained an almost traditional way of life despite the advent of tourism and its adjuncts. Among both men and women, heavily beaded jewellery was worn, their earlobes long and stretched from the weight of the earrings they wore. Most noticeable among these were black plastic film cannisters pushed through the hugely pierced holes. In towns the urbanised Masai and other tribespeople looped their pendulous lobes back over the tops of their ears for tidier effect. During the afternoon the track disintegrated at points into soft sand, and on the inclines we had to push harder than I liked. It was now badly hot and I was scared of overheating and subsequent seizure, so Mopsa and I turned back to Nairobi, leaving Paul and Vic to deal with the conditions as they saw fit. We would meet up again later.

The bike had, fortunately, coped well with this outing but still needed some other attention. The weld from Qatar which held the duplex frame together had broken again, so it was fixed in an Asian workshop. While I dealt with this and

With Paul and Vic at Magadi Lake, in Kenya ▶

The hazards of stopping for hitch-hikers in Kenya ▼

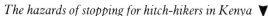

had the electrics checked over at the Lucas agents, Mopsa undertook the more difficult task of obtaining Sudanese visas – we had, by now, decided to ship the bike from Mombasa for our old friends OCL had offered us passage on a container ship to Port Sudan. Neither of us relished the idea of turning back in the direction we had come, before battling through Zaire and across the Sahara. Bureaucracy, however, almost got the better of us. The visas were only available on presentation of an airline ticket in and out of Khartoum. Would a shipping ticket do instead? No, there was no facility for such a circumstance. Mopsa remained in the office for several hours, she asked to see a higher authority, she pleaded, she wept, she acheived nothing. Still she remained. "Are you still here?" asked the doorman. "What else can I do?" she asked, "How else can we get home?" The first secretary passed by. "Are you still here?" he asked. He promised to telex to Khartoum, would let her have an answer in three weeks. "But the boat leaves in six days," Mopsa pleaded. He promised to do his best. Frustrated and far from confident, Mopsa left the office, close to tears. On the steps of the building she passed Mother Theresa of Calcutta, on a visit to East Africa and also planning to go to Sudan, who held out her hand to her with a twinkling eye. "She seemed," Mopsa told me back at Mrs Roche's, "to hold all the power and wisdom and humour and suffering of the world in her eyes. I think we shall get our visas." And so we did.

The air in Nairobi as we packed up to leave was hectic and febrile. Strange still winds would spring from nowhere, going nowhere. Desultory rains fell, settling the dust and bringing out the smell from the rotting piles of garbage which lined the roads. The sound of the traffic, the call of the communal taxi drivers, the fumes and the frustrations and the wasted time all combined to make us long to get away. Paul had hepatitis, he and Vic would be going home by the Saharan route, we would see them in six months or so. We rode through torrential rain towards Mombasa, churning up mud, and warming to the sight of the Arab influence which appears towards the coast. It seemed to carry us a little nearer the beginning and the end of our journey.

Once again OCL had done us proud. We had a suite aboard the MV Ubena and we took great delight in daily hot showers, varied and regular meals, and idling our time away in the sun, sometimes swimming in the tiny swimming pool on deck. There had been drama and bustling activity in port in Mombasa when first a container load of 947 poached elephant tusks was found by the customs, and then two stowaways were routed aboard the ship.

It was a peaceful voyage north around the horn of Africa that took us from the predominantly orange and green hues of Kenya to the blinding whiteness of the Sudanese desert. Port Sudan hung low on the horizon, pale squat buildings with occasional minarets and wandering camels. After accepting a hefty deposit for temporary import of the bike, and telling us how to get our circulation permit so we might drive in the country, Mohammed Abdelgadir Hassan, Chief Customs Officer for the port, had our breakfast brought to his office and together we discussed our plans. He told us our options were basically two: there was the long road to Wadi Halfa, two thousand kilometers of sand and little chance of obtaining petrol once we had left the port, or a two-day journey by train across the Nubian desert which would cost less than the petrol we'd need to go by bike, were it available. The train journey looked the only viable alternative and also very tempting, but we had learnt not to make decisions while travelling until all possibilities had been explored. I had heard that it was possible, although there was no road as such, to travel up the Red Sea coast into Egypt. We would visit the Egyptian consul before any decision was made. Conversation moved on. Mohammed had studied in both the USA and England, and preferred the former.

"Britain is very conservative" he said. "I returned there after ten years – nothing had changed." I wondered how he felt about his own country, and indeed his department, labouring under the weight of bureaucratic systems partly inherited from an Imperial and conservative Britain. The breakfast of flat bread, sweet black tea and spicy beans took me back over three and a half years to our first experiences of the Arab culture. The feelings were not unpleasant. Almost full circle now.

The Egyptians told us it impossible to enter their country by the coast. The border was closed and the way dangerous. "You take the train to Wadi Halfa," the consul said. "And when you arrive in Aswan you will feel very, very happy." Discretion being the better part of what they say it is, we decided on the train. It was several days before the next train left and we spent them wandering the town, drinking in the atmosphere, enjoying the changes. We tried to find reading material for the journey, but the only English language books available were either heavy volumes on the Sudanese economy or prosaic simplifications of classics of English literature: Wuthering Heights and Oliver Twist without the language. Absurd, we thought, since this suggests that the story is what makes literature, rather than the way it is told or the language it employs. While lying under a canvas shelter outside the beachside youth hostel where we stayed, we were suddenly assailed by a wall of sound. Howling and wailing filled the air, as news travelled through the area of the death of a patriarch of a local tribe of seafaring nomads. Mopsa was not well that week, and I quickly fell into being at home in the Arab culture – becoming one of the male part of the population, taking part in soccer matches on the beach, chatting in tea houses, rather than being the friend and partner Mopsa expected me to be. It was very easy, whilst amongst such charming and hospitable Sudanese men, to assume a cultural mantle that was not my own.

The train pulled out of the station, through the sprawling shanty town, the bald stoney hills and out into the desert. The outfit had been separated and its two parts were securely wedged between tyres, bales and packing cases in a goods van. We had found our seats and tried to make ourselves comfortable. The only luxury we had paid for in electing to travel first class was space: the seats which had once been upholstered in red plush over foam pads were now a tangle of metal frame and disintegrating rubber. There was no light bulb, the fan did not work, it was dusty and grimy, but at least it wasn't too crowded. Out in the corridors people and bundles lay two or three deep, all of which were uprooted every few hours when the train stopped for prayers. Our travelling companions took delight in feeding us at every opportunity from bags of fruit and bread, and we in return shared cigarettes and stories. Our sleep was fitful, disturbed by stations and duststorms and yet we remember the journey with pleasure. The only real problem was the call of nature. I could jump out of the window at stops, but Mopsa wasn't confident that she would be able to climb back in so she fought her way down the crammed corridors treading with as much delicacy as she could muster on the hands, heads and backs of sleeping forms to reach the lavatories. At one point the toilet at one end of the carriage was packed with baggage, and the other was full of sleeping people who clearly had nowhere else to go. Desperate, she returned to our compartment and sought my help. Together we made our way to the connecting door at the end of the carriage and stepped gingerly out onto the couplings. There in the night air, with the wind rushing by and holding fast to my legs she was able to find relief.

Most of the train's passengers were, like us, bound for the ferry up Lake Nasser to Aswan in Egypt. Ignorant of the situation in Wadi Halfa, we were in no hurry to leave the train when we arrived, and found we were too late to get one of the very few hotel rooms in town and so like the majority of the others, we lay down in the sandy street on that cold desert night to sleep. The following morning we walked back across the dusty, wind blown square to the station to arrange for the off-loading of the motorcycle. The station master had not yet arrived but his assistant was delighted to be able to practice his limited English. He showed us the old polished wood telephone board. "British – very good." Then pointing to the more modern telephone "Japanese – very bad." The engine of the train was American and merely good. The second and third class carriages, Japanese and very, very bad. The first class carriages, however were British again and very, very good. Despite having been well wedged in before we had left Atbara the bike was thrown around the wagon on the bumpy ride north

Re-attaching the sidecar in Wadi Halfa, Sudan

and the tank was dented and the screen cracked. Thankfully, the damage was only superficial and after re-attaching the sidecar we rode the bike away. A breakdown had delayed the ferry so we spent three days waiting for it, arranging to export the motorcycle, reclaiming our deposit and battling for tickets for the boat. Although the ferry was solely a passenger-carrying vessel and had no facilities to take vehicles on board, motorcycles had been allowed in the past. We were assured that our larger outfit would be no problem. We had emptied the bike of all but a minute amount of petrol before loading it on the train, so we tried to get some more.

"You return tomorrow," the attendant at the petrol compound told us, "Maybe I give you one litre." They had yet to unload the supplies that the train had brought in and most of that had already been assigned to the fleet of battered trucks and Land Rovers that ferried the train passengers through the desert to the port. In any event we had enough to get us to the port at the lake's edge. Port was the rather grand term for what was essentially a wooden pontoon tied to the lake shore in the middle of the desert. We waited there while six hundred odd passengers embarked and then the captain sent us a message. He wouldn't take the bike, he was already overloaded. No amount of arguing would change his mind and we felt utterly dejected as we watched our only means of exit from Sudan slowly pull away. We had no Sudanese money, no way of getting any, no petrol, no food – just tickets for a ferry which wouldn't take us. We had been stamped out of Sudan, and our single entry visas had been used. The harbour master of this tiny port was more sympathetic:

"Comes another ferry on Saturday, the captain is a kinder man," he smiled reassuringly.

Fed on bread and Nile perch brought to us by the fishermen who lived by the pontoon, we sat and waited for Saturday, and the captain was indeed a much kinder man.

Once we had docked in Aswan we were taken, with the other half dozen or so non-Sudanese on board, off the boat first and after changing the required $150 each into local currency, returned for the motorcycle. The other passengers were now disembarking. The rough disdainful treatment that was being meted out to the kind and unassuming Sudanese who had befriended us on our journey north by train and boat, did not immediately endear me to the Egyptians. A stocky sergeant with a thick stick controlled the line, letting one man off at a time and smashed their passports from their hands and onto the floor if they were not opened at the requisite page, before sending them to the back of the queue. The sidecar had been detached from the bike for loading and both parts were parked in a narrow corridor. With the reluctant help of some Egyptian soldiers we manhandled them across the shaky pontoon and onto the wharf. As we hastily refixed the sidecar one of the soldiers kept glancing at his watch motioning at us to hurry up. They were off duty in five minutes and the port was preparing to close down for the night.

It was a joy to be our own masters again, to not be dependent on the whim of a captain or on a delayed timetable. The seat of the motorcycle might get uncomfortable at times but at least it was our own. We still, however, had the Mediterranean to cross. There were winter ferries from Alexandria to Greece so we spent the next two weeks meandering up the intensely cultivated Nile valley, stopping only to visit the more interesting temples and bustling souks. In the spots that attracted more tourists the insistance of the hustlers made us uncharacteristically short tempered and sharp, but once out on the open road and passing through the many towns and villages that lined the route, the reception was both warm and enthusiastic. One lunchtime at a roadside cafe the English teacher from the local boy's school asked us if we would come and talk to his class. The headmaster was called and we were then introduced to the boys as two important English visitors: namely Sir Richard and Madame Popsi. After an impromptu English lesson taken by ourselves, a loud bell signalled lunch and all hell broke loose. The rest of the school, which numbered around 300, had by now heard of our arrival and were soon battering on the door demanding to be let in while others poured in through the open windows, filling the room. It was a riot. The headmaster took things in hand and with a large stick cut a swathe through the excited crowd who pressed forward on all sides, desperate to touch us and shake our hands. Somehow we managed to make it back to the motorcycle in one piece and roared off, leaving a tattered line of cheering children running on behind.

In Alexandria we found that it would be far cheaper for us to take a ferry from Haifa in Israel to Pireus in Greece; that would allow us eight days in which to reach Calais for a boat across the channel on Christmas Eve. It seemed that after all the frustrations and delays of the last few months we would make it home in time for Christmas Lunch. We crossed the Suez canal and rode across Sinai, entered Israel at Rafah and rode up to the hills around Nazareth, to spend a quiet two days on the farm of the Hadas family whose son we had met in Nairobi. On the morning of Sunday, 14th December, we set out for Haifa. There was snow on the highest ground and we felt the chill of a European winter sweeping down from the north. During the short ride to the coast the bike started to misbehave in a way that was unfamiliar. If I let the clutch out too fast at slow speed or low revs the engine uttered a series of low grunts and juddered to a stop. When it first happened I felt my stomach drop. It seemed that we might yet fall at the final hurdle. For the first time on our long journey an intense frustration brought tears to my eyes. When the emotion subsided I played around with the clutch adjustment and things seemed a little better but I wasn't at all sure we had solved the problem. We made it to Haifa without further incident but the seeds of doubt had been firmly planted in my mind. Emotionally we had begun to psyche ourselves up for the last mad dash across a wintery Europe, to Christmas and home.

Chapter Ten

Full Circle

THERE ARE moments you expect to be special. I had thought that the first step onto European soil might be one such, but Piraeus was scarcely different from Haifa – ports by this point seemed to merge into one. It was only later, as we sat in a pavement café with the sun low in a winter sky, the coffee steaming milky and European, definitely European, not the bitter spicy version we'd become accustomed to in the Middle East, that a warmth rose in my heart, in my throat. I looked across at Mopsa and found that she too had felt the moment – it was one we could savour and share.

We reached Piraeus on 17th December, early in the morning. There were eight riding days till Christmas and London was just over 1200 road miles away. At the café we fell in with a group of other Western Europeans from the boat, on bikes and in cars. There was an atmosphere of good cheer as we all planned to be home for Christmas after varying lengths of time away. We lingered over the coffee and the white doughy bread, small pleasures not missed but appreciated on re-meeting. Messengers were sent out to discover the times of ferries to Italy: the news was good: the ferry left that evening and we had ample time to reach Patras, whence it departed. It was all so easy: people knew, took the responsibility of telling you, we didn't have to wait, we didn't have to come back tomorrow, or later, or at all. Full of confidence we set off in a relaxed convoy across the Peleponnese.

Mopsa and I led. The sidecar was a little slower than the other vehicles, wearier and more misused, so when the others stopped at a bank to change money we pushed on alone. The road outside Piraeus widened into an empty undulating stretch of smooth tarmac. The sky was pale and the sun warmed our shoulders if not the air. The views to our left, over the indented coastline, constantly changed. Boats and ships varying in size from small wooden fishing boats to the slowly rusting hulks of redundant oil tankers lay at random moorings in the bays. The country was tinged with gold, winter had not removed all the gilded autumnal leaves from the vines whose stems and tendrils curled dark red over the dry grey soil. But as the sun passed its meridian the optimism of the morning began to fade. From the motorcycle the loud graunching sounds we had first heard in Israel grated on our nerves yet again. After several stops and restarts it continued and I found that it was impossible to change out of second gear. We managed to make it to a petrol station on the Corinth Canal and there I resignedly pulled out the tool bag, to start on work on the clutch. When we had left England over four years ago I had been a mechanical novice, but now I knew this engine well enough to be able to take it apart confidently by the side of the road. Having removed the primary chaincase cover I found that the whole clutch housing and the main drive shaft had worked alarmingly loose and that in all probability the gear pinions had become unaligned. As far as I could tell nothing had broken, but I would have to strip the gearbox down to its component parts from the other side of the bike, the difficult side to get to because of the sidecar, and then rebuild it on a retightened mainshaft. To do this I would also have to completely dismantle the clutch and primary drive. The afternoon had all but disappeared when we got down to serious work. At seven the petrol station closed. We moved the bike and the half dismantled engine into the light that shone out from the adjoining cafe. At eight the owner's wife brought us huge mugs of steaming coffee which we sipped with a dish of rice and sardines that Mopsa had prepared on our camping stove. At ten they left, expressing concern at how cold it was getting, but they left the cafe lights on so we could continue to work. By twelve it had become bitterly cold, well below freezing, and Mopsa and I put on all the extra clothes we could find, to the extent that our movements became cumbersome and slow. By two I was ready to start putting the gears back in place. The cause of the loosening had been found – I pulled out the mangled remains of a spacer, replacing it with something almost the same size that Mopsa found amongst the screws and washers we still kept in a small tin, ready for just such emergencies. As the tiredness began to numb our brains and the cold our fumbling fingers we slowly rebuilt the gears, Mopsa working from the manual and handing me the gear pinions in the correct order. It took us three attempts before they were meshing smoothly. At four Mopsa slept while I continued. At five I collapsed, to snatch an hour of fitful slumber. At seven, as the eastern sky began to lighten, the cafe owner returned to wake Mopsa with yet another cup of steaming café-au-lait and by ten-thirty the job was complete. As we rode away the bike ran perfectly and the sun rose high and cast a shadow of perfect efficiency at our feet. We had lost our friends. We had missed the boat, but as we arrived in Patras we found there was another one that evening, one that would even save us a day's riding by taking us to Ancona, five hundred miles further up the Italian coast. Christmas was still within view.

It was sometime after five o'clock when we bought our tickets and on a far hill snow from last night still rested on the northern slopes. Boarding commenced at ten and we were both very tired, in need of a good meal and to rest. A shining grey motorcycle passed by, slowed, turned around and returned.

It was a Triumph which then drew alongside. The two bikes were as different as it was possible for two bikes to be: the one gleaming, glossy, flawless, tended and polished. The other dulled, scratched, dented, used and abused. Andreas was an enthusiast and we were taken back to his apartment where his wife Georgia prepared bean stew which was followed by coffee and whiskey. Andreas then insisted on a beer, so out we went, first to a bar, then a restaurant, then another bar to finish off the evening with two large bottles of retsina. Thus fortified we felt ready to board the boat. The line of cars waiting to embark seemed hardly to move. The loading was haphazard and excruciatingly slow. This was not how we had remembered Europe. At five in the morning we finally staggered aboard. Arrival time in Ancona was set for eight in the morning on Saturday, 20th December. But the seas were rough and the going slow and we lost another twelve hours and a full day's riding.

In Ancona disembarkation was rapid, smooth and courteous, the night air almost balmy after the freezing temperatures in Greece. We decided to ride into the night to make up for lost time. We had four days to reach Calais. It was autostrada almost immediately and we found we were covering distance with disconcerting ease – something we were not used to. At two we stopped at a service station to buy sandwiches and coffee, then curled up in our sleeping bags on a grassy verge in a far corner outside, lulled to sleep by the purr of the refrigerated trailers alongside which sheltered us from the cutting wind.

At seven o'clock on Sunday morning we woke to find the sun already melting the night's frost that had settled in our hair. It was a fast and easy run to Bologna where Mopsa telephoned home to warn them of our impending arrival. Her sister, Louisa, was to set out that night on an 1100 cc Yamaha for Paris. We would meet under the Arc de Triomphe at noon on Tuesday 23rd.

The road curved and wound its way up into the Alps. It was especially beautiful in the stark December light and the gathering clouds hardly seemed menacing at all. We climbed steadily, the air became correspondingly colder, clearer and then quite suddenly snow swirled wetly around us. We stopped to seal the gaps in our protective clothing and continued. As whiteness cloaked the mountain sides, rapidly settling on the road, the spirit of the season came upon us and with the isolated villages taking on the appearance of Christmas cards, we spontaneously broke into song. Muffled by the stillness, our rousing carols carried us on through the ever thickening snow and ever greying sky, until we reached the frontier. We needed only to show our passports, no more, and then came some temporary respite from the weather as we rumbled through the Frejus tunnel, the sound of our engine spiralling into the distance behind us. As we emerged from the tunnel we saw that things had progressed. Night had progressed, winter had progressed and far below us shone the dim lights of a village covered in snow. Otherwise all was darkness and our headlights picked out the rush of the snow which swept horizontally across our path. My hands by now had lost all sense of feeling, my clutch and throttle control was clumsy. It was not the freezing of them that was painful but rather the thawing out. All the way along the Italian autostrada we had stopped frequently at the service stations where I could plunge my hands under the hot air of the hand dryers and in this way I had kept frostbite at bay. We began to slide on the corners and our back wheel to spin. Although we had hoped to make Chambery that night it was time to stop. We detoured into the village of St. Michel de Maurienne, where, although there are four hotels, only one remains open in winter. They wouldn't accept our foreign currency or our plastic card and we had no francs. We pushed on through the snow to St. Jean de Maurienne, some fifteen kilometers, and there the Hotel de Roi was more welcoming. They only had breakfasts available so after several cups of warm milky coffee and crisp bread we sank into sleep.

The following morning, Monday, 22nd December, at eight o'clock, after brushing several inches of snow off the bike, we wheeled it out into the street. It refused to start. The battery was languishing, the electrical wiring damp and the oil old and thick. After sliding it down a long steep hill the engine stirred, coughed and fired up. The motorway was hazardous, trucks and cars speeding by too fast and we were drenched in a continual shower of slush. The electrics began to suffer and the firing became erratic. In the service stations where we stopped often for coffee and to warm our stiffened hands in the stream of the warm-air blowers, men and women climbed out of their cars, the French middle classes on their way to Christmas with family and friends. They were pink faced and festive, wrapped in fur and leather and wool, and stamped their feet and clapped their gloved hands against the cold. I felt a certain superiority in our greater suffering, our great distance covered, and yet to go. We bought insulating tape and attempted to dry out and then bind the electrical connections. Mopsa took off her glasses to do some close work, placing them behind her on the ground. Work complete, she stood up and stepped back. We used the last of the insulating tape to stick them back together. In central Lyons we stopped to buy money at American Express. Mopsa did the business while I continued to tinker with our fast ailing bike. We had lost the inspection cap to the primary drive some miles back and oil had been splashing out over our left feet and legs. I found another use for one of the large NGK spark plug stickers we had carried from Los Angeles and with it fixed a thin metal plate over the hole. When I had finished I gave the outfit a cursory all round check. Fate, it seemed, had decided to be as nasty as the weather – I found that one of the sidecar fixing bolts had sheared. When this had happened in Zaire, and we had no replacement, we had improvised but here in France we felt sure we could find a replacement of similiar size. We found none and were forced into a welding shop where we eventually persuaded the reluctant owner to fashion us a new one, using the thread of the old. His reluctance stemmed from his fear that if his work was not strong enough and we had an accident we would soon be back to sue him. We promised not, explaining that our whole motorcycle was held together by improvised weldings from Africa, South America and Asia. After a three hour delay the bolt was back in place and as the street lights came on we squirmed our way out through the rush hour traffic to the autoroute north. If we drove through the night we might still reach the Arc de Triomphe by twelve next day.

It was a crazy thing that we were doing, rushing headlong back to England through a Europe deep in winter. Our view of the world while travelling, like that of the long straight roads we'd ridden, had always been from the base of a triangle with the future contained within two converging lines. As the end approached so our vision shrank. What I had envisaged should be a time of quiet reflection as we slowly motored home became instead a stubborn struggle that had our tired and fraught emotions careering between excited expectation and unhappy despair.

Back on the autoroute the traffic was much heavier and the snow began to fall in sheets. We stopped at every service area now, incapable of travelling more than the brief distances between them before the pain of the cold and the wet was too much to bear. The engine started to misfire again and then as the lights failed I pulled silently onto the hard shoulder. Speeding vehicles flashed past, throwing up a thick spray which swirled with the falling snow in the oncoming lights. The shoulder was not wide and we felt very vulnerable in such low visibility. Without light I fumbled to find an obvious fault but it seemed a vain attempt. I kicked over the engine and it roared into temporary life but the timing had somehow become so out of synch that the fuel mix was igniting in one of the exhaust pipes which made it glow red hot in the blackness. It was a depressing moment as we decided what to do next. Mopsa, overcome by tiredness, quietly wept, but once her tears had dried she resigned herself to the fact that we were now extremely unlikely to be in Paris by tomorrow or to spend Christmas at home. I, on the other hand, was still stubbornly refusing to accept defeat, unable to even contemplate, after so many miles, and so much effort, that we could fall at this late stage. Mopsa took things in hand and trudged off to find the nearest emergency telephone.

It was eleven o'clock when the tow truck deposited both us and the outfit outside a motorcycle workshop in a cold, white side-street in Mâcon. It had stopped snowing and the street lights burned bright. There was enough light to work by. Mopsa didn't agree. She knew that it would be stupid and foolhardy to attempt to continue by working into the night and then, if we managed to fix it, to ride on to Calais. Me? I pulled out the tool bag yet again and started to work. It took a further two hours before the cold, the tiredness and the reality burnt through to my conciousness. I was too physically and mentally drained to think logically about the engine. Was it electrical? Was it a sticking valve? Was it something more serious? I had spent two ineffectual hours stumbling around and was no nearer the answer. I slumped back against the wall where Mopsa sat huddled in her sleeping bag.

"Well, have you accepted it yet?" she asked coldly. I was looking at the motorcycle as she spoke. It stood defiantly metallic and inanimate in a pool of harsh light, a scattered array of tools surrounding it. I had laboured so long over that bike. Hours, days, weeks, years, spent riding it, cajoling it, pushing, maintaining, repairing. It had been as much a part of the journey as we had, had been our constant friend and the means to the end. Now it was all over. I felt bereft. Turning to Mopsa I slowly nodded.

Journey's End – With Roy Richards at the National Motorcycle Museum

Retirement for Tommy

"Perhaps we should find a hotel."

It wasn't the end, of course. We still had somehow to get back to England, with or without the bike. The next morning we found that sleep had restored our sense of perspective. We had broken down before and had then, philosophically, taken what action was needed to get the bike running again and ourselves back on the road. We had let a desire to get to our destination as quickly as possible take over from the journey itself. The motorcycle, however, had thought differently, as we had so painfully found out. The workshop, outside which we had been so ignominiously dumped the previous night, opened its doors at nine and they allowed us to wheel our frozen bike into warmer surroundings. It took their mechanic and I just half an hour to trace the faults – broken and wet connections from the alternator, a duff battery and suspect spark plug leads. While I started to put right the mess, Mopsa phoned home, only to be told that Louisa was snowed in just outside Calais and didn't expect to reach Paris until later that day. If all went well we would meet her the following evening – Christmas Eve. With the pressure off we slowly began to relax.

Christmas day was wet and blustery. With Louisa we rode the bikes up to the Arc de Triomphe and under its looming arch shivered as we posed for celebratory photographs. We drank champagne that evening which we chilled with snow scraped down from the eaves of our hotel room overlooking the Seine.

On Boxing Day we rode to Calais. The ride was subdued and monochrome. And then, as we neared the port in the late afternoon, a weak and lowering sun broke through the wintery clouds and cast the elongated shadow of our travelling forms onto the frozen ground. We glanced for the last time at an image that had followed us over so many miles of road, and as darkness fell we crossed the sea to England.